ONE NATION UNDER

DOG

ONE NATION UNDER

DOG

America's Love Affair
with Our Dogs

Michael Schaffer

A Holt Paperback
Henry Holt and Company
New York

Holt Paperbacks
Henry Holt and Company, LLC
Publishers since 1866
175 Fifth Avenue
New York, New York 10010
www.henryholt.com

A Holt Paperback® and ⑰® are registered trademarks of
Henry Holt and Company, LLC.

Distributed in Canada by H. B. Fenn and Company Ltd.

Library of Congress Cataloging-in-Publication Data

Schaffer, Michael
One nation under dog : America's love affair with our dogs / Michael
Schaffer. — 1st Holt Paperbacks ed.
p. cm.
ISBN 978-0-8050-9146-5
1. Dogs—United States—Anecdotes.   2. Dogs—Social aspects—
United States—Anecdotes.   3. Pet industry—
United States.   I. Title.
SF426.2.S313 2010
636.700973—dc23
2009051087

Henry Holt books are available for special promotions and premiums.
For details contact: Director, Special Markets.

Orginally published in hardcover in 2009 by Henry Holt and Compnay

First Holt Paperbacks Edition 2010

Designed by Meryl Sussman Levavi

Printed in the United States of America

1   3   5   7   9   10   2   4   6   8

To Keltie

If you pick up a starving dog and make him prosperous, he will not bite you. This is the principal difference between a dog and a man.

—MARK TWAIN, *Pudd'nhead Wilson*, 1894

What will it be today? Beach bag or fur-trimmed overcoat? A day of basking on a Caribbean shore or a plush night in by the fire? Slumber party or ski adventure? This winter, it's up to the pups, whose versatile fashions are jet set for it all, rain, shine, snow, or sand.

—*The Pet Elite* magazine, 2007

Contents

ONE NATION UNDER

DOG

From Doghouse to Our House

By the time we finally saw Murphy, we'd driven the two hours of highway from our house in Philadelphia to what felt like the last rural place in all of New Jersey. We'd nosed through the town—over a pair of railroad tracks, past a warehouse, down a short road. And we'd gingerly tiptoed past the chain-link fence that held Boss, the massive Saint Bernard at the shotgun-style home opposite the town's small-scale animal shelter. My wife spotted him first, an oddly undersized example of the same breed running around the muddy melting snow in the kennel's yard: "It's Murphy!" she exclaimed.

We'd spotted the pup a few days earlier on Petfinder, the Web site that lets prospective adopters eye hundreds of thousands of potential adoptees from shelters all over the United States. For a long time, we'd visited the site as a diversion, a way to kill time at work staring at snapshots of wet noses and wagging tails and drooling jowls. We'd e-mail links back and forth, each of them attached to a heartbreaking story of how this particular dog was a sweetheart who really needed a place in some family's happy home. Eventually, we got to thinking that it was about time we became that happy family.

And then we stumbled across the page that featured Murphy, his tongue drooping, his watery eyes staring cluelessly from inside a cage that turned out to be only two hours away. When we arrived that morning, we'd been talking about him long enough to feel like he was already part of our household. The woman who ran the shelter mashed a 100-length cigarette into an old tin of dog food as she led him over. As they got close enough for us to see the matted dreadlocks on Murphy's back, Boss began growling. "Don't mind him," the woman said, as the guard dog's growls turned to angry barks. "Boss don't like other dogs."

Murphy, though, was another story. He was sweet and cuddly and goofy, exactly as we'd wanted. Of course, we tried to stay skeptical. Knowing little about dogs when we started thinking about getting one, we'd searched for wisdom in a book on how to adopt an animal. Don't let those heartbreaking shelter stories trick you into getting an animal you can't handle, it warned. Put them through the paces now, or suffer later. So in the ensuing half hour, we tried the book's suggested tests as best we could. We put food in front of him and then snatched it away. No growling. A good sign. We put more food in front of him and then pushed his face away as he ate. No nipping. An even better sign. The shelter manager gazed with dismay at this spectacle of anxious yuppiehood: one of us reading reverently from the book, the other vaguely executing its tests on the befuddled dog, neither of us quite sure what to do next.

Following the book's instructions as if they were holy writ, we asked how Murphy had wound up in the shelter—and then steeled ourselves against what we'd been warned would be a maudlin spiel designed to undercut doubts about a potentially troublesome pooch. The dog, we were told, had been brought to her kennel twice. First he was turned in by someone who the manager suspected hadn't been able to unload this especially runty runt of his litter: Murphy was eighteen months old and 63 pounds at the time; ordinary male Saint Bernards can weigh in at 180. Next he was returned by a woman who couldn't housebreak him.

"But she was some kind of backcountry hick," said the shelter manager. "She didn't even know what she was doing." Ever since, Murphy had been waiting in a cage next to Boss's yard, staring up at people like us. "Look," she said. "I don't much care about you, but I do care about him. And if he goes and bites someone, someone like you will put him down, right? Since I don't want that to happen, I'm telling you: He don't bite."

The logic was pretty good.

The dog was pretty sweet.

The time was pretty right.

And so we said yes, signing some not quite official-looking paperwork—the adoption document identified the dog as "Murfy"—before forking over one hundred dollars and agreeing to take into our lives a Saint Bernard with fleas and dreadlocks and a stench somewhere between warm bunion and rotten tripe. The shelter manager whipped out a syringe, planted what was purported to be a kennel cough shot into Murfy/Murphy's snout, and wished us well. We coaxed the dog into the backseat of our Honda, where he promptly fell fast asleep.

As we began the drive home, we felt a bit proud of ourselves. Not for us the fancy breeders sought out by so many in our sweetly gentrified corner of upscale America. Not for us the genetically perfect beagles and bassets and Bernese mountain dogs whose poop is sanctimoniously plucked from city sidewalks in recycled blue *New York Times* home-delivery bags. We'd gotten a dog, yeah, but we weren't going to become, like, *those people*—the ones who shell out for the spa days and agility training and homeopathic medicine for their animals, the ones who laugh it off when their puppies frighten children away from the neighborhood playground, the ones who give up vacations and promotions and transfers in order to save pooches with names like Sonoma and Hamilton and Mordecai from having their lives disrupted. No, not us.

That's what we were telling ourselves, anyway, when the PetSmart came into view along the edge of the highway. "We should go in—get some food and stuff," said my wife. "It'll just take a sec." Thus began our unwitting journey into the $41-billion-a-year world of the modern American pet.

It didn't take long to realize that the line between sober pet owner and spendthrift overindulger wasn't as clear as I'd imagined.

I started thinking about that very subject an hour or so after Murphy nosed his way into the PetSmart—at around the time the exhausted-looking staff at the in-store grooming salon told us there was no way they could attend to our filthy new pet today; we ought to have made reservations a couple of weeks in advance. My wife, who'd grown up with a dog and had roughed out a budget when we started thinking about adopting one of our own, hadn't been aware that salon grooming was such a standard piece of contemporary pet owning that chain stores had weeks-long waiting lists. Still, without having to shell out for a wash, we made it out of the store that day for under $200. Murphy had a new bed, a pair of collars, an extend-o-leash that expands up to twenty-five feet, a variety of chew toys—that he's never used—and other goodies. The spending seemed like basic, ordinary stuff.

But as anyone who's read one of the dog-owner memoirs that seem to occupy about half of the weekly *New York Times* best-seller list could confirm, it was no onetime expense. It's a basic law of pet storytelling: Just as the romantic comedy vixen must wind up with the guy she'd vowed not to marry if he were the last man on earth, so too must the beloved dog stomp and scratch and poop on your very last nerve—and chow down on your shrinking wallet—before weaseling his way into your newly receptive heart. No surprise, then, that four years later Murphy has gone through a variety of ever newer beds (he seemed not to like the old ones) and redesigned collars and leashes (we wanted to try the special ones that are said to keep dogs from pulling too hard) and still more chew toys (we have a PetSmart discount card now and live in the eternal hope of finding one he likes). He also owns Halloween costumes (too adorable to resist), reindeer antlers (ditto), and a picture of himself with Santa (alas, ditto once more).

He has been implanted with a LoJack-style microchip that will help us find him if he gets lost.

His food—or should I say "foods"—comes from that burgeoning market sector known as "superpremium."

He's stayed at an array of upscale local kennels—sorry, pet hotels—when we've gone out of town.

On other trips, when we took him along, he got to stay in our hotel room. One place left a doggie biscuit on his doggie bed and sent up a babysitter when we went out.

Did I mention he's on antidepressants? The vet diagnosed his anxious howling when left alone as "separation anxiety," and it turned out there was a pill for it.

Or that he has a professional dog walker? In fact, the current one is his second; the first dropped him because she had too many clients.

Or that when we tote up the numbers, he's proven responsible for an eerily large portion of our social life? Dragging us into the neighborhood park on a daily basis, he's introduced a wealth of new neighborhood characters into our life. One of them was a cat whom Murphy—to his lasting regret—found shivering in a hollow tree. We brought her home and named her Amelia. And then there were two.

Then we decided to add a human baby to our flock. We'd known this would mean prenatal treatments for my wife. It was a bit of a surprise, though, when other prenatal attention focused on treating Murphy. Worries about how the dog would react to that new child sent us scurrying into the pricey orbit of one of our city's best-known dog trainers for six weeks of private lessons. Unfortunately, her take on canine behavior was so different from that of the guy whose classes we'd first taken upon adopting Murphy that we went scrambling to the massive pet-care section of our local book superstore, where we have purchased a veritable library of books about how better to raise pets.

In fact, both pets hover around all sorts of other spending decisions, poking their snouts into our deliberations on things like furniture ("I like it, but Amelia would rip it to shreds") and—most painful of all—our purchase of an SUV (between a new baby, a Saint Bernard, and a Honda Civic, something had to give).

Despite all those early vows of pet frugality, I've not felt especially strange about any of the choices we have made. At the time, each of them seemed mundane and obvious: A dog needs walking when his owners stay late at work; furniture and cars ought to match a household's needs; and, particularly with a baby in the mix, it makes eminent sense to work on a large animal's behavior. I would say that the story of Murphy and us isn't the story of a couple whose priorities were upended by a heart-meltingly adorable animal but, rather, the tale of a household engaged in what has become the normal way to raise a four-legged member of the family. And yet when I tote it all up, the truth stares at me with its own big, wet eyes: I've seen *those people*, and I'm one of 'em. If you have pets in contemporary America, you probably are, too. Pleased to meet you.

There are an awful lot of stories about pets in the media these days, but nearly all of them fit into two basic categories.

Category number one is that old standard: the tearjerker, the tale of the abused and the abandoned, the victims of indifferent owners or dire shelters or youthful sociopaths or simply the cruel hand of fate. The years I spent researching this book were a big period for such stories. In Pennsylvania, a high-profile political campaign focused national attention on puppy mills, the high-volume, low-standards facilities where dogs are often kept in gruesome conditions as they churn out litter after litter of merchandise for the nation's pet stores. In Virginia, the indictment and imprisonment of Atlanta Falcons quarterback Michael Vick on federal dogfighting charges turned into a full-blown media circus as reports detailed the dozens of pit bulls brutalized at Vick's Bad Newz Kennels. And all across the country, the deaths of hundreds of cats and dogs who ate tainted pet food pulled back the curtain on an ill-regulated multibillion-dollar industry that happened to feature some of the world's biggest corporate names.

The sob stories stand in dramatic contrast to the second, and possibly even bigger, category of pet reportage: the pampered pet tale, the gape-jawed peek at the animal kingdom's most coddled critters—and the masseuses, chauffeurs, and pet-set fashionistas who cater to them. Whether they take the form of a local newspaper detailing the opening of, say, Duluth's first luxury doggie spa, or of a sober national magazine like *BusinessWeek* dedicating its cover story to the booming U.S. pet industry, the pampered pet tales feature amazement—and hints of disdain—at what many pet owners now see as ho-hum basics of life with an animal. Yet while there's a small army of activist groups, and no shortage of scholars and reporters, who have dedicated themselves to uncovering the root causes behind the sad and often criminal stories in category one, there's far less material examining the dramatic cultural and economic changes that underlie the zany stories in category two.

This is a book about those changes. It's a story about how America's housepets have worked their way into a new place in the hearts, homes, and wallets of their owners. In a relatively short period of time, the United States has become a land of doggie yoga and kitty acupuncture and frequent-flier miles for traveling pets, a society where your inability to find a pet sitter has become an acceptable excuse to beg off a dinner invitation, a country where political candidates pander to pet owners and dog show champions are feted like Oscar winners. Sure, some tales of pampered pets still have the occasional ability to amaze us. Take hotelier Leona Helmsley's will, for instance, in which the "Queen of Mean" left $12 million to a lapdog named Trouble while giving nothing to several of her own grand-children. Such far-fetched stories are part of what scholar James Serpell calls the *roi s'amuse* tradition of pet tales: *The king amuses himself*. But for the country's 70 million non-Helmsley pet-owning households, other examples of everyday luxury, once unimaginable, seem de rigueur. Yesteryear's table scraps have been replaced by this year's home-delivered doggie dinners.

What happened? It's not like the animals have changed much. As any nostalgic pet-owning memoir will illustrate, the party in the relationship that changes is inevitably the human. Historians tell us that we've always been suckers for that doggie in the window. But exactly how that love manifests itself, and just who gets to go to the barnyard dance, has evolved dramatically. Compared to our subsistence-farming ancestors, we're all kings now. So compared to *their* ancestors, our pets live like princes.

Tales of pet keeping can be traced back to ancient societies. Tales of animal pampering are nearly as old. In China, the Han emperor Ling was so enamored of his pets that he elevated them to the rank of senior officials in his court. Ling's dogs got the best foods, slept on ornate carpets, and were given personal bodyguards. For most of history, though, ordinary people had to be spectators for such amusements. They always had animals around, of course, like cows or chickens. But for the most part, even the animals who weren't there to be eaten had work to do, herding sheep or pulling carts. Until recently, few people could afford the variety of animal classified as a pet—the one with no productive job whatsoever.

And so it was up to the blue bloods. Members of the Athenian aristocracy were said to pay twenty times the price of a human slave to buy especially esteemed dogs. In Japan, the seventeenth-century shogun Tsunayoshi so loved dogs that he made it illegal to speak of them in impolite terms; he instituted unpopular new taxes to pay for his own collection of one hundred thousand canine friends. In Uganda, the despotic nineteenth-century king M'Tesa's love for dogs prompted courtiers to curry favor by keeping their own pets. In Britain, the lapdogs in the entourage of Mary, Queen of Scots were clad in blue velvet suits; she snuck one of her beloved brood to her own execution, where it was discovered after Mary was beheaded. King Charles II, whose passion for dogs was such that he once placed a newspaper ad after one of his pets went missing, became the namesake of his own line of Cavalier spaniels. After the Glorious Revolution placed William and Mary on the throne, the couple sparked a new fancy for pugs from William's native Holland. The British Empire has waxed and waned over the centuries, but Queen Elizabeth II still travels with her pack of corgis.

The connection between pet keeping and power remained true even as royals gave way to tycoons atop society's pecking order, and as pets began to prowl the fault lines of class conflict. Nineteenth-century Parisian pet-keeping fashions, with a proliferation of books, coats, collars, bathing outfits, and the like, might have put even contemporary Manhattan's pet scene to shame: Could fancy doggie day cares compete with wealthy flaneurs walking pet turtles through public arcades? But even as Europe's newly rich were embracing an ever-changing set of pet-keeping fashions, there were great concerns over the supposedly dangerous animals that belonged to the urban underclass. Moneyed types worried that the blue-collar dogs had picked up what they saw as the violent, unclean customs of their human companions. The solution to this alleged problem: exorbitant animal taxes intended to put the squeeze on proletarian pets. Only rich pet owners would do.

Well-tended animals also became standard upper-crust accoutrements in the new nation across the Atlantic, where all people were supposed to be able to reach the top, and to bring their animals with them. As early as 1899, Thorstein Veblen, the great student of American pageantry and pomposity, sussed the secret meaning of pet ownership for the Gilded Age's elite: Pets were living emblems of conspicuous consumption. "As he is also an item of expense, and commonly serves no industrial purpose, he holds a well-assured place in men's regard as a thing of good repute," Veblen wrote in his celebrated *Theory of the Leisure Class,* the book that brought us the term *conspicuous consumption.* I'm so rich, the industrial dandy's logic went, that I can afford to feed—and house, and bathe, and clean the tumbleweeds of shedding fur from—this totally unproductive creature. In an age when many people still forced their children to sing for their supper, or at least work in a factory for it, this was quite a concept.

This is not to say that pet keeping was limited to such consumers, or that it could always be ascribed to such cynical motivations. American pet keeping existed, often in fairly elaborate forms and at spots up and down the social ladder, well before Veblen took on the pet-owning leisure class. The inhabitants of pre-Columbian America hunted or domesticated a variety of animals, but what we now understand as pets came across the Atlantic with the Spaniards. Diaries that predate the Constitution tell of beloved family cats. In the mid-nineteenth century, there was a craze for imported caged birds. By the twentieth century, pets were a way for powerful politicians to make themselves look more down-to-earth—the exact opposite of Veblen's notion. President Franklin Delano Roosevelt's Scottie, Fala, was a national celebrity, traveling with him to war conferences and visiting defense plants; the dog's breeder published his own book in 1942. Presidents ever since have deployed pets the same way—although FDR was probably the only one threatened with congressional investigation over pet pampering, the result of false rumors that he had dispatched a destroyer to retrieve the dog after Fala was accidentally left behind in the Aleutian Islands.

Pet keeping continued to evolve with the country, following each era's ideas about kindness, domesticity, and comfort. The lapdog in the millionaire's mansion became the golden retriever in the suburban backyard; the kitten from the litter of your neighbor's tabby became the kitten you took straight from the SPCA adoption center to the veterinarian's spaying practice. Everyone knows dogs are supposed to teach you about love and loyalty and fun. But I found something I had never expected when I first glimpsed my dog's sweet, dopey face: the story of modern America. In the chapters that follow, I travel to diverse corners of our pet kingdom to experience the often surprising ways that pets like Murphy serve as a fun-house-mirror reflection of our changing notions about such universal subjects as family, health, and friendship—and more historically specific topics like bureaucracy, justice, consumerism, and the culture wars.

Maybe the most telling change involved a very small piece of architecture, once ubiquitous, which I saw very little of as I journeyed around the new world of America's pets, pet owners, and pet businesses: the doghouse. Yes, one firm makes a $5,390 structure modeled after a Swiss chalet. But for the most part, though we still talk of people being sent to the doghouse, the physical structures have disappeared from our landscape. Their occupants have moved indoors, to be with their families, in far bigger doghouses: ours.

ONE

The $43-Billion Fur Baby

Meet the Pet Industry

The fans on hand to watch the San Diego Padres face the Los Angeles Dodgers that summer day in 2006 included a two-year-old black Boston terrier named Bandit. With dark glasses covering his big, buggy eyes, and a Padres bandanna around his neck, Bandit—a performing dog who rode on a motorbike in a parade before the game—was likely the coolest dog in the stadium. There was plenty of competition: The crowd included a pug sporting one of the squad's blue road jerseys, a golden retriever clad in a throwback 1980s-style uniform, and a lumbering Newfoundland wearing a Padres terry-cloth towel to collect his ample drool. Baseball and hot dogs, indeed. The "Dog Days of Summer" game is part of a national trend in pet-friendly ballpark come-ons. You can watch the national pastime. And see some baseball, too.

To get a real sense of the economic muscle of America's pets, though, take a look at the name of the stadium where the Padres play: Petco Park. As pet owners in forty-nine states and the District of Columbia know, Petco sells kitty litter, chew toys, birdseed, and dog collars. There's an enormous market for such wares: Roughly 60 percent of U.S. households own pets. That translates into 68.5 million households, up 12 percent in only six years, more than twice the rate of human population growth. Thus, when the Padres opened their new stadium in 2004, the hometown retailer was able to spend the $60 million it took to plaster its name on the ballpark for two decades to come— riding America's love of Maine coons and Boston terriers all the way into a club that includes venerable Fortune 500 names such as AT&T, Bank of America, and Ford Motor Company, as well as new economy titans like Qualcomm and Hewlett-Packard.

San Diego—named America's most canine-friendly city by *Dog Fancy* magazine in 2007—hosted a still grander exhibit of pet industrial might during the 2008 off-season. For three days in February, it played host to the Global Pet Expo, America's biggest annual extravaganza of four-legged retailing. Before arriving, I'd thought nothing could top the previous year's Global Pet Expo in Orlando. That one had 2,300 display booths, one of which featured a troupe of actors dressed as Roman centurions to promote a new line of dog chews. The 2008 show was bigger still: With 800 exhibitors and 2,400 display booths pushing everything from scratching posts to retractable leashes to ferret hammocks, it filled a building whose floor space is the equivalent of eleven and a half football fields. The expo's new-products showcase alone contained over 800 brand-new innovations, inventions that may either turn some entrepreneurs into our next pet-industry millionaires or—and here I think of whoever was responsible for the $704 stroller specifically designed for promenading with large-sized macaws—make them wish they'd invested their money in Enron instead. The show drew some five thousand wholesalers, distributors, and buyers representing old-fashioned mom-and-pop pet stores and burgeoning big-box chains alike. Roughly 30 percent of the buyers came from outside the United States. They may not drive our cars anymore, but they love our doggie designers.

The 2008 expo was billed as a fiftieth anniversary celebration for its sponsor, the American Pet Products Manufacturers Association. Back in 1958, the new organization consisted of sixteen businesses; APPMA president Bob Vetere said their first show featured only a handful of wares displayed in a single room in New York City. The room, he said, was about as big as the three aisles of space at the 2008 expo that were covered in hot-pink carpeting and dedicated to the booming, bling-filled "boutique products" sector. For all its history, though, the industry's most dramatic growth didn't come during the domestic 1950s or the dynamic 1960s. According to Vetere, the real boom came at the end of the twentieth century and the beginning of the twenty-first. In 1994, APPMA's first survey of nationwide pet spending put the size of the pet economy, including food and medical care along with the goofy gewgaws that capture the attention of uninitiated expo visitors, at $17 billion. In 2007, when the group released the latest edition of its survey, that number had risen to $41 billion.

Of course, those are the self-generated figures of an organization with every interest in making lavish pet spending look mainstream. But even a skeptic of the industry says they aren't far off. Independent analyst Mike Dillon, who writes the *Pet Industry Weekly* blog and makes his living producing reports for actual investors in the industry, argued that the business had taken a tiny dip in 2006 and only a small boost the next year. Nonetheless, his figure remained a hefty $39 billion, far above what it had been a decade earlier. Much pricier studies by the respected market-research firm Packaged Facts—corporations pay thousands for its advice on retail trends—predict at least 7 percent growth each year until 2011. If Vetere had any doubts about the figures, his triumphal tone didn't let on. "That's bigger than toys, that's bigger than candy, that's bigger than hardware, that's bigger than jewelry," he said. "If it were treated like a single retail segment . . . it would be the eighth-biggest retail segment in the United States." (I checked the industries he compared pets with, and he's right, even if it does depend on a fairly narrow definition that manages to exclude titans like Home Depot and Lowe's.)

With that degree of economic heft on display, I might have expected to be surrounded by crack reporters from the *Wall Street Journal* or the *Financial Times* when Vetere held a press conference on the expo's second morning to roll out the trade association's latest estimates. Instead, the audience consisted mainly of scribes from *Pet Product News, Cat Fancy,* and *Pet Business*. There was a certain amount of trepidation about the 2008 projections. The previous year had seen a high-profile scandal over tainted pet food, whose casualties included hundreds of animals as well as the reputations of several respected pet-food brands. The national economy was also in trouble, with a mortgage crisis that had led to an uptick in foreclosures. (One consequence: new cases of pet homelessness when new landlords forbade animals.) On day one of the expo, *Pet Business* reported that a survey of customers showed serious new worries about spending. Could the dog run be over?

Apparently not. Vetere unveiled new figures that showed the industry galloping along once again. He placed the projected spending for the year ahead at $43.4 billion, another 6 percent bump.

"Pet Market Proving Recession Proof," declared *Pet Business* on the convention's second day.

Self-cleaning litter boxes. Aquariums that can be hung like picture frames. NASCAR-branded pet beds. Snoop Dogg–themed pet hoodies. Birdcages shaped like castles. Talking food bowls. Dog kimonos.

Leashes that blink. Leashes that beep. Leashes that glow in the dark.

Organic dog treats. Kosher dog treats. Australia-themed dog treats. Dog treats sponsored by Dick Van Patten. Dog treats made from desiccated bull penis. Dog treats made from desiccated bull penis and then kneaded into yard-long braids.

GPS devices. Electronic doggie-door keys. Radio-controlled doorbells that ring when puppy wants a walk. Electric treadmills—a bargain at $499—for when you don't want to take him on one.

Gear that's proudly made in the USA. Gear that's sold under a sign that reads SHENZHEN HUACHENG SCI & TECH DEVELOPMENT CO.

Dog mineral water.

Cat mineral water.

Hamster/guinea pig mineral water.

Still more pet mineral water—but from Iceland! And in brushed-metal bottles, lest your animal absorb contaminants from the plastic!

Products to combat shedding. Products to combat "tear stains." Products to combat the smell of pet excrement. Products—"scientifically tested"—to combat the smell of pet excrement before it is even excreted.

Pet swaddles. Pet strollers. Pet diapers.

And I think I mentioned the ferret hammocks, right?

This, of all the subsectors of our vast economy, is the one that makes shoppers brave recessions? How could this be the industry that actually got a boost from calamities like the September 11, 2001, terrorist attacks or 2005's Hurricane Katrina? In my mind, much of this can be explained by a popular term I first heard at a Global Pet Expo: *fur baby*. "So many baby boomers like myself are getting pets to take the place of children who have walked away, gone to college," Vetere said. "We replace them with fur babies." What a leap: The conspicuous ornament of Thorstein Veblen's Gilded Age has become the twenty-first century's junior human; the faithful companion of old has turned into the furry ersatz child of modern times. Who better to hold on to when the world seems frightening?

People have always adored their pets, but a sheaf of survey statistics points to a striking change in what that love means. In 2001, 83 percent of American pet owners referred to themselves as their animal's "mommy" or "daddy." The number had been 55 percent as recently as 1995. In 2007, an authoritative survey of pet ownership by the American Veterinary Medical Association (AVMA) reported that half of American pet owners considered their pet a member of the family. APPMA's own survey the same year revealed that just over 70 percent of pet owners listed "like a child/family member" as a key benefit of dog ownership; cat owners were only slightly less enthusiastic. In 2008, the shrewd dog-culture magazine *The Bark* announced that 72 percent of its 110,000 subscribers regularly sing to their dogs. Even the names we give modern pets have followed their trajectory from man's best friend to America's fur baby. In 2007, VPI Pet Insurance, the nation's leading issuer of pet policies— more on that later—released a list of top names among the 450,000 animals it insures. So much for Fido, Spot, or Fluffy; VPI's policyholders, it turned out, had abandoned traditional four-legged monikers in favor of Max, Molly, Chloe, Lucy, and Jake, the sorts of names you might hear thrown around on the playgrounds of fancy Manhattan preschools. (Two of the top dog names, Jake/Jacob and Bella/Isabella, actually made the Social Security Administration's list of the year's favored human-baby names; Sophia/Sophie ranked ninth for females of both the human and feline species.)

By 2008 the quasi-parental self-conception among some

pet owners was sufficiently well known that San Francisco public health authorities launched a Web site called www .dogsaretalking.com. What did the adorable dogs pictured there have to do with human health? Nothing. But, the campaign argued, owners who got sick might prove unable to care for their fur babies: "Dogs need their people to go in for regular checkups, too." That same year, VPI celebrated the first "Pet Parents Day" on April 22.

Modern demographics have helped the trend along. As Vetere noted when we talked, the emptying nests of the baby boomers play a big role in the modern pet boom. So do the unfilled nests of folks like, well, me and my wife back when Murphy ambled in and took his place as the object of all our nurturing energies. Call us the DIPPies: Double Income, Pampered Pets. In 2007, some 70 percent of pet products and services were purchased by households without kids, up from 45 percent in 2000. The proportion of parents who have pets dipped slightly between 1991 and 2006; pet owning among singles and childless couples saw a bump. Compared to the cost of real kids, though, even the most coddled of the DIPPies' fur babies is a bargain. "They don't need the car, don't need gas," Vetere said. "It's actually a pretty good trade-off in the long run."

That's especially true for members of Vetere's organization. When 29 percent of pet owners report that they buy birthday presents for their dog and 42 percent say they buy Christmas presents for their cats, it's a good time to be in the pet industry. "Somebody pointed out to me yesterday that we no longer feel good rewarding them as pets," Vetere said. "That's not enough, because of the role they play. We have to reward them as humans. That's what makes us happy. Pets are happy. I could throw an old tennis ball to my golden retriever and he'd be thrilled. But *we* need more." Pass the organic dog treats, Pops.

The floor of Global Pet Expo turned out to be a rare place in pet-loving San Diego where pets were not welcome. No wonder: the row after row of new dog-treat lines could be enough to send even the most placid old hound into a tizzy. The human guests working the 250,000 square feet of exhibition space tend to be less excitable. As professional buyers for pet retail outlets, they're looking for products that will sell well, not those that smell well. Of course, there are a few random outsiders. We're easy to pick out. We're the ones walking around gaping at the spectacle of dog bed coolers and cat furniture warmers, the ones likely to receive mildly patronizing stares when we ask, say, why a certain line of Disney-themed canine clothing boasts about its "pre-faded" Mickey Mouse T-shirt. (The answer: "Well, the retro look is in.")

Actually, some of the people working the show look baffled, too. Word of Americans' pet spending habits spread in recent years like news of gold at Sutter's Mill in 1848, drawing people from all sorts of other industries who now shake their heads in amazement at their own customers. According to one market study, more than thirty "human-only" companies have entered the pet economy in recent years. At one pet-goods show I met an Indian entrepreneur whose Chicago-based business sells the stainless-steel bowls and plates used in subcontinental *thali* dishes. He has rebranded them, complete with bone imprint, as classy food bowls for pets. "When we ship it, Indian customs still lists it as utensils," said Shel Singh, who has thirty employees in his factory in Punjab state. "There's no category for pet goods." Singh said the workers back home are incredulous that Americans would spend $12.95 to feed their dogs out of dishes that Indians use to feed themselves for about thirty-five cents. And they're not the only ones. "I will tell you, my sister is married to an army officer, and in India we think of army officers as very sophisticated and worldly," Singh said, roaring with laughter. "But when they saw this dish, they took it to their house and put it on the table with curry and sauces!"

Odd though his new industry may seem to Singh's relatives, it is as firmly entrenched in the slipstream of globalization as any other. Its goods are the product of often complex international trade. Its retailers are increasingly likely to be national chains engaged in their own cutthroat competition, slashing prices to beneath anything a mom-and-pop boutique could afford. Don't let the big, wet eyes of the puppies in the TV commercials fool you; this is two-fisted capitalism for four-pawed customers.

On the production side, despite the occasional made-in-America boast, a huge proportion of the items displayed are made in China. That includes not simply food, where Chinese ingredients have been a source of much recent controversy, but all sorts of less controversial products: the mitten-shaped doggie clean-up bags, the bouncy balls that promise hours of fun playing fetch in the park, the Paris Hilton–style carrier bags for toting small dogs—Pekingese, even—around town. "You pretty much can't not do business with China" was how toy manufacturer Keith Benson, who travels from the Texas Hill Country to spend a couple of months a year at his Chinese facility near Shanghai, put it.

One big reason for that can be found in who's doing the buying from folks like Benson. While the expo may draw lots of mom-and-pop pet store operators, the sector has in the past few decades joined in the chaining of America. Petco, which was established as a mail-order veterinary supplies firm in 1965, opened its first retail store in 1976 and expanded outside its San Diego home base in 1980. A decade later, it hired a former Toys"R"Us executive and began gobbling up other regional pet-supply chains—twenty-one in all—as it expanded across the country. By 2000, when Petco broke the 500-store mark, it had $1 billion in sales. In 2008, it had 850 stores. Its Arizona-based archrival, PetSmart, has grown even bigger even faster. From two stores in 1987, it zoomed to nearly a thousand stores by 2008. About a quarter of them have added in-store veterinary clinics. Its shares are listed on NASDAQ. In 2007, it was six spots shy of a place in the Fortune 500.

The two titans make up 27 percent of America's nonfood pet-gear sales, compared with 18 percent for independent stores and lesser chains. Combine that with the additional 28 percent that shop at national mass merchandisers like Target and you have an enormous amount of power in a small number of firms—either cruelly squeezing the beloved indy pet store down the street or happily passing on savings to ordinary pet owners, depending on your view of these things. Either way, it's not easy for most stateside manufacturers, paying American wages, to hit the price points the mass retailers demand. Like our human babies, our fur babies are more and more likely to play with toys that come from China, low-budget workshop to the world.

Whether handmade by stateside artisans or mass-produced in Chinese factories, pet gear has existed about as long as pet keeping. In her wonderfully exhaustive history *Pets in America,* Katherine C. Grier notes that stores selling cages and collars, in addition to the animals themselves, proliferated in American cities as early as the 1840s. Subsequent decades brought other innovations we now take for granted. Mass-produced pet food dates from the 1870s, though it took a while to become widely popular. The first bag of kitty litter was produced in 1947. And postwar prosperity brought with it a whole host of new products, worthy and otherwise. A 2005 exhibit at the University of South Carolina's McKissick Museum, curated by Grier, featured examples of retro pet consumerism that would look right at home in a pricey vintage boutique: a purse-shaped plastic cage made of the Monsanto Corporation's "Lustrex" styrene plastic, its clean lines a fine example of space-age style; the Comb-a-Flea "Atomizer" comb, which promised with all the scientific optimism of that era to kill fleas and ticks; Hart Mountain brand hamburger-style horse meat for dogs, a perfect pet food for the age of TV dinners and Sunday pot roast.

You can find evidence of contemporary history in today's vastly larger pet aisle as well. Nearly any trend in human consumerism will soon appear in the animal market. Over the time I spent traveling for this book, this happened right before my eyes. In 2006 and 2007, as the national fascination with puppy-toting celebutantes crested, pet strollers and pet carriers, often in luxe tartan fabrics, were all the rage. A year later, amid fears about our environmental and nutritional health, it was all about being green, with every last food and treat and litter brand, and at least one line of stuffed animal toys, tarted up, honestly or otherwise, with words like *organic, holistic,* or *natural.*

A historian from the future, with no surviving evidence to go on save the inventory of a Petco superstore, would have a relatively easy time figuring out the tastes, needs, and neuroses of our human society, from contemporary takes on health and nutrition (all those novel "all-natural" vitamins and supplements suggest our wallet-emptying passion for wellness is tempered with a certain suspicion of traditional medicine) to modern concern with home aesthetics (you'll never go broke selling products that hide litter boxes in sleek-looking side tables, purport to reduce kitten fecal odor, or promise to keep your dog permanently off that nice new sofa).

There's a single, defining tension at the heart of the whole $43-billion tab: a three-sided conflict pitting anthropomorphization versus atavism versus solipsism, the desire to treat pets as humans versus the interest in allowing them to live as close as possible to what we imagine to be their natural state versus the less altruistic inclination to have the whole experience be easy for our human selves. That would be the fancy way of describing the interplay between the "fur" and the "baby" and the human holding the leash. Folks in the business of buying and selling use different language to describe the same phenomenon. One afternoon at the show I joined a roomful of retailers to listen to an industry analyst named David Lummis gaze into a crystal ball about what the Next Big Thing for pets might be. Rather than scouring the list of upcoming Hollywood movies for trendy retail ideas, he suggested focusing on a single illustration of pet owners' motivations. His PowerPoint presentation flashed a slide with three intersecting circles: One was marked *humanization*. Another was marked *health*. And the third was marked *convenience*.

The sweet spot for the would-be pet mogul, naturally, was right in the overlap.

TWO

Man's Best Friendster

Partying with the Queen of Pet Social Networking

Penny Lane Russo's doggie shower may not have been the absolute fanciest such affair in recent New York history—there's a lot of competition for that honor —but it was awfully nice all the same. There were two different cakes: a simple pink number with a yellow rubber ducky on top, and an architecturally elaborate delicacy shaped like yellow-and-pink play blocks arranged to spell out the word *baby*. Both, naturally, were chicken-flavored, Penny Lane's favorite. There was a lavish array of cookies as well, in all kinds of fun designs: baby-blue butterflies, girlish pink umbrellas, milky white baby bottles. The party favors included cone-shaped hats emblazoned with the image of the guest of honor, a four-month-old chestnut-and-white Cavalier King Charles spaniel with enormous black eyes. "I asked for everything you can think of," explained Rose Russo, the event's hostess and self-described mom to Penny Lane.

Penny Lane, Russo said, is "a real princess . . . She's like a little girl, packaged in a dog's clothing." For the party, Penny Lane was clad in a frilly pink sequined tutu with a tulle under-skirt and matching pink bows over her floppy ears. Her outfit coordinated perfectly with the cakes and the cookies. The dogs that had come to fete her were equally stylish. There were tuxedos and neckties, velvet dresses and festive sweaters. Considering that the menu also included servings of doggie ice cream, the pricey sartorial choices involved some risks, but when you're throwing a doggie shower you need to maintain certain standards.

At any rate, the two-legged guests had a buffet that could ease jitters about ice cream stains—or fights, or poop on the floor, or any of the other anxieties that might arise when you gather thirty or so dogs for a party. "The human guests got bub-blegum cigars, and the dogs got dog chewing cigars, and it was just the best party," said Elaine Lewis, who attended with a Chihuahua named Crystal. "We had a nice little spread with champagne and mimosas," Russo recalled. "Of course, that was just for the grown-ups. I mean, the humans."

At first glance, Russo may not fit the image of the sort of person who dresses her puppy up in frilly clothes. A forty-year-old former New York police detective, Russo grew up in Brooklyn, one of eight kids. But she always loved dogs. A vari-ety of them—as well as several cats and a chicken—used to wander in and out of her family's apartment, often "rescued" from the streets by one of her brothers. Later, as a detective, she took to strolling with police dogs while making undercover drug buys. Dealers, she said, would assume she was a local walking a dog and looking to score. She left the force in 2003, for health reasons, and decided to give the dog world a go. She set up a little dog-training and dog-grooming business in sub-urban Westchester County, where she moved with her new husband.

Not long afterward, one of Russo's clients was throwing a birthday party for her dog. Amused by the concept, Russo tagged along. She and the caterer, a woman named Ada Nieves, who had a part-time business hosting dog parties, struck up a conversation. Russo was eventually hired to work with Nieves's four Chihuahuas. The women became pals, which is easy to do with Nieves, who greets about every second person with the endearment "my love." (The others are greeted with the no less effusive "hon.") When Russo adopted Penny Lane a couple of years later, Nieves offered to throw her a party. It'd be fun, she said. Russo could invite her clients, and Nieves could invite some of her friends. They might drum up some business for each other, or at least make some new friends.

"It was my very first dog, so she threw a baby shower for me," Russo said. "Now everybody sees me and associates me with Ada. She's Penny Lane's dogmother, her godmother. She's the greatest."

If you own a toy-sized dog in the general environs of New York City, and you have an Internet connection, Ada Nieves may require no further introduction. From a studio apartment on the Lower East Side of Manhattan, the forty-three-year-old Puerto Rican has over the past few years emerged as the key interpersonal connector for a burgeoning canine social scene—a social director to the four-legged set. Among other things, she presides over the Manhattan Chihuahua group, with about eight hundred members, on the social-networking Web site Meetup.com. In this capacity, she organizes monthly get-togethers for owners of the small pooches. The gatherings began around 2002 with about a dozen people meeting in a park. By 2006, when Nieves organized a Chihuahua Christmas party that featured a Santa Claus and a mariachi band, they had blossomed into enormous affairs held in rented indoor dog runs. That same year, her Chihuahua group joined a handful of other small-dog online groups for a Circle Line cruise around

Manhattan that drew 250 pets and their owners. "It was all on the Internet," Nieves said. "Everyone found each other because they were searching on their dogs."

Offline, Nieves is no slouch, either. Most weekends find her at some event or other with one or more of her own dogs. It's not easy to converse at length with her at such gatherings. Nieves is constantly greeted by friends asking after her animals by name: Cinnabon Bon, Vanilla Salt, Tabasco Chili Pepper, and Tequila Bon. Her Web site is full of pictures of the pups, in various costumes, at gatherings all over the city: the Broadway Barks Benefit, the Times Square Dog Day Masquerade Contest, the Small Dogs Group Ice-Cream Social, the Barking Beauty Show, the Paws for Style Fashion Show and Celebration. At the 2006 dog prom in Tompkins Square Park, Cinnabon Bon won the award for best stud. At the Chi-loween Costume Parade a few months later, she and the foursome appeared in *Wizard of Oz*–themed outfits. One of the judges was a producer on Martha Stewart's TV show. Nieves was invited to appear on the show the following week; also-rans from the Chihuahua group were invited to come sit in the audience.

"There's just so much going on," she said. "It's like a social whirlwind having a Chihuahua. I feel like I know everybody."

So when Russo brought home Penny Lane in 2007, Nieves knew just what to do. She credits herself with having thrown New York City's first puppy shower a couple of years earlier. Since then, she'd started marketing the skill, throwing parties—sorry: "pawties"—and showers for owners across the city, and charging up to $1,500 a pop. But this was a friend. "I'm her godmother," she said. "Of course, I have to throw a party."

A year later, when I first met her at a Nieves-organized Chihuahua Christmas party, Russo's social world—and her professional one—had been transformed. "She has told her customers about me," explained Nieves. "I have told my friends and my customers about her. In the beginning we had completely different sets of people. And now, we have a friendship, so she has introduced me to her customers and her clients and her friends, and vice versa."

Russo isn't the only person whose sense of community has been shaped by a four-legged companion. It just so happened that the woman she befriended is an especially good example of one of our petcentric era's most interesting phenomena: pet social networking.

By the time Nieves shows up for the Chihuahua Christmas party, a couple of minutes before its scheduled start time at noon, there are already a dozen or so people, and a slightly larger number of Chihuahuas, milling about in the Greenwich Village doggie day care whose playrooms she has rented for the affair. Everyone lights up when Nieves trundles into the room. Her husband, Edgar, trails behind, lugging party supplies. He'll play Santa. Ada tells the assembled to sit tight and proceeds into the windowed playroom that will host the food and the Santa pictures. She sets up a cheese plate for the humans and a table topped with doggie treats. Edgar changes into a Santa getup; he's joined by a couple of young women who serve as Santa's helpers. Outside the play area a line of fifty or so Chihuahua-toting partygoers winds around a corner and through the aisles where the day-care center displays pet supplies available for purchase. "Merry Christmas!" Nieves exclaims.

Soon the festivities start in the center's "Jungle Party Room." Nieves stands at the door and takes admission—five dollars, to cover the rental cost for the facility—as the guests file in. By the time even a dozen dogs have entered, the space has descended into Chihuahua chaos, with a roomful of dogs running, jumping, humping, pooping. (The jungle room's trees may be fake, but the dogs don't always act like it.) The pet guests, for the most part, are dressed up: a Santa outfit here, a green "I've been naughty" sweater there, enough argyle in the small space to blind a cat. The humans are less elaborately decked out. But most of them are outfitted with at least one key accessory: a digital camera. As the room fills up, it makes an irresistible tableau for the photographers on hand—seventy tiny dogs, all in one place.

What do you do at a pet holiday party? Well, nothing all that different from what you'd do at a human holiday party. You chat with friends in the room, introduce yourself to strangers. There's always something to talk about. Indeed, after three yuletide hours with the Chihuahua folks, I had yet to overhear any conversation that veered very far from the particulars of dog ownership. There was a lot of cooing over outfits. *Oh my gosh! Look at Joey's holiday collar! Where did you find Barbie's sweater? Puppy is to* die *for today!* At least one such conversation got so involved that a participant didn't notice that his Chihuahua had snuck past Nieves and out onto Lafayette Street. After Nieves raised the alarm, one of the elves ran out and chased down the runaway.

I first bumped into Russo while I was gawking at the Chihuahua clambering over Santa's lap. She seemed to sense I was a newbie. "Have you ever seen anything like this before in your life?" she asked.

I had. I first met Nieves about six months before the Christmas gala. Back then, it was a hot and muggy New York summer weekend. Which, naturally, meant she was hosting a Chihuahua pool party. I'd spent the day hanging around Manhattan's sole canine swimming club, a small indoor pool in Chelsea. It wasn't quite the example of over-the-top Manhattanite pet-owning luxury that I'd earlier imagined it might be. Most of the dogs on hand were old and arthritic or otherwise hobbled; aquatic exercise was the only way for them to avoid becoming obese. Perhaps sensing my disappointment, the manager suggested I stay until a little later in the afternoon.

"That's when the Chihuahua people are coming," she said. "They tend to be memorable."

A few hours later, Nieves showed up with a doggie ice cream cake (made from rice milk, yogurt, and cream cheese) and a cabload of Chihuahuas. Before long, about forty other guests joined her in splashing around the pool with a similar number of dogs, several of them outfitted in stylish swimming goggles. Most of the swimmers came from a demographic—more *The View* than *Sex and the City*—whose members tend to be a bit hesitant when it comes to stripping down to a bathing suit before several dozen people in the middle of a big city. But the goofball pets, and the bond of ownership, seemed to help override those concerns. The party turned into something of a celebration for a Chihuahua named Eli, who had recently won a contest where owners submit pictures of their dogs and the winner appears on a box of Milk-Bone biscuits. His owner, Karen Biehl, had appeared alongside the dog on the back of the box; she wore a slinky blue dress, he a tuxedo. Nieves, perhaps unsurprisingly, counts Biehl as a dear friend. "Eli is our own celebrity," she gushed.

In Nieves's circle, pretty much every dog is a celebrity. The June crowd and the December crowd overlapped significantly. So, I'm told, did the Chi-loween crowd, the Thanks-Chi-Giving crowd, and the Saint Chi-trick's Day crowd. And each of those events, before too long, started to look like a Hollywood premiere, with flashbulbs popping.

"Oh, I never miss these things," explained Valerie White, a forty-eight-year-old illustrator who was at the Christmas party with her husband, Danny, fifty-one, and a seven-and-a-half-year-old Chihuahua named Zeena. Zeena came clad in a snowflake sweater, a Christmas gift from one of the other group members, part of a smaller group with whom she schedules doggie playdates on non-Meetup weekends. "I've been coming since the beginning, pretty much. Since 2002 I think it was. I've become good friends with Ada, and with Karen, who's Eli's owner, and Elaine and Angela and Beatrice. And the dogs. There's Bambi and her sister Daisy, and there's Puppy, with those great ears. And Sadie. And there's Petie over there in the military gear. And some of them are new. Oh, but there's Joey and Spock there, I know them, too. And Vanilla, of course, Ada's dog. We always get together with the dogs. We do a lot of e-mailing, about our lives and about the dogs. We're pretty close. We sort of come here more for us. Zeena seems to care less."

In another corner, Beatrice Kozak and Gail Margulies were deep in conversation. They were among the ten or so people who gathered in a park for one of the first Chihuahua gatherings, which they attended with their respective dogs Joey and Spock, so named because of his prominent—even for a Chihuahua—ears. Since then, Kozak, forty-five, and Margulies, fifty-two, had come to consider each other friends. After getting off work from her job at a radiology clinic, Margulies regularly walked over to Kozak's apartment to visit. "We had a lot in common, the same kind of personalities," Margulies said. "And it turned out we had to walk back in the same direction from one of the parks, and we just said, well, I'll see you next time. And we had ice cream at one of the places, with the dogs, on the way back from one of the Meetups. And then we just said, you know, why don't we get together sometime after one of the Meetups, and we got to be friends."

It's a story you hear all the time in Chihuahualand: urban anomie overcome by something as simple and obvious as love for a nice sweet dog. Nieves herself, the ultimate social animal, tells a similar tale: "I was invisible before the dogs. Now I never have any time. It's like a new family, all the Chihuahua people."

As Kozak and Margulies and Spock and Joey were making their outings to the pet-friendly ice cream parlor, both academia and big business were focusing some of their biggest craniums on the very phenomenon these owners and their dogs were acting out: How and why do people wind up in one another's orbits?

The dynamics of social interconnectedness have lately been a source of American worry and fascination. In 1995, a then-obscure scholar named Robert Putnam published *Bowling Alone,* an essay chronicling the decline of the clubs and institutions that knit society together. His titular example was bowling. Although the number of people who bowl had increased over the preceding two decades, the number of people who bowl in leagues had shrunk. Putnam argued that the decline of such forms of association heralded a hemorrhaging of the country's "social capital" in an age of mass media and suburban sprawl. The book-length version of the argument, published in 2000, became a best seller. Putnam was invited to Camp David to chat about the subject with President Bill Clinton.

The rise in rates of pet ownership—indeed, the fact that urbanites like Kozak and Margulies even have dogs—may be connected to the same trend. The University of Pennsylvania's James Serpell, who studies interactions between humans and animals, has argued that the explosive growth in the number of Americans who get pets is tied to the crumbling of other social support structures. He traces the acceleration in pet population to the mid-1960s, the same point at which Putnam's story of eroding social capital begins. Before then, pet ownership rose in ways that essentially mimicked population growth. If the decision to get a pet were simply a function of postwar prosperity and home ownership, the uptick might have commenced earlier.

"Social networks fragmented over forty years—there's more living alone, more divorce, more childless people, fewer people living in close geographic range of their families, and less community involvement," Serpell says. "And there has been a dramatic increase in pets . . . As we lose social support, as our relations become fragmented, we are using dogs to fill the gap."

How do they do so? Research going back decades shows people lean on pets for the obvious reason of keeping themselves company—and to very good effect: One study showed that pet-owning heart attack patients were four times more likely to survive than petless patients. Another experiment on hypertensive stockbrokers demonstrated that those who'd been given dogs as well as medication performed better on subsequent stress tests than those who'd only gotten the drugs. Other research shows that social disconnectedness even shapes the way we think about animals. In a fascinating 2008 article, University of Chicago professor Nicholas Epley and three colleagues determined that subjects who were less socially connected were more likely to attribute human characteristics— thoughtfulness, consideration, and sympathy, none of which are within the canine skills set—to pets. The same tendency to anthropomorphize helps sell everything from doggie sweaters to Nieves's catered birthday bashes.

Animals can also provide a way to overcome that same modern isolation—another thing researchers had noted well before Tequila Bon and the gang showed up in Nieves's apartment. One 1979 study of Swedish dog owners found that four in five of them agreed with the statement "The dog makes friends for me." Nieves's era, though, has seen a more organized approach to petcentric togetherness. In the first decade of the twenty-first century, anthropologist Lisa Jane Hardy spent two years in her neighborhood dog park watching people interact, using the research for a dissertation and a documentary film project that sketch out the full richness of a self-conscious dog-owning subculture. Hardy describes a world of complex rules, rituals, and archetypes. It's a place where people fall in love, make friends, do battle, and develop unique identitities. And you look mighty weird there if you don't have a dog.

In particularly dog-friendly areas, savvy businesses capitalize on the same phenomenon. With a dose of entrepreneurial moxie, the unsurprising idea that people befriend the folks they see every day at the dog park can be turned into something like the jam-packed "Yappy Hour" I visited one otherwise quiet summer night in Austin, Texas. Recognizing the college town's evolving style of dog ownership—you can't seem to sit down for a cup of coffee in the Texas capital without tripping over a leash, which itself is frequently attached to a dog who at that moment is slurping from the outdoor café's doggie water bowl—the bar's owner had figured out a way to turn dog owners' daily ritual into a moneymaking social spectacle: let the dogs in. So I met Todd the vizsla and Biscuit the (mostly) Lab. I'd come to a place where everybody knows your dog's name.

While idealists have fretted about social capital, capitalists have been trying to harness it. The questions of who transmits ideas, and how they get transmitted, helped turn Malcolm Gladwell's *The Tipping Point* into one of the most influential books of the new century. Among other things, Gladwell described a viral spread of ideas, and identified certain people as "connectors" who, intentionally or not, bring worlds together. "Sprinkled among every walk of life . . . are people with a truly extraordinary knack for making friends and acquaintances," Gladwell writes. "They are connectors . . . The closer an idea or a product comes to a connector, the more power or opportunity it has." Gladwell's "connector" is a perfect description of Ada Nieves.

Of course, Nieves's style of networking isn't simply about meeting people in the physical world. She happened to get her dogs during the decade of Facebook and Friendster and MySpace, the once-obscure social-networking Web site purchased by Rupert Murdoch for $580 million in 2005. It didn't take long before such sites developed their veterinary analogues. Take Fuzzter and PetCrash, both of which follow the

basic social-networking model of allowing users to create pro-
files and then link up with like-minded users to swap pictures
or arrange playdates. Naturally, the sites are laden with ads for
pet goods and services.

The granddaddy of the pet social-networking Web sites is
Dogster.com, which launched in 2004 and by 2007 had sur-
passed half a million users. Users post a lengthy profile of their
pet, complete with a description and a list of likes and dislikes.
They can search for acquaintances and list them among their
dog's pup pals. That done, users can also "leave bones" for special friends or use their credit cards to buy still more virtual
treats. By the end of 2007, the site hosted over 3 million pet pictures, uploaded by users. Some twenty thousand users had also
uploaded video of their pets to the sites; Dogster also had at least
ten thousand different affinity groups dedicated to different
breeds and regions. Advertisers steer users to everything from
dog-friendly hotels to local dog walkers.

The people in charge of Meetup, though, claim the point is
to bring people together face-to-face, as Nieves has used the
site to do. They've brought her in a couple of times as a consultant. "[There are] thousands and thousands of pet Meetups a
month in small towns, big towns, medium towns," said CEO
Scott Heiferman. "I've poked my head into some of these
Meetups . . . It's not that the people want to meet new people.
In fact, in today's world people want to avoid strangers. But
the dog is sort of the excuse. They come for the dog but stay
for the company . . . Dogster doesn't let the dogs sniff each
other's butts."

The night before the Christmas party, Nieves got about three
hours of sleep. She says she doesn't make any money from orga-
nizing the Meetup.com group or from any of her other pet social
scene appearances. Instead, Nieves makes her own relatively

modest living from catering dog parties, selling dog cakes, and occasionally hiring out her own pups as four-legged models. She also sells doggie couture; she's particularly fond of Chihuahua tuxedos. For the ladies, she's also designed, sewn, and sold canine knockoffs of outfits stars have worn to the Academy Awards ceremonies. Other than Oscar Night, Christmas is her busiest season.

Nieves had stayed up until three in the morning baking dog treats in the small kitchen of the fifth-floor walk-up she shares with her husband, Edgar, an army sergeant. The treats tend to look a lot like the goodies she used to make in a previous incarnation as a baker of specialty cakes for children's birthday parties: bright and shiny and sweet-looking, crafted into novel shapes. Over the years, she has made dog cakes shaped like footballs, cowboy hats, hot dogs, and a whole roast chicken. For one birthday dog, who was alleged to like nibbling on his owners' pasta, she made cupcakes topped with imitation spaghetti and meatballs. She's particularly proud of one cake creation that was shaped like a fluffy Maltese dog.

The contents would probably displease the average eight-year-old birthday party host. Her cakes are made of whole wheat and chicken broth, with an icing of cream cheese and honey. She says she has the recipes tested for safety at a lab. Lately, she's been trying to cut out wheat gluten, to which some dogs are allergic, by using oat flour. "Since I couldn't find any oat flour, what I'm doing is I'm grinding my own oatmeal. I'm just doing it in the kitchen. There's not much room for other things."

Nieves's home-entrepreneurial efforts go beyond her kitchen. The sewing machine and bolts of fabric are for her fashion line. The computer is for maintaining her Web presence, which includes the Meetup site, a Web site advertising her dogs' modeling skills, pages dedicated to selling her pet desserts and canine couture, and a page linking to video clips of her growing résumé of dog-oriented TV appearances. "I bought her a dog because I was going to Iraq" was how Edgar explained it. "I came back to this."

After waking up at six to finish the baking, Nieves was out the door, taking a taxi to an apartment building on Park Avenue to drop off a $160 dog birthday cake. "They're having their own party, so I'm delivering a cake." Next stop: Bryant Park, the ornate green space behind the New York Public Library. One of the merchants who set up shop in the park during the Christmas season sells Nieves's dog treats; she dropped off ten pounds of star-shaped, chicken-flavored cookies. Then it was into yet another cab for a ride to a boutique in SoHo that also sells her goodies.

The business part of the day done by late morning, Nieves went back home to get the gear for the sixty-five Chihuahuas who had RSVP'd for the Christmas gathering. Once it was finally under way, Nieves smiled, exhaustedly, from the doorway. She fielded a barrage of questions from partygoers on all sorts of Chihuahua-related subjects: food, fashion, behavior, training. She also spent much of the afternoon playing traffic cop for still more picture taking, this time with Santa and his helpers. Two days later, the whole Santa photo collection was up on her Web site.

Beneath the parties and the goofy fun, you can catch the occasional idealistic view of dogdom's social possibilities. The Chihuahua socializers are not upscale socialites or frivolous pet-obsessing spendthrifts. They're perfectly ordinary people, often far from wealthy, who've found community via tiny pets.

As the party wound down—Edgar had taken off his Santa costume and was busily repacking the unclaimed doggie treats—I spoke with the one guest besides myself who wasn't accompanied by a Chihuahua. Elaine Lewis's dog had died a month earlier. A medical-school administrative staffer, Lewis had been attending Nieves's Meetups, as well as gatherings of both the "small dog group" and the "tiny dog group," for a couple of years. I'd spotted her even before the party started, accepting hugs and good wishes from other guests milling around the kennel.

"I had a little black Chihuahua named Crystal who died November 15, heart failure," she explained. "Now I have two older dogs at home. I'm thinking I might also look into adopting another older dog."

Lewis said much of her social life was tied up with the pet groups, and that the dog people were "really supportive" after her recent shock. "It's a wonderful network of people."

Lewis recalled the day of Crystal's death: "First she had trouble breathing, and I took her to Fifth Avenue Vet, the emergency vet, and they tried to bring her around. They told me she was in heart failure. An hour or an hour and a half later, they said she wasn't going to make it, and I needed to come say good-bye. And I called Ada. I was crying, and she was crying.

"She sent out a mass e-mail," Lewis continued, welling up anew. "I got over one hundred e-mails and calls. People who I didn't even know knew me. They called, and people have sent me cards and brought me gifts—someone brought an urn, and they took her pictures and blew them up. I didn't think I could have gotten through it without all these people."

Just then, Nieves interrupted what had become a fairly intense chat. "Okay, everybody," she shouted. "I've got some extra stockings, with treats. Who wants extra treats?" Finding no takers among the stragglers, she plopped the stockings back in her bag. "Merry Christmas to me," she said.

THREE

It's Me *and* the Dog

The San Francisco Dog Wars and the Pet–Friendlying of America

For Adonis the rat terrier and Kelli the poodle and Brando the chow mix and Harold the Tibetan terrier mix, the cliffs and trails of San Francisco's Fort Funston are a slice of doggie paradise—a place to escape short leashes and concrete sidewalks, a wonderland of sniffing and scampering and exploring. On a sunny Thursday morning in January, I watched the four pals, who've been visiting the park together for years, frolic in the California sun. Above us, the sky was cloudless. Below us, the Pacific was sapphire-blue. And in every direction around us, nearly every square foot of the Northern California terrain was covered with dogs.

Dogs galloped in the parking lot. They wrestled on the lawn outside the old battery gates. They scampered along the hiking trail leading down to the beach. Pawing and digging, they traipsed right past the bollard-and-chain dividers meant to keep visitors off fragile indigenous flora. With small dogs and big ones, purebreds and mutts, energetic puppies and slowpoke seniors all romping free, the scene could serve as a television commercial for an especially wholesome line of pet food—a picture guaranteed to melt any heart.

Except, apparently, Matt Zlatunich's. To hear Zlatunich tell it, the old fort whose sixteen-inch guns once protected San Francisco from foreign invaders has been seized by a dangerous new horde, one that now threatens to overrun the entire city: Adonis, Kelli, Brando, and Harold, and thousands of other off-leash dogs.

A city firefighter and an avid bird-watcher, Zlatunich took me to Fort Funston to watch the invasion in action. Though it was a weekday, there were probably a hundred dogs in view, including six who were lapping water from six different stainless-steel bowls laid out in front of the drinking fountain. Don't let Zlatunich catch you cooing at them, either; the way he sees it, the dogs—or, rather, their human owners—have spoiled what ought to be a pristine home to threatened species like the bank swallow, the Forster's tern, and especially the endangered western snowy plover. "Just look at this," he said, sighing as we stared down the trail to the beach. "Look at that collie, on the wrong side of the fence. Where's the person who's the guardian? I don't even see a person there. The bank swallows are right beyond the fence. Look at those pawprints, they go right in there, right where you're not supposed to go. You can see it's not just a single, isolated incident. It's a daily thing. Part of the park experience is the sounds you hear, the aromas. What do you hear? If the dogs weren't barking, you'd hear the ocean. And what do you smell? . . . You can see how much of the habitat is not really viable habitat anymore. I haven't walked these trails for years. A lot of bird-watchers used to come here, but you can't do anything else because of the dogs."

Indeed, over several visits to the park, I counted exactly two visitors who weren't accompanied by a pet. One was Zlatunich. The other was me. "It's like dog camp here," he concluded. "They've completely taken over."

Fort Funston is the archetypal example of what Zlatunich and an array of allies see as the canine takeover of San Francisco. But it's hardly the only one. Zlatunich and I spent the better part of a morning in his beat-up Jeep Cherokee visiting spots where man and dog squabble over urban real estate. At the beach off Crissy Field, in the picturesque former military base known as the Presidio, we stared through his high-powered telescope at a plover, one of a dwindling number of the endangered birds that roost in the city over the winter. A conservation group had placed a color-coded band on the bird's leg to identify it. One of the group's volunteers was on the beach doing a bird survey, something Zlatunich regularly does as well. "Oh, that's lime-white-red-red," said Zlatunich, peering through his scope. "Have you seen lime-white-yellow-yellow today?"

Unlike the situation at Fort Funston, everyone agrees that the area where lime-white-red-red stood was off-limits to off-leash dogs, though Zlatunich said the rule is regularly violated. For an example of what would happen if such zoning were dropped entirely, he turned his scope toward the eastern edge of the beach, where dogs are allowed: no plovers. "It has such an effect," he said.

The battle is even fiercer down the coast a couple of miles, at Ocean Beach, the sandy stretch where the city's Richmond and Sunset neighborhoods meet the Pacific. Though signs warn visitors to leash their pets, the handful of dogs on the beach today ran free. In the past, people have been ticketed for such offenses, only to have activists take their cases to federal court, where the citations were overturned on technicalities. The rules have since been clarified, but Zlatunich said authorities remain gun-shy. From a boardwalk, we stared through the telescope at a group of plovers. The birds, Zlatunich explained, were supposed to be resting and fattening themselves up before flying off in the spring; anything that might cause them to abruptly take flight thus serves to further endanger them. As we spoke, a surfer and his off-leash black Lab bounded past, causing birds to scatter. "Imagine that twenty, thirty, forty times a day," Zlatunich said. "It destroys their habitat. The dog people think they're for the environment. But what they're doing is not natural at all. And it's just against the law. That's all we're saying: Obey the law."

The leash fights also extend to ordinary city parks where the clashes concern recreation preferences, not threatened species. In the Sunnyside neighborhood, one antidog activist has been known to watch through binoculars until someone improperly unleashes a dog, at which point the police are called. In vest-pocket-sized Duboce Park, the divide over dog issues was so bitter that the neighborhood association hired an outside mediator—something it never had to do for any other issue. On the windswept hilltop of Bernal Heights Park, the professional dog walkers who drive in with six or eight dogs at a time are convinced that a recent redesign that cut most of the parking spaces was less an effort to free up extra parkland than an underhanded scheme to force them out. The list goes on.

Zlatunich, defender of the bank swallow and the western snowy plover, is also a character type that locals have come to know well in the last decade and a half: a foot soldier in the Great San Francisco Dog Wars. Over the past decade and a half, battles over dogs have convulsed the city's politics, leading to several federal lawsuits, a 1,500-person march on city hall, and an array of allegations that one or both sides of the conflict are guilty of racism, pollution, homophobia, environmental extremism, child endangerment, Big Brotherism, and puppy hatred. Not to mention the failure to pick up poop. Mayor Gavin Newsom joked that "we'll probably solve the issue of homelessness before we're able to solve the dog issue."

Neither a lawyer nor a politician, Zlatunich has nonetheless engaged in his share of combat. Over the years, he's filed some seventeen police reports having to do with the animals. (He gave me a list of them, complete with notes such as *"4-15-2007: Two off-leash Laberdoodles* [sic] *harassing injured Western Grebe in WPA at Crissy Field. Owner refuses to leash uncontrollable dogs. Necessary to kick lunging dog. Police called to scene. NO CITATION ISSUED!"*) He's attended meetings, written letters, and spent hours at the far end of his telescope as he helped the Golden Gate Audubon Society compile voluminous reports that detail the threat to the plover. (One report he showed me outlined the canine menace in clinical, mathematical terms: 2.35 disturbances per survey hour, as opposed to 0.35 from human walkers and 0.3 from human joggers.) Zlatunich—who strikes me as someone not to be messed with—claims he has been regularly menaced by dog owners for his trouble.

Zlatunich is just one of a number of leash-law proponents who have felt the wrath of dog owners. Activist Arnold Levine told a reporter in 2007 that dog excrement had been thrown on his lawn and in his car as a result of his advocacy; he eventually left the city.

Off-leash proponents also feel like victims. They accuse folks like Zlatunich of wanting to leash up humans along with pets. The Ocean Beach Dog organization's Web site depicts an ideal day at the beach—with dogs frolicking in the water—beneath a stirring quotation that Thomas Jefferson probably never imagined would someday apply to dog recreation: "When the people fear the government there is tyranny. When the government fears the people there is liberty." Like combatants in actual war zones, the dueling sides sometimes have the same targets. Where antidog activists blast the park service for being too pusillanimous vis-à-vis off-leash scofflaws, off-leash activists depict its rangers as jackbooted thugs on a "jihad," ever scheming to remove four-legged family members from its terrain. In standard local-politics fashion, the criticism gets intensely personal, with the park superintendent Brian O'Neill derided on one activist site as "Lyin' Brian."

At times, the sloganeering—I saw more than one bumper sticker at Fort Funston that read I HAVE A DOG . . . AND I VOTE—has given the impression that the policing of unleashed dogs is San Francisco's single biggest political issue. Even if that's not true, it may be the most volatile one. "It's the third rail of city politics," the local Animal Control director, Carl Friedman, told me. "You don't even want to touch it."

San Francisco is named for the patron saint of animals, Saint Francis of Assisi, and dogs have played a significant role in its modern politics. In the 1970s, Supervisor Harvey Milk—the first openly gay elected official in any big city in the country—rose to prominence on the prosaic issue of getting the government to do a better job cleaning up dog poop. Though they mirror similar controversies elsewhere in the country, the twenty-first-century battles over leash laws feature a level of fury that no other municipality has matched. At the root of the Great San Francisco Dog Wars are a few demographic facts that make the city by the bay unique. For one thing, it is one of the few big cities on earth where dogs outnumber children: City officials estimate that there are 120,000 canines within its 46.7 square miles. Census figures cite 110,233 human children in the same chunk of territory. That's around 14 percent, about half the national average, and enough to certify San Francisco as DIPPie paradise. Without children to care for, all that free-floating nurturing energy has to land somewhere.

Enter Adonis and Kelli and Brando and Harold.

Another reason for the exodus of children also helps explain the passion around dog issues: San Francisco is a very expensive city. With average home prices that hover around $800,000, it's not an easy place to bring up a brood even if you want one. The city's wealth and its tradition of social tolerance leave San Francisco with fewer examples of the sorts of topics—crime, blight, discriminatory laws—that grab activist attention elsewhere. Without urban war zones or social bigotry to obsess over, all that free-floating political energy also has to land somewhere.

Enter Adonis and Kelli and Brando and Harold's need to romp in the park.

It's easy to see the dog wars as a case of a liberal blue-state oasis veering toward self-parody: Where else but the Bay Area could environmental groups wage political war against the Society for the Prevention of Cruelty to Animals? How left-coast do you have to be for civil libertarians to view a *park ranger* as a modern-day Bull Connor? But San Francisco's dog politics are not some patchouli-scented vestige of Haight-Ashbury. Rather, they date to the 1990s, as the region underwent a tech boom, the country underwent a radical upgrade in how it treats pets, and the creaky wheels of local government struggled to adapt. For all the revolutionary language, San Francisco's dog wars are to a large extent a classic case of different groups grappling over a scarce resource—in this case, space. It's the basic stuff of urban politics, the type of thing that has occupied ward pols dating all the way back to Boss Tweed's New York.

Not that the circus that followed the 2001 proposal to change city leash laws reminded anyone of old-time machine politics. The first proposed change in thirty years involved identifying up to eighteen new spaces for fenced-in dog runs beyond the seventeen already designated dog parks within the city system. But it also included plans to start cracking down on those who let their dogs off leash in the city's 174 remaining parks. The idea came about after prodding from people such as Marybeth Wallace, who worked with a youth-advocacy group.

"No one else could use the parks with all the dogs," Wallace told me. "It felt unsafe to a lot of people."

But, as the census figures indicate, evoking kids doesn't necessarily make good politics in San Francisco: 2,400 public comments flowed in over a single month, many of them furious. "I completely oppose the draft dog policy and I will not allow my dog and [me] to be penned in like criminals," wrote David Kulick, a resident of the area around Mission Dolores Park, itself a hotbed of controversy about off-leash dogs. "I pledge civil disobedience before I will be degraded in such a manner." The San Francisco Dog Owners Group (SFDOG) organized a march on city hall on top of its bimonthly "Critical Mutt" rallies (motto: "Speak Now or Forever Hold Your Leash"). The initial proposal was shelved, but a year later the city's recreation board again took up the idea. Some one thousand people filled the chambers while others watched on video from an adjacent room as the board's chairman tried in vain to silence an enraged, epithet-shouting crowd. After the controversial new rules were finally adopted, a pro-dog member of the Board of Supervisors—San Francisco's city council—introduced a measure to redesignate all city parkland legally off-leash. It didn't get anywhere. But the next citywide election saw the emergence of DOGPAC, a group influential enough that local pols vied for its endorsement.

For all the passion displayed over neighborhood parks, an even bigger struggle has involved an area officially beyond the bureaucratic control of those local pols, the stunning Golden Gate National Recreation Area (GGNRA). The canine battles in the federally owned terrain that includes Fort Funston, Ocean Beach, and Crissy Field involve the trickier question of whether the environment can handle the contemporary wants of dog-loving humans. Instead of a simple tug-of-war over space, it's a scientifically complex, philosophically charged debate about human stewardship over the earth, and what sort of sacrifices that stewardship demands. The basic disagreement is this: Dogs, say environmentalists, are particularly destructive park visitors, digging up fragile shrubs and chasing delicate wildlife. Predictably, that doesn't sit so well with many owners, who view an outdoor romp with the pup as a solidly green pastime, a respite from our pollution-belching daily lives. That they're both partially right hasn't made the struggle any easier.

Thus did the environmental portion of the dog wars open with the odd spectacle of the ASPCA tossing brickbats at the Audubon Society. When a ban on off-leash dogs at Fort Funston was first proposed in 1995, no less a figure than the then head of the city SPCA said dogs were being unfairly blamed for erosion actually caused by storms. "We get angry when we hear that dogs are responsible for the weather," Richard Avanzino said at one meeting. "And we would like to point out that these are urban parks in the middle of a city. This is a 'recreation area,' it's not the 'Golden Gate National Pristine Environment.'" Longtime local Audubon Society leader Arthur Feinstein told me that what dog lovers had done to the park was "an insult." The park service backed down, for a time. Predictably, Avanzino was not much more charitable two years later, when officials floated the idea of banning off-leash dogs from Ocean Beach, something they said was crucial to protect the snowy plover. Decrying the park service's "gross arrogance," Avanzino vowed civil disobedience. "You can come visit me in jail," he told the *San Francisco Chronicle*.

The controversies have more or less followed the same lines ever since. Outside environmental groups such as the California Native Plant Society and the Center for Biological Diversity press for dog bans in the name of threatened flora and fauna; off-leash enthusiasts push back in the name of freedom and recreation—and speculate that ban advocates are playing environmental Chicken Little simply because they don't much like dogs. The park service, stuck in the middle, has embraced, waited on, or dropped a series of policies in the face of protests, lawsuits, and logistics. When I visited San Francisco in early 2008, advocates were gearing up for a battle over yet another proposed set of leash arrangements. There was little reason to assume it would be the final word: Over a decade of engagements, off-leash advocates have been remarkable for their willingness to fund pricey federal court challenges to various short-lived park service policies. As early as 1997, the movement acquired a martyr of sorts, Michelle Parris, a professional dog walker who was stopped by rangers after letting five dogs off leash in the Presidio. An argument ensued, then a twenty-miles-per-hour chase of the car in which Parris and the dogs were traveling. She was ultimately convicted of knowingly breaking the law, but only after a trial that prompted a protest march to the federal office building and so many spectators that it had to be moved to a larger courtroom.

One measure of how hard it would ever be to curb off-leash recreation comes via a DVD given to me by Sally Stephens, the current president of SFDOG. The footage depicts a January 2001 meeting of a GGNRA advisory panel. The body is debating yet another set of proposals on dogs and leashes. It's a rainy night, and yet an overflow crowd has showed up. You can see some of them outside the windows, in the rain. Chants of "Let Us In!" and "No Leashes!" drown out some of the witnesses. Speaker after speaker attests to the vital importance of the park's off-leash areas, particularly Fort Funston. Skeptical board members are jeered. Eventually, a member of the city Board of Supervisors stands to offer a blunt warning: If the feds boot off-leash dogs out of GGNRA, he says, city hall might decide to repossess the land and evict the feds instead. The crowd goes wild, chanting his name: "Gavin! Gavin! Gavin!" It's Newsom. Two years later he was the city's mayor.

"I'm not saying it was directly connected or anything," Stephens told me. "But it was pretty cool."

By Saturday morning the weather was even better, and there were probably four hundred dogs at Fort Funston. I was there for a hike with Linda McKay, Karin Hu, and Anne Farrow— the companions, respectively, of Brando and Harold, Adonis, and Kelli. All three women, and all four dogs, are veterans of the Great San Francisco Dog Wars. McKay, who leads the Fort Funston Dog Walkers group, was among the stomping masses at the pivotal park advisory board meeting ("It was like a rock concert"), helped organize DOGPAC ("We had a meeting . . . and all these candidates were there, hat in hand—it was incredible"), raised tens of thousands of dollars for legal fights, and still runs monthly cleanups at Fort Funston ("After I've spent five hours serving coffee, buying doughnuts, and doing the cleanup, don't let your dog poop in front of me").

Nothing so dramatic was on the agenda today. We were simply taking a walk with the pups: down a trail toward the beach, up and around a couple of hills, underneath a canopy of old Californian trees, and back to the park entrance, with its postcard ocean views. Everyone had fun, especially the dogs. But I had to ask why, with all the problems of the world— even with all the problems of the world's canines—they would sink so much time and money and passion into a quarrel over leashes. McKay is an information technology professional who commutes an hour every day to work and back; Hu is a college teacher; Farrow is retired ("until I got into dog politics"), but could have picked a pastime involving less interpersonal rancor. How much is a canine walk in the great outdoors worth?

Their answers point to a relatively new development that makes the leash issue so confusing to outsiders: the centrality of dogs in the lives of ordinary people. "My life would be completely different without someplace like this, where I can come up here at nine-thirty and just stay for hours," said McKay. She cited sociologist Ray Oldenburg's *The Great Good Place,* a book about the importance of "third places" in people's lives. "You've got your work, you've got your home, and you've got this other place where everybody knows your name. It's like *Cheers,"* McKay explained. "This is our life," said Hu. And, they've decided, it's a life worth fighting for.

That's the sort of talk that drives leash proponents bonkers. To Brent Plater, an environmental lawyer who has repeatedly clashed with McKay's group over the years, the issue is a straightforward matter of land use; turning it into an emotionally loaded question of preserving one's way of life, he maintains, is an elaborate dodge. "Here it is framed as a civil rights issue, where animals have some inherent right to run off leash," said Plater. "If the dog is not allowed to run off leash, then not only are the dog's rights impacted, but [owners'] rights to even be present are impacted. So that if leash laws are required, we're excluded from the park." (Plater insists he's a softie when it comes to dogs. As I interviewed him in his law office, he cuddled Charlotte, a disabled white Chihuahua-terrier mix he adopted from a rescue group.)

In a way, the fight represents a liberal, urban analogue to the National Rifle Association's battles against all gun control or the snowmobilers pushing to open up Yellowstone National Park to their gas-guzzling vehicles. It's a case of people making one activity central to their identity, and viewing all efforts to regulate that activity as un-American plots to control their very identity as a class of people. It's a short hop from that view to the Bill of Rights rhetoric that often dominates both the national debate about guns and the discourse of the Great San Francisco Dog Wars. And it's a rhetoric that makes compromise especially difficult.

Two days after Newsom's star turn at the park advisory board meeting, San Francisco was transfixed by the gruesome death of a local woman named Diane Whipple, who was mauled to death by a pair of Presa Canarios who lived with neighbors in her apartment building. A ferocious breed of guard dogs, with cropped ears and massive heads, Presas are also known as "Canarian Dogs of Prey."

Objectively, Whipple's death was unrelated to the leash-law issue. She was killed indoors, not in a park; one of the killer dogs was even leashed at the time. But as the horrific details of the mauling came out—the dogs were being raised for an Aryan Brotherhood member then serving prison time; their guardians had ignored previous complaints about their aggressiveness—critics saw a rhetorical opportunity. The deadly dogs had, at times, been allowed to romp, sans muzzles, in local parks. Couldn't that strange dog in your neighborhood park be equally dangerous?

That tone of some of the antidog talk mirrored standard conservative criticisms of libertine San Francisco. As with sex, so it might be with dogs: Society abolished all the rules, and look what they got? Teen pregnancy and STDs; poop in the park and bites on the face.

The more nuanced truth is that the city's structural responses show a place grappling to create structures that would let it deal pragmatically with the enhanced status of pets in modern society. As such, it may well prove yet another example of Californian trend setting. During the years of San Francisco's dog wars, the rest of the country has also seen all sorts of institutions, from hotel chains to emergency-response agencies, from workplaces to battered-women's shelters, rewrite their rules to deal with contemporary pet keeping—a coast-to-coast phenomenon you could call the pet-friendlying of America.

Take the travel industry. For years, one downside of having a pet was that it made it harder to take off for the weekend. It's much easier now. Responding to the customer, numerous upscale hotels now permit dogs. Seeking out the fanciest of them, I blew a hefty chunk of my book advance for a night with Murphy at the Loews Regency on Manhattan's Park Avenue. Our $619 tab included a $94 charge for the hotel's in-house pet sitter. (The doggie biscuit on the doggie bed was complimentary.) Previous guests, a concierge informed us, included a much more famous Saint Bernard: Beethoven slept here. For less stratospheric budgets, the popular Web site pettravel.com lists more than thirty-five thousand pet-friendly accommodations from coast to coast. In 2005, Midwest Airlines became the first airline to offer pet frequent-flier miles—three round-trips earn a free flight in the pet-friendly skies. One good destination might be Phoenix, whose Sky Harbor airport has its own dog-walking area for pet-toting travelers. One Saturday afternoon, I watched a brown schnauzer named Cherokee amble toward the run, accompanied by a seventy-seven-year-old Minnesotan named Tim. A snowbird who winters in Arizona, Tim was headed back to Minneapolis for a funeral. Why take the dog with him? "Where else would I put him, a kennel?" Tim said. "He travels with me."

The nonvacationing world has also made its adjustments. Pet-friendly offices, once the stuff of 1990s dot-coms that also featured break-room pinball machines and free ice cream sundaes, became common enough by 2006 that the job-search Web site SimplyHired.com added a filter that allowed job hunters to seek out work that would let them bring their dog along. The trend, or at least a portion of it, had reached far from Silicon Valley. I visited the offices of the industrial-services corporation DBI, which builds and maintains grassy highway islands, on 2007 Take Your Pet to Work Day. A manager told me the annual June spectacle was sufficiently morale boosting, and sufficiently nondistracting, that it could become an everyday thing. The company is located in Hazleton, Pennsylvania, better known for a stridently anti-immigration mayor than for creative-class businesses.

Institutions that deal with catastrophes have also shifted their rules to reflect the pet-smitten world of the people they're supposed to be helping. In 2008, the American Humane Association announced Pets and Women's Shelters (PAWS), a new initiative to open up women's shelters to pets. Researchers had found one reason given by women for not leaving abusive households was that they couldn't take their animals with them. Shelters by and large didn't permit pets, and many women were afraid of what violent spouses would do to the animal left behind. The Shelter for Abused Women and Children in Naples, Florida, reported that a hundred pets a year stayed at the pet-friendly facility it opened in 2003. In 2006, Maine became the first state to authorize judges to include pets in domestic-protection restraining orders.

Likewise, the realization in the wake of 2005's Hurricane Katrina that many people refused to flee because they were forbidden to bring animals to shelters or on evacuation vehicles prompted Congress a year later to pass a law requiring local and state disaster plans to include provisions for pets. The situation shouldn't have surprised anyone who closely followed events after the September 11, 2001, terrorist attacks, when the closure of lower Manhattan left many pet owners terrified that animals stranded in apartments would starve to death. Three days later, a shuttle that was supposed to escort the frantic owners to pick up their pets was delayed by President George W. Bush's arrival in the city. "It's not like he has a cat down there or anything," a woman named Christina Coleman said.

Back in San Francisco, where the dog wars were in a relatively quiet stage during the second half of the decade, activists think future troubles can likewise be averted through enlightened new government policy. In the city parks, a commission had helped sort out some new geographic arrangements to mollify off-leashers and anti-off-leashers alike. Duboce Park, where dog acrimony once drew a documentary film crew, was finishing off a $200,000 renovation that delineates (but doesn't fence) dog and nondog areas. The park's old nickname—Dog Poop Park—is fading. The cops still aren't writing a lot of tickets for off-leash dogs, but the fine for dog poop is up to $319. (The human variety will cost you only $90.97.) Either way, officials say, the complaining has ebbed. And out in the GGNRA, the plans of officials and environmentalists to forbid off-leash dogs are now moving slowly through a complex public-comment period.

Stephens, the leader of SFDOG since 2005, predicts things will get hot again once that period ends, but in the meantime she's hoping to harness the power of the dog lobby to get the city to invest in dog education. Good-bye, "don't fence me in." Hello, "petiquette lessons." "There should be accessible and affordable dog training for everybody," she says. "Every recreation center should be having dog training and dog safety classes." The goal would be a new form of government licensing—a "canine good citizen test"—where certified dogs would be allowed off leash wherever their owners wanted. It may sound like a bureaucratic nightmare, but federal pet-evacuation plans seemed weird not so long ago, too. For Stephens, it's an exit from the dog wars. "My whole thing is, education is the way out of a lot of these things."

But as Stephens and I visit Mission Dolores Park, that still seems a ways off. A compromise, she says, has led to a rough leash-law peace: The pooches are supposed to be in one of the upper corners of the park, up the hill from picnickers and kids. For the most part, the rule is observed. At least it's being observed more carefully than marijuana laws during our visit. A cloud of smoke billows by as we stare down at the park, where an errant small black mutt has run into one of the supposedly off-limits areas and is sniffing around a couple who are lying on a blanket. They shoo the pup away and go back to sleep. "We all accommodate," Stephens says. "That's what it's all about. Well, until the next big fight."

Of all the institutions San Francisco has erected to help navigate the controversies of this new pet-friendly world, the most celebrated is probably municipal dog court. Though it doesn't deal with park poopers or leash scofflaws, the court—technically known as the San Francisco Police Department's Vicious and Dangerous Animal Unit—is supposed to head off tomorrow's dog maulings before they happen. I visited the courtroom for one of the weekly hearings shortly after my ride-along with Zlatunich. The scene could not have been more different. In a couple of hours, I'd gone from a PBS nature documentary to an episode of *Judge Judy,* complete with family feuds, neighborhood warfare, and various accusations of drunkenness, insanity, not caring for ailing parents, and living in an eyesore. "We see it all here," said police sergeant William Herndon, who conducts the sessions.

The hearings, mandatory for any dog that has been the subject of police reports about aggression, are no joke; for animals deemed incorrigible, Herndon has the death penalty at his disposal.

One of the day's cases involved Jose Barcelo, whose neighbor had complained to Animal Control that Barcelo was unable to control his allegedly threatening dog, which Animal Control had taken into custody. The dog turned out to be a Chihuahua named Pita. The neighbor hadn't shown. In court, Barcelo spoke through an interpreter. Herndon asked him if the charges were true. A long response followed. Though Barcelo spoke in Spanish, his body language, notably the circling motion he made with his finger at the side of his head, was international. "He's claiming that he has been told that this person has mental problems," the interpreter said. "Well, please tell him this," Herndon said. "Just ask him to make sure to be as diligent and careful as possible around this person, to try to keep his dog as far as possible away from her." With that, he ordered Pita released without official conditions; she was produced, in a cat carrier, from a back room. Barcelo left with the dog under his arm.

The matter of Jaws, Anthony Kim's pit bull, was less open-and-shut. Walking on a leash, the dog had lunged at and gashed another dog. Though Kim had paid the other dog's veterinary bills, its owners now wanted Kim's dog muzzled. Kim explained that his dog was raised to be a sweet boy who would never hurt anyone. "Well, how did he get the name Jaws?" Herndon deadpanned. He ordered a professional behavior evaluation. "Something's happened, something is triggering this behavior with your dog, so we're going to have the behaviorist at the shelter look at him. She's going to give a report, tell you what's happened, and recommend some things for you so you don't have these problems again. It's actually a good thing," Herndon said. He told Kim to keep the dog muzzled for the time being. "I'm not going to order him euthanized . . . If I get a report that something's happened and he's not muzzled, you're going to have a much bigger problem."

Evaluations were also ordered in the case of Kodiak the rottweiler (one brother had brought a vicious dog complaint against another; the testimony soon devolved into family acrimony about who was spending more time caring for a sick parent) and Ted the mutt (that session included allegations by one neighbor of improper home renovations carried out by another, who happened to own the dog) and Fat Boy the German shepherd. Fat Boy had bitten an eight-year-old named Antonio "on my bottom," according to the boy. Fat Boy's owner wasn't home at the time, but her two sons were. Antonio, who was first to speak, identified the lads as his friends Peppy and Poppy. He explained that he'd gone out to play with the friends and encountered the dog in the street outside their house. "Peppy and Poppy were throwing little rocks at him to get him off me." A neighbor called 911; Animal Control showed up to file a complaint against the dog's owner, who testified that Antonio hadn't been allowed to come over and play. Perhaps recognizing that Antonio wasn't the one on trial, she added that Fat Boy was a nice dog. Herndon wasn't convinced, prodding the owner about where she kept the dog (the backyard, though he was said to be allowed in the house) and how the dog had gotten out (an accident). In the end, police were ordered to Fat Boy's house to make sure the fence was secured. His owner was also instructed to keep the dog muzzled when he was out of the house. But the dog was spared, at least for now. "We might see this one again" after the evaluation, Herndon said later.

Could something like dog court also solve the leash wars? A fifteen-year veteran of the animal beat, Herndon told me he never wants to add that portfolio to his workload. For him, dealing with people whose dogs have done actual, verifiable harm is tough enough. "People treat them like it's their kid," he said. "And you get some kid that's out of control in public, you'll think twice before saying something to the parent. Same thing here. So it takes a court to talk about it."

Animal Control chief Friedman sees the desire for new animal laws, both the pet-friendly sort and the not-so-pet-friendly sort, as part of a modern tendency to police things that were once informal. A native New Yorker, he arrived in San Francisco fresh off an involuntary tour of duty in Vietnam. Freedom was in the air. Jimi Hendrix was playing in a park. Daily life here, unlike back home, didn't seem to be buried under a thick membrane of nitpicking regulations. As we talked, he explained the changes as logical and maybe even appropriate, but he still sounded wistful. To him, the dog wars are a sign of his beloved city becoming more, not less, like the rest of the country. "Growing up on the East Coast, the first thing you see when you get to the beach is a sign that says NO," he said. "No fires, no camping, no nothing. It was different here. But now we're a little less live-and-let-live. There are a lot of reasons for that, safety and it's crowded here and so on. But that's what's going on with the leash thing." Even the freedom to run free, it seems, requires a complex web of rules.

FOUR

Trading Up

Who Says You Can't Teach an Old Dog New Luxury?

I'll happily go out on a limb here and declare Manfred of Sweden the world's most fashionable Yorkie. His outfits run the gamut from blue fleece hoodie to red tartan coat. One day you might find him in his khaki M*A*S*H jacket, the next day in a leopard-print robe and silver KumKum necklace. As a veteran of runway shows from his native Scandinavia to Japan to Los Angeles, he also affects the nonchalance of the jet-setter. When I first met him, at a Pet Fashion Week cocktail party in Manhattan, the four-year-old superstar looked not at all fazed by the pulsing pink lights or throbbing music, or by the fact that the fashion line bearing his name was about to debut a colorful new leather look inspired by the Beatles' *Sgt. Pepper's Lonely Hearts Club Band*. "Feel the leather," Manfred's owner and biggest fan, Bjorn Gärdsby, told me. "It's like butter, or a woman, whatever your preference is."

For years, two-legged versions of Manfred have been the toast of the town during the annual—human—fashion week in Bryant Park, where they strut their stuff each September before audiences that include celebrities and fashion royalty. Since 2006, their pet-industry analogues have gathered in late August a few blocks to the south. During Pet Fashion Week, hip designers like Gärdsby dominate a surreal parallel universe where strip-mall behemoths like Petco and PetSmart fade from view. Cosponsored by the crystal maker Swarovski, the show features jewel-encrusted canine kimonos in museum display cases, one-hundred-dollar Parisian dog collars, merino-wool puppy sweaters, and doggie beds modeled after yoga mats. It's the place to be if you want to learn the season's big pet-fashion color (purple) and fabrics ("metallic"). There's enough pet bling to blind a guide dog.

"A woman who wants a Chanel or Gucci piece is not going to put their pet in something from a department store," explained Mario DiFante, the show's organizer. "We're showcasing the Chanels and Guccis of the pet fashion world."

The two-legged fashionistas on hand include Lina Asselien, a Montreal-based designer behind the Romy and Jacob line of pet wear. Asselien's wares include a lamb's fur parka and a chocolate fleece housecoat, both for dogs. "What we're selling is luxury lifestyle," she said when I visited her display. "We have greyhound owners and whippet owners who custom-order fur coats in very large sizes. It doesn't matter who you are. People who want luxury are willing to spend for it."

Another star is Chicago-based designer Janet Lee, whose pet carriers look like high-end handbags. "We wanted it to look more like a pocketbook than a pet carrier," said Lee, thirty-four. "At the time, there was only one other company making them, and they were going for bright colors. We wanted something that would look like couture. We coordinated with the kind of materials you might see in a Marc Jacobs bag." Lee told me she does $1 million of business a year. Her bags are in Barney's and Nordstrom's. In a country living beyond its means, pets' accessories are part of the same spiral of human gluttony. In 2008, months before the financial crisis, an academic study linked excessive spending on oneself to excessive spending on one's pets. Rather than simple, if misguided, altruism, the expenditures are viewed from the ivory tower as a way for shopaholics to keep on pampering themselves. Doggie perfume in my nose, fashionable doggie beds underfoot, I'd reached the plush heart of modern pet excess. We're all Mary, Queen of Scots now.

But even here, the backstory of Lee's business demonstrates that $1 million of doggie-handbag sales is about more than an irrational desire to shower status symbols on animals who remain wonderfully unconcerned with any cosmopolitan pecking order. The real driver was the upgraded status of pets—the same social promotion that sent San Franciscans to the barricades over dog parks. "Back ten years ago no one thought about carrying their dogs," Lee said. "They stayed at home. But then, with Paris Hilton, everyone started thinking about carrying them, and carrying them well. So now you're going to get a nice bag that looks like it's on the runway. It's going to coordinate with what you're wearing." In other words, you can take part in the pet-friendlying of America, and look posh, too.

Just as the casual Fridays in the workplace pushed Americans to upgrade their chino wardrobes, so too has the opening of restaurants and hotels to pets motivated stylish types to upgrade their leashes and their pet carriers. Lee's next project indicates that the bespoke pet's more precise equivalent isn't some royal doggie of yesteryear but a creature a bit closer to home: the (nonfur) baby, for whom accessories can also reflect parents' fickle tastes as much as the child's actual needs. Lee recently adapted one of her classy pet carriers into a diaper bag. Just because she's carrying baby gear doesn't mean she has to ditch her fashion sense in favor of rainbows and bunnies. "It's the same thing," she said. "You're out in public, and you're a stylish person, and you should be able to stay that way."

At the kickoff cocktail party, I quietly sipped a puptini for about twenty minutes as I waited to introduce myself to Gärdsby, whose wife and business partner, Ann, stood next to him holding a bored-looking Manfred. A crowd of people surrounded the Swedish trio; there was no break in sight. For an early minute, I was convinced that Gärdsby, the impresario behind the Manfred of Sweden line of canine clothing, was a non-pet-world celebrity that I was supposed to recognize. Could he be some long-lost member of Abba? But then it dawned on me: With the shag haircut, the thick square glasses, and the open-necked collar, Gärdsby was a dead ringer for Austin Powers.

In contrast to Janet Lee, Gärdsby didn't offer quotidian pragmatic explanations for the phenomenon of Pet Fashion Week. That worked well for him. At a trade show whose organizers were eagerly trying to demonstrate the pet world's move beyond crocheting, corgi-owning grandmas, he was a chain-smoking, Euro-accented, umlaut-festooned gift straight from central casting—the guy who could convince the world that pet keeping and personal glamor need not be mutually exclusive. He looked like the quintessential fashion star.

Gärdsby's pet fashion saga began one winter in the southern Swedish city of Malmö. Manfred was cold. Gärdsby said the local pet stores didn't sell anything that fit the little dog. So Ann went to work on one of the old leather jackets from Bjorn's rock years (he wasn't in Abba but did record an album called *On the Line,* the cover of which features Gärdsby posing next to a neon light). Strolling around with their newly hip-looking dog a few nights later, the couple ran into a Panamanian transplant who was unhappily struggling through her first Swedish winter with her dog. She asked about the jacket, and the conversation led to an order: She wanted one, too, only maybe with some bling on it.

Having moved from musician to producer ("I was already well known in Sweden"), Gärdsby had a knack for self-promotion. He placed his jackets in a few boutiques, found his way into some magazine pieces, and repeated. Within a couple of years, he said, his work was shown at the "very famous international design museum" in the western Swedish town of Göteborg. He then broke into the American market in classic form. At a charity pet-fashion show at an upscale Los Angeles doggie day care, he put Manfred and the brand that bore his name front and center. B-list Hollywood stars (a woman from E!, a costar from *House, MD*) took turns walking well-dressed puppies down the catwalk. "We're in so many countries now: England, Japan, everywhere," he said. "I brought a lot of the thinking from the record company into this business: branding from beginning to end, keep it simple, make sure you accompany everything with the right music."

The most revealing conversation I had at Pet Fashion Week wasn't about pet fashion at all. It was about the unlikely subject of paper.

It wasn't just any paper, mind you—certainly not the recycled newsprint new dog owners might use to housebreak their puppy. The stuff in question, in creamy white, was unlike any form of dead tree I'd ever felt. Sturdy enough to support a Himalayan rope bridge, soft enough to swaddle a colicky baby, and with the ever-so-slight give that you might associate with the jogging oval at an upscale health club. At Pet Fashion Week, though, it held a bottle of dog shampoo. Or, to use the brand's preferred terminology, "Canine Grooming System."

"Just feel the boxes," said Mary Rech, the director of salon and retail sales for the two-year-old shampoo manufacturer Isle of Dogs, who was staffing a display booth designed to look like the entrance to a sophisticated hair salon. "They're so soft. It's called 'Curious Touch.' There are only about two people who use it in this country." The paper—whose British manufacturer likens its feel to "the skin of a peach, a new baby, or a Camembert cheese"—isn't the only luxurious thing about the new line of grooming goods. Nearly everything in the firm's Pet Fashion Week display area telegraphed exclusivity: the names of the shampoos (Evening Primrose, Royal Jelly), the typeface on the bottles (a sans-serif look that you might find on the bottles in a high-end beauty parlor), the partnership with the W chain of boutique hotels (Isle of Dogs shampoos are complimentary for canine guests at the pricey hotels), and even the company logo's tasteful evocation of Britain, which perhaps distracts from Isle of Dogs' less glamorous actual home—Milwaukee. "If it didn't say Isle of Dogs, you would think it was a human brand, wouldn't you?" asked Rech.

The prices were luxurious, too—say, $28 for 250 milliliters of Isle of Dogs formula number 12, Veterinary Grade Evening Primrose Oil Shampoo. By contrast, a twenty-ounce bottle (that's 591 milliliters for those of you who might prefer Isle of Dogs' fancily European units of volume measurement) of Johnson's "No More Tears" baby shampoo costs $4.99 at my local drugstore. The prices even dwarf the burgeoning field of specialty pet shampoos. Earthbath Mediterranean Magic Rosemary Scented Deodorizing Shampoo, a midmarket line that comes in plain old bottles lacking the extravagant cardboard boxes, sells for $9.99 for a sixteen-ounce bottle, proving that even the proles who troll through the aisles at Petco might want to bathe their pets in "the scent of a lush Mediterranean garden." Isle of Dogs, though, doesn't seem to want those customers, however many of them there might be. A hint comes from one piece of reading assigned to staffers by Isle of Dogs' marketing vice president, Carlos Tribino. Rather than tasking them with a book about pets, or even pet stores, he explained that he put them on to a volume about Viking ranges and high-end golf clubs and beautifully sculpted $750 vacuum cleaners: the hugely influential business tome *Trading Up* by Michael J. Silverstein and Neil Fiske.

Staring at the American consumer brain, in its pre-2008 form, at least, Silverstein and Fiske discover a schizophrenic nation whose citizens drive $40,000 all-terrain SUVs to buy bulk discount goods at Costco, folks who will pay thirty dollars for a small bottle of shea butter lotion to moisturize skin that is washed with plain old Ivory soap. The aging baby boom and the wealth explosions of the 1980s and 1990s, they write, created a mass market for artisan craftsmanship. But few can go top-of-the-line for every purchase. Rather, they pick and choose based on both their own values and other, more easily manipulated tastes and needs. An expensive imported-cacao chocolate treat or Italian-recipe coffee concoction might make one customer feel sufficiently special that he doesn't mind spending three times what he'd pay for a Hershey bar or cup of Folgers. For another, it might be the exclusivity that comes from walking the blond-wood floor of a Williams-Sonoma rather than the teeming aisles of a department store that, upon inspection, is selling similar cookware. For yet another, the satisfaction might lie in feeling the rush of generosity and nurturing that comes with serving a farmers'-market dinner to guests or children— or, perhaps, pets.

"For sophisticated and discerning spenders, New Luxury goods provide a rich and broad vocabulary with which to speak—without saying a word," Silverstein and Fiske write. By the time their book came out, in 2003, New Luxury logic was already tiptoeing into the pet industry: Purportedly scientific foods were jostling with plain old kibble, elaborate extend-o-leashes finding a niche in what had been a very simple market for dog-walking tools. But it took folks like those at Isle of Dogs to bring this spending to the next level with a playbook that came straight out of *Trading Up*. The strategy was to eschew big-box pet stores, targeting Isle of Dogs sales to boutiques, both pet and human. Catering to humans who see themselves as their pet's parent, the firm created a Web site where would-be buyers can enter specifics about their animal's look and then be directed to the most chemically appropriate line of shampoo. The $50,000 trade-show display, Tribino noted, was designed to conjure an aura of exclusivity. Isle of Dogs also sponsored the Pet Fashion Week runway show.

"People are spending more on their pets, but not as much as they could or as much as they would like to, if given the right products," Tribino told me later, after he'd moved to Europe and taken a job with a luxury brand consultancy. "Pet luxury remains a bit of a silly, cottage industry, for the most part. At Isle of Dogs we broke that mold. We launched a true luxury brand, not a wannabe, with luxury credentials, luxury quality, luxury packaging, and luxury pricing." Never mind the demands of fashion; the emotional force of Tribino's argument is evident even to the owner of a drooly Saint Bernard. Don't I owe this sweet and loyal pal something better? Doesn't he deserve the best wash and the fluffiest fur and the softest coat and the sweetest smell? I'm a guy who tends to believe all pet shampoos are created equal, but after chatting with Tribino, even *I* was starting to think I was giving Murphy a raw deal by not buying him Isle of Dogs. Pet fashion may not be for everyone—especially in troubled times. But in a world of ever more smitten pet people, a little bit of trading up might well be.

Across the pet industry, a lot of very bright people in 2007 were betting that Bjorn Gärdsby's Yorkie—so fashionable, so well kempt, so brand-conscious—was the shape of pups to come. Or at least some pups to come. One morning during Pet Fashion Week, I watched Tribino deliver a presentation about the consumer trends of the year ahead. Once a general manager of the firm Brand Architecture International, Tribino had an idea about the shape of the contemporary consumer economy, a place where the Whole Foods Markets of the world are thriving while the Safeways struggle. In his presentation Tribino summed up his approach with a neat visual trick. "Why pay thirty dollars for a bottle of wine . . . ," he asked via a PowerPoint message. Hands shot up: We do it because it makes us feel special, or because the wine is good, or because we want to impress someone. Then the second half of the question appeared: " . . . when you can pay a lot more?"

The Isle of Dogs presentation may have surprised some of the smaller-time pet-store owners who turned out for Pet Fashion Week's marketing lectures, but the firm was hardly alone in noticing the new upscale niche in the industry. Like so much of the rest of the economy, the world of pet stores was becoming less democratic, with galloping growth at the top of the market. As chain retailers like PetSmart gobbled up the middlebrow market, local pet stores might have gone the way of the mom-and-pop hardware store in the age of Home Depot. Instead, according to industry consultant Mike Dillon, they moved into a lucrative new niche that sits roughly at the intersection of pet necessities and human accessories, a universe of gourmet foods and bespoke fashions—the universe on display at Pet Fashion Week.

"The entire industry is really being driven by high-income earners. Seventy thousand dollars a year and above is driving fifty or sixty percent of the whole industry," Dillon said. "That's what's pulling in the luxury." According to one study, $70,000-a-year consumers represented 51 percent of total pet spending in 2005, up from 28 percent in 1995.

The wealthy and the childless are the market for fancy new pet boutiques with names like Bonejour or Chic Petique or Doggy Style or Rex and the City. The share of all pet products labeled as "upscale" more than doubled between 2002 and 2006, from 19 percent to 43 percent, according to the same study. To be sure, that's based on manufacturers' self-generated descriptions of what constitutes "upscale," and many of those manufacturers wouldn't be able to get through the doors of Pet Fashion Week. But it's a good indication of where things are headed. "What you see here in this entire show is maybe the equivalent of a week of sales at Wal-Mart," Craig Rexford, publisher of the trade journal *Pet Business,* said as we walked the floor in New York. "But it's where the action is."

In 2006, Rexford got ahead of this trend by introducing *The Pet Elite,* a high-end spin-off from *Pet Business*. Printed on thick matte paper and featuring a tiara-wearing French bulldog on an early cover, the magazine billed itself as "the only business publication written exclusively for luxury pet product buyers." But a few months after Rexford launched his tony new magazine, rival *Pet Products News* added its own upmarket brand, *Pet Style News*. And then *Pet Groomer* rolled out a third upscale title: *Pet Boutique*. There will be no shortage of coverage for Isle of Dogs.

The upscale firms, in turn, are returning the favor with advertising and branding efforts that, they hope, will pull still more people into the luxury-pet universe. Traditionally unregulated, the world of pet grooming has long been associated with, say, the nice old lady down the block who might offer to wash your dog in her musty basement. But Isle of Dogs' display advertised seminars about the move "from groomer to stylist." At Pet Fashion Week, the company sponsored a visit from an all-star grooming team from Bangkok's Starwood Arts of Dog Grooming School ("5 Thailand Champions with HRH Princess Bajrakitiyabha's Trophies," explained the business card of the school's director, Sathit Suratphiphit). Starwood's works— elaborately coiffed white poodles, their manes dyed orange or green or purple—were displayed on the runway, carried by models dressed up to look like statues from a Buddhist temple. The 'dos had as much to do with an ordinary canine look as a couture show might have to do with what you'd wear to the office, but the sense of a new market for commerce came through all the same.

"We're telling these groomers, you have to transform or you will not survive," Rech said. "Most of the spending decisions today are being made by women, and in the last ten years they have gotten used to spas. I go to one, even in Milwaukee. And they are not going to want to take their pets to a noisy, smelly groomer." Cold-pressed evening primrose oil conditioning mist, anyone?

In the process, the boutiques have figured out the formula for the excess-laden modern pet industry. Under the fancy wrapping is a message that appeals, simultaneously, to customers' desire to stand out and their desire to be nurturing, even though the nurturee in question could hardly care less whether he's bathed in rosewater or tapwater. "Purchasing typically is grounded in emotion and justified on logic" was how Vicki Lynne Morgan, a marketing consultant who works with pet products, put it. "You just have to figure out who your market is and supply them with a logic that fits."

Most residents of America's 70 million pet-owning households have probably had an idea or two about some product or service that might be convenient or simply lucrative. The gut I've grown because I've given up the gym in order to take my morning walk with Murphy has me convinced there's millions to be made by starting a health club with its own dog run. But of course I'm too cowardly and too lazy to do so myself. The boutique wares at Pet Fashion Week, though, provided a surprising showcase for small-time entrepreneurs with more pet-business moxie than me. These are the petrepreneurs.

What makes someone decide that his or her pet idea might be the next big thing? One spring night a few months before Pet Fashion Week, I visited a classroom in northern New Jersey where a dozen hopefuls had paid thirty-five dollars apiece to hash out their own plans for pet-oriented commercial success. The class was called "Owning a Successful Business in the Pet Industry" and taught by Morgan, whose firm, Animal Brands, advises industry heavyweights and wannabes alike.

Many of Morgan's eleven students described themselves as unhappily employed in corporate America, realizing they'd rather work for themselves doing something they loved. Just as foodies might dream of opening that small neighborhood café, so Morgan's class of pet lovers dreamed of ditching the boss in order to play with the dog. The students told of plans to start pet-sitting businesses, become pet personal shoppers, mass-produce homemade treats, and otherwise give up the rat race in favor of the pet chase. Morgan's class provided a useful corrective for the more romantically motivated of the assembled (the pups may be cute, but this stuff is hard work) as well as a lengthy primer on how to crack the multibillion-dollar code. Today's petrepreneurial paradigm: think fancy. "Back in 1989, we had a futurist come in, and he said a lot of polarization would come to the pet industry," Morgan said. "My suggestion to you is to become a niche player."

While most of the questions focused on the basics of starting businesses—getting loans, getting customers, et cetera—one pair of women was well ahead of the bunch. Sue Dolbow and Mary Lou Sparano, friends since high school, had started work a year earlier on an idea called Retro-Pup. The business plan was simple enough: Make dog beds that you wouldn't want to hide when company came. They would find fabrics bearing the midcentury modern designs the women preferred, then have them sewn onto large cushions. "Everything out there is so ugly, in pink or with bones all over it," Dolbow said. "The dogs don't care. So why don't we have something you'd actually want in a nice living room? If you pay a million dollars for a house—not that I did or anything—you don't want something you have to stick in the closet." As with many trends in the pet business, it's about the humans.

When I met them, Sparano was still working part-time at the Morris County Library. Dolbow described herself as a "woman of leisure." After work, Sparano would dash over to Dolbow's house and they would spend the rest of the day on Retro-Pup business, checking on orders or looking for fabric. The firm was doing about $60,000 in business every year, they said, turning a small profit with items like the $280 Eames-print dog bed. But Sparano and Dolbow were aiming for bigger things. "We're going to Pet Fashion Week at the end of the summer," Sparano said. "You should come, too."

I checked in on Retro-Pup a few times in the ensuing months. The "news" section of their Web site reported a string of the minor sorts of successes that can make businesses like theirs. Take this item: *You will find Retro-Pup dog beds in the home of Sally Hershberger, owner of the white-hot SALLY HERSHBERGER SALON in New York City's Meat Packing district. "I absolutely love the dog beds!" says the style maven and hair designer to the stars.* Good news. Or: *VH1's new show, THE FABULOUS LIFE OF CELEBRITY PETS selected one of our beds for their premiere episode.* Even better. Pet Fashion Week, here we come!

In a normal, non–*Trading Up* retail economy, the next dream might have been to land that big chain-store contract that keeps the dollars rolling in month after month. But in the world of pet fashion, where necessity long since stopped having anything to do with it, the calculus is different. Thus when I stopped by Dolbow and Sparano's Pet Fashion Week booth to ask if they were on the lookout for the buyers from PetSmart and Target, they said it would be a mixed blessing. The money might be good, but it could complicate the rest of their business.

They weren't alone. Kate Ross, the designer behind a preppy sweater line called Tartan Hound ("We call ourselves kind of the J. Crew of dogs"), told me that if it ever came to it, she'd make a whole different product for the big chains, while leaving current best sellers like the puppy rugby sweater ("it's kind of a classic look") to the roughly five hundred small boutiques that sell her stuff and desperately need to maintain a distinction between themselves and the big-box stores. As if to underscore her point, as Ross briefly talked to me in her sales booth at Fashion Week, a boutique buyer perked up, turning away from the array of striped sweaters to ask, with alarm: "You're selling to PetSmart?" Ross assured him that she wasn't.

Despite the *Access Hollywood*–caliber news on their Web site, Dolbow and Sparano's reality remained a lot closer to the unglamorous hard work Morgan had predicted. They came to the show under their own power and accompanied by an entourage of exactly one: Dolbow's husband, Kyle, who drove them to Manhattan in his silver Dodge SUV and then erected their advertising display on the show floor. They wound up getting a fair amount of attention and an award nomination, but no big score that would land them in the big time. Yet.

To get a sense of how their would-be buyers among boutique owners think, I took a stroll through a trade show with Seth Kaplan, the realtor turned owner of a pet boutique on the north fork of Long Island. Kaplan's evaluations had a lot to do with the basic rule of boutique ownership. Once an item is associated with the big chains, he told me, he won't stock it anymore. "Take Hartz, which has made some really neat products," he said, waving a dismissive hand toward a mammoth display for the pet-health conglomerate. "I absolutely will not touch their stuff because of the association with supermarkets. I don't want to be compared to them."

Kaplan's store, Pet Pantry, in the suburban town of Roslyn, has been in business for a quarter century—or, as he put it in pet-retail terms, "since back when Nutri-Max was the top of the market." Despite the proliferation of big-box pet stores, the shop has stayed in business, he said, by offering a combination of much-desired expert advice and continuously hopping to higher-brow brands. Kaplan, who speaks in a heavy New York accent and was smart enough to wear running shoes to the show, swore me to secrecy before he identified the New York–area celebrity who frequents his store.

Kaplan had been at Pet Fashion Week, but I first met him among the mass-merchandisers of Global Pet Expo. As we walked the trade-show floor, it didn't take long for Kaplan to start separating himself from those masses. Soon enough, we passed a Chinese trading concern that imports cheap-looking food bowls. "I'm a high-end sort of store, so that eliminates a lot of the plastics and that sort of thing," he said, without breaking stride. "The Chinese prices are so out of line with Americans. But the quality—oh, boy. The price, for my customers, is not an issue. They've decided that their pets is an area where they'll just spend what it takes. And also the Chinese always get the sizing wrong."

Similarly unacceptable was a booth pushing a chemical "grass saver" dietary supplement, its brochures depicting a suburban lawn whose deep green hue is unblemished by any bleaching from the family dog's liquid excretions. "My customers are very suspicious of anything that's going into the animal," he said. "So am I." That suspicion extends to something as simple as rawhide. When a vendor told Kaplan his chews were mainly imported, Kaplan promptly lost interest. "My rawhide is American," he said. "Most of [the others] are imported from South America and treated with formaldehyde."

And don't even get him started on the big food firms. "There's Purina," he scoffed as we turned a corner and came face-to-face with the conglomerate's towering display. "It's by-products and preservatives. See what we're up against!" Kaplan grabbed a bag of Beneful, one of the firm's lines that is marketed toward the health-conscious buyers who frequent Kaplan's store. "You would think this stuff is amazing," he said, pointing to the ingredients. "But look. Ground yellow corn is the first item on the list. Chicken by-products is the second. I mean, come on!"

By contrast, Kaplan positively glowed when approaching the colorful display area of Redbarn Premium Pet Products, manufacturers of Bully Sticks, dog chews made from the roughly half-million inches per week of bull penis that might otherwise go unused by America's meat industry. "It's the number-one, all-natural, best dog treat on the market," Kaplan declared. Without evident fear of double entendre, he proceeded to enumerate the unconventional goodie's benefits: It is hard, like a bone, which makes it good for a dog's teeth and appealing to his chewing instinct; it can be long, up to a few feet in length, meaning a dog can chew on it all day; and, of course, it's a lot tastier than a rawhide. Redbarn has since expanded the Bully line to include braided Bully Sticks and Bully Sticks twisted into the shape of pretzels.

According to Kaplan, his clientele doesn't include any of the lowbrow boors—like, um, me—whose theretofore subconscious castration anxieties are triggered by the sight of a wall full of twisted and knotted animal penises. "People want it," he said. "They're educated. They like to do the best for their dogs."

Kaplan, of course, helps them do just that. One sweltering summer day, I trekked out to Long Island to visit his store. It felt at times like a rolling seminar for the customers whose Range Rovers filled his parking lot and whom he directed to various nutritional, educational, and otherwise animal-uplifting products on the shelves. During a quiet moment, he almost looked sad when I asked him about the passion he'd displayed:

Isn't the relentless focus on top quality a little over the top when you're talking about dogs and cats? "Aw, no way," he replied. "It really mirrors what we're all about. Burger King used to be totally acceptable. And now you might think twice about even doing that annually. But you'll go get a really nice burger and not feel guilty at all."

Whatever glamorous aspirations the Pet Fashion Week promoters had, there remained a clash with the reality of the industry—even its high-rent district. At the runway show, many of the buyers who had paid to be there were still people who sold at pet stores in Birmingham or Memphis, far from Manhattan's dizzying orbit. At a press conference, Alexa Cach, the show's fashion director, puzzled some visitors with statements like "Designers are what makes us grow" and "We're styling the pets based on trend visions for spring 2008." Among the visions: *android* and *muse,* the latter of which she defined as "like something you found in the attic."

"They all reflect what's going on in the fashion industry and should reflect what the pet industry is doing," Cach concluded, the glittering lights behind her flickering from orange to purple. One reason for the general befuddlement may have been that her media largely comprised features producers from morning TV shows and trade writers for pet publications. Catching on to this disconnect, Cach opened the show with a set of instructions her colleagues in Bryant Park likely never have to deliver. "Look at the line sheets in front of you. Cross off what you like. See how it moves on the models. And then go talk to the designers."

The models were even more happily dissimilar to the human variety. Eschewing politically incorrect show dogs, Pet Fashion Week featured rescue dogs of varying sizes and often undeterminable breed backgrounds from local shelters. Using runway rookies can be risky: At another show, I heard, there had been an, ahem, accident on the runway. The Amazonian human models who paraded alongside the dogs were another story, as glamorously self-confident as could be imagined. When one of the dog models froze in a moment of anxiety under the klieg lights, I was particularly impressed at the aplomb with which one scantily clad model snatched the offending beagle into her arms before its evident stage fright could lead to a repeat accident.

Few notes were being taken as the pups hit the runway. Music blared while the bewitching models walked or carried the fabulous pooches down the catwalk. Out came the digital cameras, just like at one of Nieves's parties. Never mind looking for the android theme, or eyeing the way the Dog in Paris line of collars complemented the model's retro attire, or noting the tasteful look brought forth by big-time pet-wear designer Emma Rose. This was cute! A Doberman in a pink winter coat! A standard poodle staring into the spotlights! Have you ever seen anything like it? The "awwwws" rose above the pulsing soundtrack. Next to the deejay table, to the right of the zigzagging stage, the designers' faces seemed to fall a bit as adoring giggles erupted from the audience.

Pet Fashion Week may yet convince the world that a stylish pet is a key accessory—we're well on our way—and Gärdsby may eventually make millions off that belief. Someday deciding how to dress your pet may come with the same layers of identity and anxiety as deciding how to dress yourself. But not yet. At Pet Fashion Week, even America's priciest boutique owners agreed that New York's most stylish pets remained cute. No amount of *Bright Lights, Big City* lighting, no snarl on the face of a model improbably sporting a bald wig, no deliriously soft piece of canine couture could distract from the essential, sweet doggishness of the whole affair.

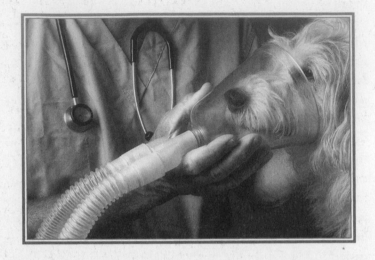

FIVE

Hip Replacements and Health Plans

The Miracles of Modern Veterinary Medicine

As Ben the beagle is wheeled in for surgery, Chick Weisse is talking about how he first got interested in veterinary medicine after reading *All Creatures Great and Small*. That seems to put him in the same category as about 98 percent of practicing veterinarians. Reading James Herriot's classic collection of vignettes from his days as an English country vet, one can easily see why. The sweetly nostalgic memoir traces the career of a young animal doctor who drives around the prewar Yorkshire countryside in a rickety Hillman automobile, making house calls on a series of colorful, indecipherably accented locals, winning their undying affection with all-hours visits to sheep, pigs, horses, and a beloved Pekingese named Tricki Woo. It became a smash hit upon its 1972 release; a TV adaptation and four further books followed, each of them painting a picture of a calling dominated by kindhearted souls certain to reach retirement with a trove of zany and charming stories to tell.

Herriot's sepia-toned world was antique even by the time his first book was released. *All Creatures* opens with the newly arrived doctor inserting his entire arm deep in the womb of a laboring cow. As a dubious farmer watches, Herriot is lying on a cobblestone floor, stripped to the waist and covered in blood and snow, and struggling mightily to free a calf that has been unable to squeeze itself out into the world. "By gaw, it's alive," the surprised farmer murmurs when calf and cow both survive the hours-long encounter. It's an experience that's relatively rare for today's vets—suburbanized, pet-focused, and on the whole unlikely to spend significant periods of time with their limbs stretched to the limit in order to grope around a troubled patient's innards. But Herriot's ongoing duels with ailments like Strawberry Foot Rot or Kinky-Back seem especially distant from Weisse, who is at this moment strapping on a suit of lead padding to protect him and six other members of his surgical team from the radiation that for the next ninety or so minutes will stream from a gargantuan Siemens mobile fluoroscopy unit into Ben's diseased bladder.

"It's a couple years old, but it does the job," says Weisse, gesturing toward the machine's mobile C-arm. Like an observatory telescope that happens to be aiming in the wrong direction, the mammoth device can pivot and rotate to provide a real-time, live-action image of the patient's insides—veins, ducts, cancer-ravaged organs, and all. Next to him is a bank of computers and a pair of monitors. A radiologist with an ultrasound paddle flips open a laptop to get a third peek into the dog's body. The entire team, which includes another surgeon, an intern, a pair of veterinary technicians, and a fourth-year vet student, dons outer sets of scrubs atop their lead padding, rubber gloves over their scrubbed hands, and surgical hats and masks over their heads. They look vaguely like astronauts. And once the

lights go down and the fluoroscope comes on and the squad gets
to work, the images on the monitors look a lot like Apollo 11's
black-and-white lunar footage.

Since 2002, Weisse has been a professor at the University of
Pennsylvania's Matthew J. Ryan Veterinary Hospital—VHUP,
in the acronym-laden jargon of a research university. Along
with New York's celebrated Animal Medical Center, the
Philadelphia facility is one of the nation's premier animal hospitals. The pair have been called the Mayo Clinic and the Mass
General of the pet world, their reputations luring clients from
thousands of miles away. Less than half of VHUP's thirty-three
thousand annual patients come from Philadelphia; in a three-
year period, the hospital's 120 veterinarians saw animals from
forty-eight states for complicated and costly procedures like
canine hip replacement surgery or rounds of radiation therapy
from the hospital's brand-new linear accelerator. Heartwarming
or downright surreal cases from the hospital make the national
news on a regular basis. In 2005, a team of surgeons removed a
hunter's arrow from the skull of a dog from Washington, D.C.
In 2007, one of the hospital's oncologists developed a vaccine
that cured a dog's lymphoma and may soon wind up being used
for human cancer patients. The greatest share of ink has probably been spilled over Penn's pioneering feline kidney-transplant
program. Not long before Ben the beagle was rolled into Weisse's
operating room, Gordy, an eight-year-old black cat from
Baltimore, was the recipient of the hospital's one hundredth
transplanted kidney. That $12,500 procedure, involving two
teams of surgeons working simultaneously for six or eight or
twelve hours, now seems old hat.

Three weeks out of every month, Weisse is just another surgeon at the hospital, slicing and sewing, attacking ruptured
spleens or extracting accidentally ingested cassette tapes. Take
away the artificial respiration machine and the work might seem
familiar even in 1930s Yorkshire. Weisse spends the fourth

week focusing on a novel field of minimally invasive animal medicine he has helped create: interventional radiology. With the fluoroscope illuminating the internal goings-on, the process involves snaking wires and catheters and needles through the body's veins and organs and passageways, working from within to open up blocked ducts, shut off troubled blood vessels, or deliver doses of chemotherapy directly to whichever artery abuts a tumor. No blood, no guts, no worrying that the lily-livered journalist working on a profile of Weisse will faint in the middle of the OR. Nothing but an image on the monitor that looks like a submarine exploring distant inlets of the Beagle Bladder Sea. Forget *All Creatures Great and Small*. It's a scene straight out of *Fantastic Voyage*.

Ben's case is a tough one. Three weeks earlier, the six year old beagle was diagnosed with bladder cancer. In human and canine alike, that's one of the nastier, more aggressive varieties of the disease; Ben's vet gave him two to four months to live. Chemotherapy might extend that, but he'd still be looking at six months to a year. Chubby and playful, the dog doesn't currently look sick—unless you watch him struggling to pee, or catch a glimpse of his urine, which is full of blood. An ultrasound back home in Connecticut revealed that the tumor is sitting directly on his ureters, the ducts that carry urine from the kidneys to the bladder. One of the ducts is almost entirely blocked. The other may eventually be too, leaving him unable to urinate and destroying his kidneys. The prospect could slice the dog's life expectancy to only a few very unpleasant weeks.

Ben's local vet had wanted to open him up for surgery, though the vet offered little to be optimistic about. "He said if they find the tumor very spread, they will consider euthanizing him on the table," said Milen Velinov, who has had Ben since he was a puppy. Velinov, a pediatric geneticist, pored through the scholarly literature. "I didn't agree with that. This tumor is not operable most of the time." So he opted for an initial dose of chemotherapy, hoping it would slow or stop the tumor's growth even if the statistics showed that an actual rollback was next to impossible. Chemotherapy would also do nothing about the dog's near-term ability to pass urine. Velinov took to the Internet looking for answers. One Web site cited a novel program at Purdue University, in Indiana. He called the university to ask about coming out to get Ben some treatment. The response: Why don't you go to the folks we learned from?

Velinov and his wife, Milena, loaded Ben and a sheaf of canine X-rays into the car at dawn on a Wednesday. Stamford, where they live, is about three hours from the hospital. But it was rush hour, and New York was in between. The dog looked fine when they arrived, but Milen had about thirty-six hours' worth of stubble on his face and looked like a medical student who had just pulled an all-nighter. "This has been topic number one since he was diagnosed," he said. "I've done so much research." In one of the examination rooms, they chatted with Weisse's interventional radiology partner, Allyson Berent. Ben snuggled up to the medical team, wagging his rear end. The only indication that he might have been a bit low was that he didn't even flinch when Berent performed a rectal exam.

Exam completed, Berent had a couple of proposals. For the straining, a result of the tumor having blocked one of the two paths for urine to work its way out of the body, she suggested inserting a stent, a tube that can keep a passageway open. "You don't see it; he doesn't feel it; it's like it isn't there," she said. "But it allows the urine to go out." Berent's team had performed this procedure twenty-six times, she said, and had had fairly good luck. (She also recommended that Ben be neutered, something the Bulgarian-born Milen had resisted since they adopted the dog at four months of age.) For the cancer, Berent suggested a similarly new technique called intra-arterial chemotherapy.

For humans and—until recently, at least—for dogs, chemotherapy has traditionally been administered via IV. The cancer-killing drug then flows through the bloodstream to distribute itself throughout the body, which would be fine if it weren't that cancers live in specific parts of the body. Using the same *Deep Space Nine* approach, intra-arterial chemotherapy involves maneuvering probes to inject the medication directly into whatever artery is closest to the tumor. According to Berent, this technique gives eight to twenty times the concentration of chemo to the afflicted area, and "in theory it makes perfect sense."

But while the theory made sense, there were not enough data to provide any idea of how much time the treatment might win Ben. Berent's team had done these treatments on sixteen dogs over the past nine months, and most of the tumors had stabilized. "Stable's good, because [the tumors are] not growing. But we don't know if they would have been stable anyway," she said. One tumor had actually shrunk, though Berent said regression is very rare. In other words, the treatment might add to the year the dog was statistically likely to live. But it might not. Entering the program also meant Ben would need to make four more monthly trips to Philadelphia for each session, which would require him to be put under general anesthesia and spend the day in the hospital. And it would cost $1,500 a pop for the treatments, twice as much as ordinary chemo. On top of the roughly $2,500 the exam and stenting operation were likely to cost.

The Velinovs signed right up. "I think we're willing to go all the way," Milen told Berent. His wife, Milena, explained that the couple's kids were grown and Ben was "a very special dog."

Unfortunately, because Ben had just had his first dose of chemo at the local vet, they needed to wait a couple of weeks before switching to the high-test variety. Milena agreed to come back in two days—which would be round-trip number six—for blood tests to see whether the count had recovered. She and

Ben would stay in a hotel, and if the answer was no, she would turn around, drive back home, and put off the surgery until round-trip number seven. "We're used to driving a lot," Milen said. They weren't the only ones; out in the waiting room I noticed discarded local newspapers from Albany, Newark, and New Haven.

The tests came back clean, and so a couple of days later the dog is under the knife. A very small knife. The only cut he gets is the little nick necessary to insert an impossibly narrow probe that Weisse and Berent, safely outside the body, will guide toward Ben's bladder.

Encased in their protective garb, Weisse and Berent step up to the dog. Ben, unconscious, is a mess of tubes and wires, his throat intubated, his limbs shot through with IVs, his side shaved. Monitors are clamped to his tongue. A respirator is on hand to do his breathing for him. Without much fanfare, Weisse threads the guide-wire probe into his side. Berent works another up the dog's urethra and into the bladder from the end of his penis. On the monitor, we see the guide wire inching along through the emptiness like an imperial gunship chugging to the rescue of some endangered upriver colony. Weisse periodically asks a colleague to flush contrast dye through the dog's veins. The solution appears black against a white backdrop on the monitor. Picked up by the fluoroscope, each flush of the contrast solution briefly shows off the animal's internal road map of veins and passageways. Eventually, the minuscule probe winds past a kidney and onward toward the bladder. Contrast dye sent up through the urethra to fill the organ reveals its lightbulb shape.

Weisse, though, is having a hard time getting there. Thanks to the illness, the passage resembles an airport's Homeland Security checkpoint at rush hour: Nothing gets by. On the monitor, his guide wire's hooked end bounces again and again against an invisible impediment. "Can you mag in?" he asks one of the technicians. "We're just going to keep turning the wire back and forth to see if we can go in there." The fluoroscope zooms in closer: ureter, wire, blockage. No luck. He tries deflating the bladder by draining out the fluid that has been keeping it full. Then he has the squad refill it. (The various expelled liquids are drained into a container that, in keeping with the generally nongross nature of the procedure, is discreetly out of the way.) Another shot of contrast dye shows that the jostling has done nothing to ease the probe's passage toward the bladder. Weisse calls for a stiffer wire; a resident unsheathes it from its sterile wrapping. "Okay, this feels a lot better," he says. Another ten minutes of trying to push past the tumor ensue.

Finally, with no warning, the wire pokes right through. Welcome to the bladder. "Let's get some biopsies while we're in there," he says. On the monitor, little pincers emerge from a tube that has been passed over Weisse's guide wire; they snip off microscopic bits of organ, which are in turn pulled back through the tube, out the nick in the dog's side, and into a tiny vial for later examination.

Now that Weisse has threaded the wire past the blockage, the next order of business is to put a stent where the tumor is crushing the ureter. This, too, proves complicated. The vessel from kidney to bladder is all coiled up, meaning an especially long stent is required. If the ureter were to suddenly uncoil, the alien object could shoot off into Ben's body. Working the guide wire, Weisse sets about wedging the stent into place, adding little curlicues to each end to prevent them from sliding out from the openings of their respective organs. "What a mess," he says with a sigh. He orders the C-arm to the horizontal position, changing the monitor image to something resembling a western landscape. He manipulates the wire probe to push and pull the stent toward where he wants it. When the fluoroscope zooms in, it looks a little like a pipe cleaner being curled for some misguided elementary school arts-and-crafts project.

But eventually it sticks in place, one end curled into the kidney, the other curling into the bladder, neither going anywhere. A final shot of contrast dye goes all the way through—from kidney to bladder and beyond.

"Look at that beautiful double curl," Weisse says.

Back home, the beagle's urine is clean and the straining is eased. Milena schedules the first intra-arterial procedure for two weeks later. It has to wait that long in part because Weisse and Berent are going to be away at a conference. They regularly lecture about advances in minimally invasive procedures, something a lot of vets don't yet know about. But this trip is a little less common for Weisse. He's going to a convention in Washington to discuss some of his techniques with a human-medicine radiology group.

According to a survey commissioned by the American Animal Hospital Association, 93 percent of pet owners would risk their lives to save their animal. That 93 percent would probably also risk their savings for the pet: A *Journal of the American Veterinary Medical Association* article reported that in 2003, Americans spent $1.32 billion to fix dogs' knees; that year, more than a million dogs had anterior cruciate ligament surgery. That so many humans like the Velinovs are now willing to do so much on behalf of so many canines is one reason the veterinary profession has undergone such a metamorphosis over the past generation. About the only characters whose social role has changed more dramatically are the ones the vets treat.

Weisse got interested in interventional radiology during his residency. One day, a toy-breed dog appeared at VHUP with a degenerative disease that would eventually cause his trachea to collapse. Weisse's mother is a human-medicine radiologist; he'd heard about cool things being done with stents. So, at her suggestion, he picked up the phone and called the adjacent human-medical hospital and asked one of the doctors to come and help. They struck up a friendship. Weisse eventually got a fellowship that let him spend one day a week studying the procedures at the human hospital. "They do the stuff all the time there," he says.

"I really think this is a golden age of veterinary medicine. Every generation has one. The last time, a generation ago, was the development of specialties, with people not just training as generalists but developing specialties, oncology and so on," Weisse says. "But here it's the overlap with human medicine, learning from [the MDs] and also going the other way with translational medicine. With the disposable income people have, with having children later and caring more about their dogs, there are just so many opportunities." Even during the financial crisis of 2008, when the appetite for some pricey measures slowed, the number of pets being schlepped to high-end hospitals didn't.

As late as 1970, veterinarians were a largely rural lot, laboring on the same array of barnyard animals and handling the same skinflint clients as James Herriot. Well into the postwar pet boom, dog- and cat-oriented practices represented a small slice of a business whose customers would likely have balked at chemotherapy bills even if the treatments had been available. VHUP's feline kidney transplants are particularly amazing when you consider that the first professional journal about feline medicine was established only in 1971.

The focus on livestock was one reason veterinary schools gave for why the profession remained overwhelmingly male. In 1968, a mere 8 percent of the country's vet students were women. The old guard argued that women weren't strong enough to wrangle with, say, an ailing bull. The federal government felt otherwise, threatening the schools with a cutoff in funding under Title IX, which mandated sexual equality. By 1986 women made up 48 percent of upcoming veterinarians.

The class of 2007 at the nation's twenty-eight veterinary schools was a whopping 79 percent women, according to statistics from the American Veterinary Medical Association. At VHUP, Weisse was about the only male I interacted with during the days spent trailing the interventional radiology team—not including Ben, of course. There are a lot of theories about why women so dominate the profession. One scholar told me about research that suggests women are more sensitive to animals. But that sounds a little too sexist for my taste. Others chalk it up to financial or lifestyle factors: Though they enter with the same powerhouse GPAs as medical students, and leave with the same towering debt, DVMs get paid a lot less than MDs. A trade-off, though, is that the length of time between graduation and getting to work a normal nine-to-five life is a lot shorter for veterinarians, who don't have to do residencies and internships. Women, the speculation goes, might be more willing to accept that trade-off. But, notes veterinarian Carin Smith, who has written on the subject of gender, that rosy picture doesn't take into account the long-hour burdens of running the small businesses that most practices turn out to be.

Either way, as the profession's focus shifted to pets, a newly minted vet didn't have to assume that she'd spend her entire working life in the farm belt. And instead of dealing with clients who view each animal as an economic unit—and thus might treat the vet like a tractor repairman—they dealt with clients who loved their animals for their own sakes and proved increasingly willing to act on that love by ordering up previously unimaginable medical interventions. Vets could live in metropolitan areas, pick up lattes on their way to work, and get treated like a noble healer on the job, just like all their med-school-bound classmates back in undergraduate organic chemistry. The result was a better-educated, more worldly pool of applicants.

Which in turn helped as the field further professionalized, dividing itself into increasingly diverse specialties and subspecialties, from dermatology to toxicology to oncology to radiology, which in turn begat radiation oncology. In 1980, according to the AVMA, there were 1,981 specialists who held board certifications from twelve specialty professional organizations. By 2007 there were almost 9,000, and the number of recognized specialties had grown to twenty. (Herriot's heirs, on the other hand, are a dying breed. In 2007, amid news reports about a population crisis among small-town vets, Missouri followed the lead of Maine, Louisiana, Ohio, North Dakota, Pennsylvania, and Kansas and passed a bill that would forgive student loans for veterinary graduates who worked in rural areas.)

Pet owners in the United States spend about $10 billion each year on veterinary bills. Since the average small-animal vet's take-home pay is a relatively nonlarcenous $79,000 a year, the figure reflects a big jump in heroic procedures by doctors like Weisse and the clutch of ambitious interns that drift their way. Nearly all of the dogs I watched the team treat, Berent said, would have been euthanized were new treatments not available. There was Bubba Earl from New Jersey with his liver problems. There was Jake from Manhattan with an abnormal vein that diverted blood from organs. There was Hudson from upstate New York with an even bigger mess of the veins, known as shunts. Now there are techniques to help such dogs, and owners willing to pay for them. But the big chicken-and-egg question—not that most vets these days focus much on poultry—is whether to attribute that change to the customers or the providers.

The sinister interpretation is that vets—who in 2007 graduated with an average debt of $107,000, nearly double that of 2000 graduates—are after your money. In 2003, *Consumer Reports* dedicated a cover story to veterinary sticker shock. Packed with horror stories from customers, one of whom declares, "I was robbed," the strong implication of the piece was that rising prices were no accident. In the case of Weisse's experimental procedures, though, seeking out the profit motive becomes more convoluted due to the hospital's mission as a research hospital where doctors are empowered to think up all sorts of zany interventions without worrying whether they'll pay for themselves. A number of his colleagues have dual appointments as researchers at both the university's medical school and its veterinary school. Gail Luciani, the hospital's spokeswoman, said VHUP loses money on nearly every case. At any rate, bouts of sticker shock have yet to dent vets' position among the nation's five most trusted professions.

The real drivers for the new spending are the clients—that is to say, the dogs' owners. Like ideas about dog food or dog behavior, humans' own medical experiences shape what they think is appropriate for their dogs. Back in 1968, generalists also ruled the human medical marketplace, and the roster of high-tech interventions was far shorter. Once we started seeing those things on our own trips to the doctor, we wondered why they weren't available to our pets too. Vets ignore this trend at their peril, notes Kristi Reimer, editor of *Veterinary Economics* magazine. "As human medicine becomes more specialized and as people and their own doctors are more likely to have a treatment team—a primary care doctor and a specialist for this problem and a specialist for that problem, there's sort of a shifting expectation not only for their own health care but also for, well, why shouldn't that be available for pets as well," Reimer says. "They seek out what they've experienced on the human side . . . It used to be, well, if the dog had cancer you took it outside. Not anymore. A lot of people fight it the way they fight their own cancer."

One winter night a couple of years ago, my dog suddenly couldn't move. Murphy had spent the day with his pal Lula, a Greater Swiss mountain dog. Lula lived in an old apartment where the radiators tended to overheat. When Murphy came home, he collapsed. My wife called a friend, and together they put the dog on a blanket and loaded the blanket into the back of the friend's station wagon. At VHUP, Murphy was wheeled in on a gurney. I'd been out with friends and showed up a little later. When I got to the hospital, I sat down in a waiting room where most of the people were weeping, and the others— including me—were looking distinctly freaked out.

This is very different from human medicine. A few weeks earlier, we'd visited a human emergency room down the street after a holiday kitchen mishap. There were a few wet eyes in that crowd, but mostly we saw people fuming that they'd have to miss Thanksgiving dinner because their husband burned himself with the turkey deep-fryer. The difference, of course, is that no human-medicine doctor will ever declare that it's best to put the turkey-frying husband to sleep. The possibility of euthanasia hovers over veterinary decision making, freighting so many choices with disconcerting doses of guilt, mortality, and utilitarian financial analysis. In Murphy's case, a perplexed night-shift vet emerged an hour or so later to report that our dog was prancing around the corridors and no one could figure out what had been the matter. We pretended to be mad at him. But it still felt like a brush with death.

The second place veterinary hospitals look especially different from the human variety happens to be right next door to the waiting room: the cashier's desk. These days, most of us humans open up our wallets for the copay while our insurance company gets the itemized bill (and cuts us off if it gets too high). By contrast, even though vets have elevated their professional reputation from one step above podiatrists to a hair beneath Jonas Salk, they deliver a bill that looks like what you get after the mechanic services your rattletrap Ford Taurus. There's a deposit at the beginning. And, at the end, line items that spell out every detail of what transpired. People gape, and then they pay.

Most vets, Reimer says, hate talking about money. Breaking a medical procedure down to the grubby business of dollars and cents seems like an insult to all that scientific training. Walking through a morning's worth of interventional radiology appointments with Berent, though, I noticed she was always explicit about the dollars. Which were big. Fifteen hundred here, twenty-five hundred there, a $3,000 stent. "I always try to be up front," she said. "I even go a little high. I don't want anybody to accuse me of anything."

At times, she went out of her way to try to save people money. Take the case of Bubba Earl, the gangly and deaf white boxer who started going lame at the age of eight months. He tumbled off the couch one day, and Mark and Michelle Halmo rushed him to a vet. Six days of hospitalization, and as many theories about his condition, followed. One doctor suggested his problems might stem from a hepatic shunt, a trick vein that diverts blood that ought to be feeding the liver. He recommended that Mark call VHUP, where correcting shunts has been a big part of Weisse and Berent's practice. Now, with an eager client in front of her, the doctor said she wasn't so sure. Shunt dogs, after all, are usually not very bright because their liver troubles impair brain development; the Halmos, by contrast, had taught their deaf dog an impressive array of hand signals. Mark wasn't so happy about the uncertainty. A CT scan was the definitive way to find out, but the whole procedure could wind up running $2,500 to $3,000. Why not do some other testing first, looking at other liver problems, and then come back?

"In my line of work, I'm a diagnostician," said Mark. "I have to know now."

Mark's profession? Commercial and industrial HVAC installation. "Take note we did not bat an eyelash," he said.

It later turned out, as Berent had thought, that Bubba Earl did not have that particular condition after all.

Back home in New Jersey a couple of weeks later, Halmo estimated he'd spent about $10,000 responding to Bubba's illness, which had been diagnosed as a severe liver problem. The dog would be on about a hundred dollars' worth of medications each month for life; Halmo noted that the life could be another ten years. (Berent later told me the diagnosis was more like "ten months to ten years.") "People at work and friends of the family, they'd say, you're really going to put that kind of money into a dog?" Halmo said. "I'd say, yeah. If you don't understand that, there's no way I can explain it to you. Either you get it or you don't. Even my ex-wife had kind words to say about it."

The prospect of customers who don't bat an eyelash has helped veterinary medicine's progression toward big business. For years, its organizational chart had a small number of prestige animal hospitals up top and all sorts of individually owned practices at the bottom. The diversity within the field, in everything from office decor to technology, can be jarring. In the same zip code as VHUP's nuclear imaging gear there's a well-loved local veterinary practice where I take my own pets. Here's how the veterinary technician weighs them: She picks up the pet, stands on an old scale, and checks the weight. Then she puts the pet down, weighs herself, and subtracts the difference.

The money pouring into the field may wind up making such a bare-bones practice untenable. One glimpse of the field's private-sector future comes from driving a few interstate exits away from both VHUP's nuclear imaging gear and the beloved vet who doesn't have a dog scale. A brand-new eighteen-thousand-square-foot facility houses Metropolitan Veterinary Associates, a private local specialty practice. The building features recovery rooms with heated floors, oxygen-infused cages for ailing animals, and an MRI. I spent a day tagging along with the doctors there. I had assumed it would be a place that drew slightly more critical or complicated cases than the average vet. And in fact I did watch a surgeon—the kind that uses a scalpel and gropes around in bloody bodily cavities—extract a pair of ingested thong underwear that had wrapped themselves around a rottweiler's innards, and a colleague do a tricky $1,200 root canal on a Great Dane. But there was also a dermatology consult and a neurology consult and a cardiology consult. Much of the action would not so long ago have required a trip to a place like VHUP. Or, more likely, it wouldn't have happened at all.

The biggest vet business story is what's happening at the bottom of the professional ladder. Like hardware stores and real estate agents before them, veterinary services are slowly turning into a world of competing chains. Since 2000, firms like the VCA, Banfield, and National Veterinary Associates have been on a buying spree, snapping up smaller operations and turning them into chain outposts. Banfield, owned by PetSmart, grew from 434 locations in 2003 to 617 four years later, many of them inside PetSmart stores. National Veterinary went from 61 clinics to 99. And VCA, which since its 2001 IPO has traded on the NASDAQ exchange under the ticker symbol WOOF, nearly doubled from 230 to 438. VCA earned $844 million in animal-hospital revenue—and a couple hundred million more from its diagnostic facilities—in 2007. And while human hospitals dicker with insurance companies to get that money, VCA got most of it paid up front. Between 2002 and 2007, the stock nearly tripled NASDAQ's average. "Single-doctor practices are becoming a thing of the past," *Veterinary Economics* declared.

Likewise, Big Pharma has also grown interested in Big Vet, rolling out a slew of canine medications that mirror the stuff their owners are likely to have in their own medicine cabinets. Literally. In many cases, the drugs are only slightly altered versions of medications prescribed to humans. In January 2007, Eli Lilly, which already had an agricultural-animal division called Elanco, set up a pet-focused unit, LillyPet. Its first release was Reconcile—doggie Prozac. The same year, a Pfizer drug called Slentrol became the first FDA-approved drug to combat dog obesity, yet another new way pets are waddling in the footsteps of their owners (25 percent of American dogs are estimated to be overweight). And before the year was out, Pfizer also introduced Cerenia, the first canine car-sickness drug to hit the market. The carefree old image of the dog with his head out the pickup-truck window and his tongue wagging happily in the breeze is now available to every pup—thanks to the chemical alchemy of twenty-first-century medicine.

And the very success of veterinary medicine leads to still more growth opportunities. America's pets, like America's humans, are living longer, making geriatric care a potentially profitable new field. The dollar figures are enough of a reality that some consumers are starting to hedge against their bleeding hearts. Veterinary health insurance plans in 2007 covered between 1 million and 2 million pets. A tiny number, but one market-research study put its growth at 26 percent each year between 2003 and 2008. The largest firm, VPI, says it insures 450,000 of them alone. VPI wrote its first policy in 1982 and largely had the field to itself for years. Not that it was much of a field. As late as 2000, barely 1 percent of dogs and cats had policies. By 2010, according to association forecasts, 5 to 7 percent of pets will be covered. Since the turn of the century, the field has become crowded with new competitors: PetFirst opened up in 2004. PetsBest came online in 2005. And in 2006 and 2007, members of a team that won a business-plan contest at the Wharton School set up dueling firms, Embrace Pet Insurance and Petplan USA. Trupanion, cofounded by Starbucks Coffee mogul Howard Schulz, joined the fray in early 2008.

For those without insurance, a number of new firms have arisen to offer on-the-spot loans for pet emergencies. Care Credit, which allows customers to borrow money for a variety of human health needs, also lets them borrow—with interest, naturally—to pay vet bills.

And of course, in an age of pet love, there's always pet charity. The Matthew J. Ryan Veterinary Hospital of the University of Pennsylvania, named for a former Speaker of the Pennsylvania state House of Representatives and featuring a brand-new academic building named for a dog-loving local banker, is built on it. Even the C-arm used in Ben's procedure carries a plaque explaining that it was a gift from a northern Virginia caterer—a woman whose one-month-old Labrador, Jack, was declared as good as dead by a local vet before Weisse made him one of the first dogs he treated for a shunt. Another client, Weisse says, recently paid $150,000 for a study of liver tumors. Weisse and an MBA friend have set up their own non-profit to help with more new research to push the minimally invasive techniques into areas like heart disease.

Some charities fund needy clients as well as innovative researchers. An Internet-based nonprofit called In Memory of Magic has donated over $1 million to pets in veterinary need, pulling in small contributions from browsers who can see pictures and read stories on the charity's Web site. Jack Nadolski, a nine-year-old Siberian husky, got $2,375 toward radiation treatment for a nasal carcinoma. Dustie George, a six-year-old yellow Labrador mix, got $2,683 for tibial plateau leveling osteotomy surgery to repair a hobbled hind leg. The owners' online pleas are enough to make even the hard-hearted reach for their checkbooks. "I am also going to sell baby items on eBay to help with the cost, and I am doing a yard sale," wrote Dustie's owner, who said she'd recently lost her job and also had a cat with leukemia. Soon after, someone came through. Dustie had surgery two months later.

Luckily for the Velinovs, they don't have to turn to eBay to fund the frequent long-distance round-trips to VHUP. But they are vowing to work toward keeping Ben alive long enough to get into the geriatric market. By his first round of chemotherapy, the trip to Philadelphia and the preappointment overnight hotel stay have started to seem familiar. At home, Ben has taken to following the couple everywhere. "We're both depressed," Milen says. The kids, off at college, "call and ask about him all the time. They think about it all the time. They are traumatized as well. He is a member of the family."

Ben's condition has meant changes for the couple. Though Milena, a freelance translator—she can translate from six languages and into four—works out of the house, the Velinovs have made arrangements to never let the dog be alone. As for the money, which will likely top $10,000, Milen says, "We are adjusting our finances. He's the priority, basically. Whatever else we have to pay for is on hold. If we have to buy a car, we don't buy a car right now. That's how it works."

Weisse and Berent estimate the results will win Ben six months to a year more. For now, he's not in pain. As a scientist, Milen says he knows about the dog's long odds. But he also says he's not going to give up; cutting-edge procedures, after all, could improve Ben's chances. "I've never discussed how much time this will get," he says. "Ben is the only dog I care about. It's one thing to look at published papers with many dogs. If you care about one dog only, you can change the protocol and do more."

Back in the fluoroscope lab, Weisse and Berent are working a new set of stents through a cancer-ravaged Westie named Monty. Like Ben, he has a bladder tumor, only this one is blocking all urine from leaving, which could kill him very quickly. So he's in for a urethral stent that will let the liquid shoot right past the tumor. In addition to the implant's $3,000 price tag, the procedure also comes with a 10 to 15 percent chance that Monty will be left permanently incontinent—*permanent* being a relative term, since the procedure will do nothing to extend his life beyond the six to twelve months that the cancer leaves him. The machine comes on, the lights go down, and the doctors start threading the probes through the dog's veins and arteries. Eventually, Weisse finds the right spot and deploys the stent.

"See how snug that is?" Weisse asks. "Well seated." But as a medical procedure, all the heroics nonetheless fall into a fairly glum category. When the operation is over, Monty's family will get some extra months with their dog—tantamount to years, in canine time—but the underlying disease remains. "It's, Let's not euthanize. Let's keep him peeing. What's amazing is, this is all palliative."

"To them, that's okay, because they're doing everything, and that's what they'd do for their kid," says Berent.

"You tell some people that the animal has three to six months to live if you do the surgery, and they look at you like, 'You want me to spend four thousand dollars for three to six months?'" Weisse says. "And then the next owners that come in, you tell them you can get three to six months, and it's like the hand of God has just given them another three to six months. Everyone has their own perception. The procedures that we do, you kind of select out for the people who are like, an extra day is worth everything."

SIX

Breeding the Perfect Beast

Where Do Pets Come From?

Well before the 2008 Westminster Kennel Club dog show champion had been named, Uno the beagle had already won over the crowd. Competing with a poodle, a Sealyham terrier, a Weimaraner, an Australian shepherd, and an Akita, the brown-and-white pup with the floppy ears emerged to the roar of a capacity Madison Square Garden crowd as the Best in Show portion of the contest began. The cheering—much of it from the eighty-dollar-a-ticket "cheap" seats—grew louder with every wag of Uno's white-tipped tail. He was, his handler Aaron Wilkerson said later, "the people's dog."

Today, he was the 132-year-old Westminster show's dog, too. Beagles are the only breed to have been consistently listed among America's most popular dogs for nearly a century, but the fifteen-incher from South Carolina was the first of his breed to win the most celebrated dog show in the country. A day after he triumphed in front of the packed Garden and 3.2 million television viewers, Uno's media schedule included appearances on *Today, Fox and Friends, Martha Stewart,* and CBS's *Early Show*. In the afternoon, he posed for pictures in Grand Central Terminal. News accounts carried inside scoops about his favorite chew toy (a soft yellow duck, though he was happy to chew a reporter's microphone after the show) and his favorite airline (Midwest, which provides a dog-sized harness for his seat). He rang the opening bell on Wall Street two days later.

By the weekend, the veteran CBS newsman Bob Schieffer even made some space for Uno amid a presidential politics discussion on *Face the Nation,* summing up the nationwide beagle-mania. "When Uno the beagle took Best in Show, I cheered out loud, my wife cried real tears of joy," he said. "Beagles are the best dogs that ever were. I feel the same way about dogs that I do about food. I like my food to look like food, the meat in its place on the plate, the vegetables in theirs, not all stacked up like some cutesy piece of art. And, please, flowers belong in vases, not on my plate. As for dogs, I like them to look like dogs, not some perfumed ball of fur that resembles a powder puff. You wouldn't paint a beagle's toenails or put ribbons in a bea-gle's hair . . . America is a better place when beagles rule. Good dog, Uno."

For the record, there are some big differences between Uno and your pet, even if you're a TV host. As a show dog, he's an investment with four co-owners. Like any champion, he's the product of generations of selective breeding. The humans who create such animals work tirelessly to "improve" the breed, bringing paws and tails and snouts up to strictly delineated standards. And show winners often work as high-priced studs to further improve the next generations. By most definitions, Uno is hardly a pet. Instead of being an animal kept with a fam-ily for its own wonderful sake, he's a lucrative economic unit. *Pet quality* is, in fact, a term of derision for top breeders, used to describe animals that are not up to their standards. That Uno happens to be a true-blue sweetheart that most people would want as their family companion is nice, but beside the point.

I hadn't come to Westminster because the lives of its elaborately coiffed contestants said much about the lives of ordinary housepets. I was there because the show is America's biggest advertisement for a phenomenon that still shapes much of modern pet ownership: the desire for purebred dogs. When you think about it, the enduring appeal of purebreds is a strange thing. Dog shows rose to popularity in the late nineteenth century, with all of the creepily eugenicist principles of an era obsessed with race and petrified of miscegenation. Fanciers obsessed about genetic purity and quality bloodlines, verifiable lineage and breed standards. Mongrels were most definitely not welcome when gilded-age Manhattanites gathered to establish the club at the Westminster Hotel in 1877; since 1884, entrants have had to be registered as purebred dogs with the American Kennel Club. The dog show's values mirrored those that governed which humans were allowed into the Victorian elite. But since then, society has democratized. Elite universities champion diversity, formerly off-limits social clubs recruit minority members, even the august wedding-announcements page of the *New York Times* is downright polyglot, with Jews marrying Hindus marrying WASPs marrying Catholics. These days, when the average supermodel seems to come from Swedish-Bolivian-Japanese stock, you can scarcely read about a prestigious French chef without learning that he was born in Mozambique and also spent two years apprenticing under a Thai cooking master. And yet Westminster retains its old trappings. The show's thick, bound catalog, with its listings of sires and dams and kennels, reads like a copy of the Social Register. Mixed breeds are still forbidden. The television announcers are dressed in tuxedos.

In the stands, ordinary Westminster spectators—distinctly less likely to wear evening gowns than, say, crocheted corgi sweaters—were there for a simpler reason: It was fun! Like a day at the zoo, but with the vast diversity of dogdom close enough to touch. The show's media staff advised reporters to tell their readers that the contest is a good place for would-be dog owners to come figure out what breed they want. So long, of course, as they don't want "mixed." I spent the better part of a morning with three old college friends who'd flown in from Atlanta and Dallas to watch. "Just call us, like, 'the Gals,'" said one of them. "Don't use our names, because we called in sick at work." This induced a fit of laughter from the Gals, a delighted reaction soon repeated when a Norwich terrier gave the Gals a particularly adorable look, and after a beagle gave the Gals a particularly adorable look, and a schnauzer—"my breed," said one—gave the Gals a particularly adorable look. Don't mutts give adorable looks, too? Sure, they said. But you can see those anywhere. At any rate, the Gals were hooked. "My husband would never come to this," one of them concluded. "So we decided to make it a girls' weekend. We gotta do this every year."

In the world of purebred dogs, it's a lot more comfortable to contemplate Uno than Megan's dog's father. And yet, to critics, the two have a lot in common. Uno is the champion whose nationally televised triumph helps reinforce the idea that purebred dogs in their various breeds are objects of consumer desire. And Megan's dog's father, a breeding dog who lives in a tiny wire cage in an Amish country hutch he shares with several dozen similar dogs, helps the retail market cater to that desire.

A farmer named Elmer Fisher pointed out the four-year-old off-white King Charles spaniel one summer afternoon in the small Pennsylvania town of Gordonville. I was there with a man named Bob Baker, who had come to Lancaster County, he told the farmer, because he wanted to buy his wife a dog like the one his daughter had taken home a few weeks earlier. Fisher, a pleasant man who wore the standard black trousers, suspenders, mustacheless beard, and straw hat of Amish country, said he didn't have any dogs like it at the moment. But perhaps Baker would care to have a look at the others? We walked over to what looked like an old chicken coop. Inside, amid a cacophony of barks, there were thirty or so dogs in cages—spaniels, poodles, bichons frises, and "cava-chons," made from crossing Cavalier King Charles spaniels and bichons. The cages were a couple of feet off the ground and had wire floors, allowing the animals' excrement to drop straight onto the wood shavings below. That made it possible to clean up the space without ever having to remove the animals from their enclosures. Over years in captivity, the wire floors also dig into a dog's paws, according to critics.

Fisher showed off his current wares. There were a couple of poodles for $250 apiece and some cava-chons who would turn eight weeks, the minimum age for sale, at the end of the month. There was also an only days-old litter of cocker spaniels. Fisher opened up a box where the dogs were suckling at their mother. The pups were tiny, the size of gerbils. "Oh, that one's gone dead," he said. A boy of about eight, also dressed in Amish attire and wearing a soup bowl haircut, scooped the tiny brown animal out of the box by hand, walked over to a nearby wheelbarrow, and added it to the cart's load of discarded wood shavings and dog droppings. On the other side of the room were the breeder dogs, living in the cages where they would spend their entire lives: mothers with engorged nipples and abdomens swaying toward the ground from years of litters, dogs who would be retired—which in some places means shot—once they stopped producing the big litters the young dogs produce. And sharing a cramped cage with another spaniel was Megan's dog's father. He'd been a stud his whole life, living right there in that cage for four years. And what was his name? "I don't know," the farmer said.

Shocking to an ordinary pet owner, the scene didn't faze Baker. Rather than the vaguely clueless dog-seeking dad he posed as, he's a veteran animal-cruelty investigator with the ASPCA and was visiting on an undercover operation looking for inhumane conditions at wholesale dog-breeding operations like Fisher's. In reality, "Megan" wasn't his daughter but a volunteer who'd made a scouting visit some weeks earlier. According to Pennsylvania Bureau of Dog Law Enforcement records, the farm we were visiting housed 52 dogs at the most recent inspection; it sold 118 in the past year. That actually makes Fisher a relative small fry. One nearby breeder had 715 dogs on his property during its last inspection. The paperwork also lists numerous past code violations at Fisher's facility, including uncleaned whelping areas, excess excreta, and problems with water receptacles. Although the violations had been corrected before the most recent state inspection, Baker was now here to document the place in living color, via a minuscule hidden-camera lens sewn into place as a button on his shirt and operated with a switch hidden in his pocket. Perfectly legal but still possibly horrifying to the general public, this facility was the first of five small-time Amish breeders on his itinerary for the day. The resulting footage would be logged and cut into highlight reels for elected officials and the mass media as part of a high-profile campaign against the operations that critics call puppy mills.

The year of Uno's triumph at Westminster was, coincidentally, a big year for that campaign. Two months before the show, the Humane Society of the United States released a video tracing the origins of the pets for sale at the fancy Los Angeles boutique Pets of Bel Air. Britney Spears and Paris Hilton had been customers at the emporium, where $2,400 toy dogs lounge in baby cribs until they are sold. Humane Society investigators discovered shipping documents that showed the store purchased dogs from a series of squalid facilities in the South and Midwest, the very antithesis of Bel Air pampering. The video interspersed scenes of well-heeled Angeleno shoppers with shots of rural cages crammed full of miserable-looking dogs—dogs, a narrator reported, that were denied basic veterinary care, the opportunity to play with other animals, and a chance to go to the bathroom outside their kennel. The story quickly became national news, splashed across the pages of the *New York Times,* the *Los Angeles Times, People,* and—yes—*Celebrity Dog Watcher.* Within hours of the video's release, city officials briefly shut down the store for selling pets without a valid permit. Taken aback by the bad publicity, the pet store, which had quickly reopened after bringing its paperwork up to date, issued a statement claiming it had never knowingly purchased puppy-mill dogs.

An even brighter spotlight landed on the industry a few months later, in Pennsylvania. For years, an activist named Bill Smith, who runs a shelter outside Philadelphia, had railed against the condition of the dogs mass-produced by Amish farmers in neighboring Lancaster County. He'd gone so far as to buy billboards along Amish-country highways to raise the consciousnesses of the tourists who visit for traditional buggy rides and shoofly pie. In early 2008, he bought a billboard in a more influential location: opposite the Chicago studio where Oprah Winfrey films her daily TV show. Perhaps America's most influential animal lover, Winfrey makes her pets a regular feature of her show; over the years she's devoted episodes to all sorts of canine subjects. OPRAH, DO A SHOW ON PUPPY MILLS, the billboard pleaded. THE DOGS NEED YOU. In April, Smith got his wish. Winfrey did an entire show about the subject, dedicating it to her recently deceased cocker spaniel, Sophie. The show's footage of commercial dog breeding in

Amish country—some of it shot by Baker—was harrowing, with images of malnourished, mistreated dogs whom breeders "debark" by shoving sharp sticks down their throats. The effect was a bit like watching one of those animal-rights videotapes depicting the mistreatment of young calves at the hands of agribusinesses. Except worse. Veal, however it is produced, is something you buy to eat. A puppy, especially now, is something you buy to love. On air, Winfrey importuned viewers to never, ever buy from a pet store. To do so, she said, amounted to subsidizing the puppy-mill industry. "It is my belief that when you actually see this with your own eyes, America, you are not going to stand for it . . . the millions of you watching today, go to shelters to get your pet."

What activists call puppy mills are actually farms that raise beagles or bichons instead of, or usually in addition to, tomatoes or corn. They're not illegal—the rules are complicated, pocked with loopholes, and often ignored—but they're not pretty, either. And, because small-scale breeders won't sell dogs to pet stores, nearly every pet store in the country sells puppy-mill dogs. Baker says puppy mills are nothing new: "The term *puppy mill* has changed over the years. When I first started, it was never meant as a derogatory term or a pejorative term—it just meant anyone who was mass-breeding puppies for stores. But the conditions were so bad that the term got a reputation." A stockbroker before he got into humane work during the 1970s, Baker has done much to give it that reputation. "I went to one place in Missouri where [the owner] was getting rid of some of his breed stock because the breed wasn't selling," Baker said. "He had about thirty of these Eskimos and Samoyeds, and he took out his shotgun and was just shooting them. He was in the back field, just shooting them in the head. I said I was a salesman, selling kennel supplies, so he figured I was just in the industry and knew what I was involved with." With a Rolodex of contacts in the mass media, Baker has turned a number of such stories into national scandals; he credits himself with helping to put several retailers out of business. Though he's hardly happy with the status quo, he says the attention has forced big-time breeders to improve their practices. "Back in the early eighties, you would see dogs housed in old cars. You could go down to the town dump and get old refrigerators and washers to put them in. They don't do that anymore. And another thing you don't see is they used to take old oil drums and tie dogs to it. Now they house them better and feed them better."

Based in Saint Louis, Baker visits Lancaster County often enough that he has his own phone number in the local area code, the better to maintain his cover. He's been coming for a quarter century, since the local puppy industry was born. Until the 1980s, most of the nation's puppy mills were in the heartland, where they'd first popped up in response to a postwar boom in purebred pet sales. But wholesalers who sold puppies to stores in the Northeast were looking for suppliers a little closer to the market. At the same time, the county's Amish and Mennonite small farmers were feeling the squeeze from agribusinesses. "Many of these family farmers found it was a good way of keeping their farm," Baker says. "Start breeding litters." Today, the county has 338 registered kennels. The Amish culture, with little pet-keeping tradition, was less inclined to be stymied by the disconnect between selling an animal as a beloved family member and mass-producing it as an agricultural commodity.

That's exactly the disconnect that has turned the issue into a twenty-first-century cause célèbre. In the past, warnings against shopping at pet stores scarcely mentioned animal mistreatment. Instead, they mainly took a consumer-protection angle, arguing that pet store dogs were more likely to be sickly or ill-behaved— a bad product, in other words. But in the fur-baby era, the focus has switched from product quality to production cruelty, from consumer protection to canine protection.

Targeted at changing the spending habits of pet owners themselves, the puppy mill campaign also represents a dramatically different type of crusade than previous humane efforts. Historically, animal-protection organizations have fought to protect other people's animals—horses that pulled city jitneys, cattle that starred in country rodeos. Each of those campaigns could be seen as a political battle between separate cultures: on one side, *bien-pensant* folks who view animals as individuals who deserve consideration; on the other, people who view them as tools for pulling weight or growing dinner. The battle over puppy mills is a humanitarian campaign for the pet era. In arguing against shopping at pet stores, activists aren't butting into other people's business so much as they're asking pet people to live up to their own standards. If you love your dog as a family member, can you really be okay with a business that keeps its mother confined in a breeding hutch until there's no more use for her?

Pictures like Baker's have also featured in a new legal effort to regulate commercial dog breeding. In Pennsylvania, Governor Ed Rendell, a dog lover who used to bring his golden retriever with him to work as Philadelphia's mayor in the 1990s, channeled the outrage into a broad campaign against the puppy mills centered in the chunk of Lancaster County I visited with Baker. Rendell fired the members of the state's Dog Law Advisory Board, built a rapid-response team of kennel inspectors, and hired a feisty ex-prosecutor to make sure his Bureau of Dog Law Enforcement stopped losing so many cases. He also proposed a series of legislative changes to increase cage size, require shade, and forbid the painful wire-floor cages. The new laws would allow only veterinarians to perform cesarean sections, debarking procedures, and euthanasia. That final topic grabbed headlines in the summer of 2008 when a pair of

Amish-country breeders were reported to have shot and killed their entire population of eighty dogs after state officials ordered veterinary exams for dozens of them. "They were old, and we were hearing that they don't want kennels anymore," one of the men, Elmer Zimmerman, told the *Philadelphia Inquirer*. "The best thing to do was get rid of them." The mass killing, which took place as Rendell was prodding rural legislators to take action on his dog-breeding proposals, was perfectly legal. Hoping to capitalize on the public outrage, the governor—alongside his dog—hit a Philadelphia dog run to campaign for the measure two days after the story broke.

An ex-prosecutor himself, Rendell had by this point become sufficiently immersed in dog-law minutiae that he eventually taught a Continuing Legal Education session on the subject. One fall night, I also watched him discuss the effort before a crowd of veterinary students, winding together the byzantine details of state regulatory processes with the story of his dog, Maggie—rescued by Smith's group from the hutch where she'd spent years restrained in order to be mounted again and again as a breeding dog. "A lot of the major kennel owners view puppies as products, just like pigs or chickens," he said.

But if you're selling something for profit, what other than a product could it be? Over several days of driving Amish country roads, I spotted dozens of handmade signs advertising apparently incongruous goods like STRAW HATS/PUPPIES and HOME MADE ROOT BEER/LABS/BBQ and WELDING/POMERANIUMS (*sic*). The same was true of the electronic superhighway. One search led me to a site called cutebichons.com, laden with pictures of adorable little puppies like "Layla" ($395) and "Snickers" ($350). But when I drove to the address, it turned out to be the farm of Daniel Esh, which state records say is home to more than four hundred dogs and a recipient of repeated warnings over the years for practices like allowing a dog's open wound to go untreated and having too many dogs in a small space.

My day with Baker and Smith wound its way through the rolling hills of the county, past horse-drawn carts and old silos where drab Amish clothing was flapping on laundry lines. One result of the Amish shunning of modernity is no TV, and hence a lot less post-*Oprah* suspiciousness than I'd expected. (Smith, who joined us on the trip, steered clear of most of the farms because a photo of him had been circulated among Lancaster County breeders following his appearance on the show.) Sometimes, we didn't even have to chat up farmers; we simply walked over to puppy hutches visible from the road. In the town of East Earl, a dozen enormous rottweilers sweltered in cages on one farm's lawn. There was excrement on the floor and most of the plastic paint buckets that served as water bowls were empty. No one was around. On our last stop, in the town of Stevens, we pulled up to a farm whose sign advertised brown eggs. It turned out the farmer, who identified himself as Roy Miller, also had English mastiffs and French bulldogs. Thinking it would warm Miller up, Smith said he wanted to buy six dozen eggs. Before long, we were staring at two mother English mastiffs, massive yellow dogs in tiny hutches. The male breeding dog was on the other side of the driveway, constrained in a makeshift cage built out of pieces of fencing that had been looped together. Smith took Miller's number and said he'd call in a few weeks to see if a new litter was on its way. As we got ready to leave, the farmer took us into the barn to pick out our eggs. "The chickens, we let them run free," he said. "So the eggs are better." As we drove off, we spotted a second hutch with a quartet of brown puppies peeking out at the road.

Given the nature of our current relationships with pets, it's natural that talking about them like commodities should feel odd. But the history of dogs, especially, is intertwined with that of human commerce.

Scholars have often disagreed about how the fearsome wolf became the modern *Canis lupus familiaris*. But most of them agree that we humans had something to do with it, either by actively taming the beasts or—more plausibly—by inadvertently helping evolution tame them for us. One theory: Humans ditch their hunter-gatherer act and settle into villages. Trash dumps quickly follow, which for the nearby wolves represent the species equivalent of ordering takeout instead of doing the hard work of stalking prey. Who gets to raid this prehistoric buffet? Chances are it'll be whichever wolves are less frightened by the presence of humans, or, eventually, those more adept at sucking up to said villagers. The result is an animal tailor-made for our human conception of cuteness. Compared to his wolfen predecessors, the modern domestic dog's frequently floppy ears, soft face, and happy-go-lucky personality telegraph a perpetual childishness, the very quality that disarms humans, literally and figuratively. People like Uno, in other words, because he was made, by natural selection, to be liked by them.

But natural selection alone can't explain how, in a few short millennia, dogs have evolved into the most diverse species on earth. Creating a range of animals that includes giant Great Danes and pipsqueak Chihuahuas required more active human involvement. After a few dozen millennia or so, humans got into the breeding game, directing their now tame dogs' sexual desires in order to create four-legged tools for herding, or guarding, or chasing foxes across the English countryside, or rescuing alpine wanderers, or keeping unruly colonial subjects in line. Never mind those aristocratic studbooks. In evolutionary terms, fancy purebred dogs are measly arrivistes; dogs were a fairly indistinct species until five thousand or so years ago—a blink in planetary history—and even the earliest examples of specific breeds were not particularly common as late as the time of Christ. Most extant breeds date back less than two centuries.

When you consider the end users—us—the sudden burst of

breeds is easy to understand. The pet-era phenomenon known as dog fancy requires a trickier undertaking than simply breeding working animals: catering to the fickle tastes of those whose animals have no jobs except companionship. In the nineteenth century, this upscale hobby was quickly turned into contests like Westminster. By the twentieth century, as pet buying spread to those who had once made do with whatever stray happened along, the fanciers had spent generations crafting tails that wagged just so on a few hundred different breeds.

So much for how Uno and Megan's dog's father got here. Where dogs are going next remains a mystery; human preference in dog breeds remains as fickle as ever. Or, as one of the Amish farmers put it: "People like one kind one year, another kind some other year. I don't know why." One guy who studies that very question is a Western Carolina University professor named Hal Herzog. Herzog isn't a veterinarian; he's a psychology professor who thinks about the vicissitudes of human taste. Over the past decade, he's pored through registration data from the American Kennel Club, the country's most prestigious purebred-animal group, trying to make sense of the dizzying rise and fall of popular breeds. The Irish setter, for instance, was happily trundling along with between two and three thousand new registrations a year from the 1940s to the 1960s. Then, all of a sudden, starting in the mid-1960s, it became the Beatles of dog breeds, with exponential annual leaps in the number of new registrations. In 1974, a whopping 61,549 new setters registered with the organization. And then, equally quickly, the breed faded away. Another decade later, the number of new setters was a mere 7 percent of what it had been at the peak. Herzog found the same pattern, at different times, for breeds ranging from Afghan hounds through Saint Bernards—a sudden spike, then a sudden tumble.

What happened to the Irish setter? Did the war in Vietnam suddenly make Americans yearn for the comfort of a big red dog? Did Watergate do him in? Surprisingly, one answer Herzog's research discounts is mass media. Notwithstanding Bob Schieffer's hopes that Uno's victory might herald a beagle-dominated future, the breed of the Westminster winner does not correlate with which breed people gravitate toward over the following years. Nor, necessarily, do popular movies: While *101 Dalmatians* famously led to a run on the spotted dogs—and an equally famous backlash when the real-life animals turned out to be less sweet than their cinematic kin—other movies have had no impact whatsoever. Between 1998 and 2003, a series of popular Taco Bell advertisements brought a Chihuahua onto TV screens across the country. And new AKC Chihuahua registrations declined.

Instead, Herzog chalks up breed tastes to a complex mathematical model based on the anthropological idea known as *random drift*, the same notion that governs fluctuations in baby names or pop music charts or how many buttons we prefer on men's suits. The bottom line: people copy other people. Some people tend to adapt earlier, set a model for others, and then move on once the phenomenon has played itself out. By the mid-1970s, it seems, the Irish setter had become a little like what bell-bottoms were to become a few years later. Except, of course, that Irish setters are living things for whom the drift in human tastes had real consequences. At the start of the boom, the demand most likely meant more people decided to enter the commercial field of Irish setter production. Inevitably, some of those producers would have been less sensitive than others to the breeding animals' physical or emotional needs; still others might have raced to meet demand by cutting corners on who gets to reproduce, failing to take the time to breed out genetic problems. Whether or not any of that was what ended the dog's popularity—Herzog says he doesn't have enough information to know for sure—commercial breeders moved on, buying more popular breeds while "retiring" Irish setter bitches.

The uncertainty over breed popularity reflects one of the strangest things about the U.S. pet industry, with its $43 billion in sales and its publicly traded firms. The industry has a small army of marketing analysts who can tell us exactly how many new lines of premium cat food were released in a given year, but few people from the business side know much at all about the very first acquisition pet people make: the pet itself. The pet-production end of the industry remains largely segregated from its retail and service sectors. Purina doesn't make 'em, and PetSmart won't sell 'em. The reason boils down to a truth about our contemporary idea of pets: If you make a living appealing to the altruistic emotions of Max and Chloe's pet parents, it's bad business to simultaneously treat Max and Chloe like commodities—especially when some of those commodities are produced in sweatshops.

APPMA's own figures suggest the point of entry to pet ownership remains overwhelmingly informal. Twenty-nine percent of dogs are acquired from breeders. For all the fuss about puppy mills, just 15 percent were purchased at pet stores in 2006. Even if you assume all Internet and classified-ad sales are puppy-mill dogs—an unfair assumption—the animals remain a small minority of the pets who come home to America's families each year. For cats, the numbers are even lower. In both cases, that means the majority of pets come through nonretail channels: from friends or relatives, as gifts, as strays, from shelters, via the newspaper. "Most of the pets in this country change hands and are acquired outside of any structure," says Steve Zawistowski, who tracks the issue for the ASPCA. "All of this stuff in the media about the forty-billion-dollar national pet industry, and you realize that most people get their pets for free . . . You're really going back to the old AT&T model where it's, 'We'll give you the goddamn telephone, but we'll tell you how much it costs to use it.'"

Even at the very top of the breeding heap, the question of commerce is a tricky one. Championship breeders, of course, will take the same money as Amish farmers or the pet stores they supply. In fact, they'll usually take a similar amount of money, and for a far more reliable product. But they'd just as soon not take the money, too. Even if the way veteran breeders often talk about dogs, which can sound more like a discussion of handcrafted jewelry, is jarring to civilians, their inattention to the bottom line makes it clear that they don't see their wares as simple commercial goods.

One October morning, I took a drive out to the very center of Long Island to watch a Manhattan couple buy a dog from Beowulf Kennels, a breeder of prize beagles whose show dogs included one of the pups vanquished by Uno on his way to the crown. Beowulf is a small-scale, responsible kennel, the opposite of the mass breeders targeted by Smith and Baker. I'd been given the name by a contact at the AKC. The Web site listed a slew of titles Beowulf dogs had won. I arrived to find the unpretentious home of Ted Swedalla and Terri Giannetti, the couple behind Beowulf. About the only thing setting the place off from its cul-de-sac neighbors was the squat kennel they'd built on one patch of an already small yard. Swedalla and Giannetti spend many of their weekends traveling to dog shows across the country or conferring with other beagle folks about the next generation. They both have day jobs: Swedalla is a contractor and Giannetti works at JFK Airport.

If Swedalla and Giannetti were looking to upgrade their lifestyle via some quick, no-questions-asked commerce with the lawyer-banker couple who'd driven out from the city in a black BMW, it didn't show. Like any responsible breeder, the couple won't sell to pet stores. They won't even sell to most of the people who drive out to their home. By the time Phillip Daniel and Ritta Lee set out to see the beagles that morning, they had already filled out a lengthy questionnaire supplied by the kennel. They'd described their household (childless couple), detailed their daily schedule (workaholic professionals), and professed their willingness to have their home inspected by the kennel. They'd explained why they wanted a dog (companionship) and listed the books Daniel had consulted during his months of reading up on dog breeds (rest assured, he's thorough). They'd acknowledged that they understood how a puppy is a multiyear commitment and promised not to ever give their dog to anyone else; the kennel would take it back if necessary. (By contrast, most Lancaster County breeders offer a ten-day guarantee in the event a vet finds something specific wrong with the animal.) When Daniel had first called, Giannetti didn't have any puppies available. But she said she planned a litter in the fall, ready to be taken home in November. Perhaps they'd care to come have a look.

About a half hour into Swedalla's monologue about the finer points of beagle care, Lee piped up with what could seem to be an obvious question: "When can we see the dogs?" It quickly became clear she would have to wait a bit longer. Swedalla was getting going. "You'll see them, you will," he said. "But you must have more questions. Beagles are hounds. Do you have any questions about hounds?" And he was off. He riffed on the breed's history, its behavior, its aesthetic standards. He talked about the thirteen-inch variety and the fifteen-inch type and showed off the different sizes of crates that should be used to crate-train them until they're housebroken. He showed them how to sniff a dog's ears to check for infection. He dispensed wisdom on canine nutrition and the meaning of a dog bark. Daniel and Lee, picking up on what was expected of them, followed up with questions of their own. Should they hire a behaviorist? (Yes.) How much exercise does a beagle need? (They're flexible.) "I watch their body language," Swedalla said later. He was talking about the prospective buyers, not the dogs. "I listen to their questions. I screen out about eighty percent of people who want to buy a dog."

Eventually, Swedalla walked the couple back through the kennel area, where he keeps the adult dogs. There was Clapton, and Blush, and Justice, and Kerik. And then Tommy. "You're going to meet a very famous show dog," Swedalla said. "He was best beagle in the country in 2000. He's won many awards. He's twelve, but he's got the body of a two-year-old. The reason is diet and exercise." Appropriate, if slightly baffled, gushing ensued. "He has probably the best feet you'll ever see on a beagle," Swedalla added, warming to the subject. "They're cat feet, which they're supposed to be."

"So gentle," Lee said.

"That's the essence of a beagle," Swedalla declared, beaming.

Finally, Swedalla led them across the small stretch of backyard separating the kennel building from his house. The puppies were in a whelping area off the kitchen, the better to receive full-time attention. And, of course, they were adorable: Little Sonata, Josh, Full Round Circle, Texas, and Three White Legs. Only the boys were for sale; a female had been adjudged show quality. They tumbled over one another as Swedalla laid down a bowl of food. "You can see at this point that they're very easy to fall in love with," he said. "But just remember, there's a lot of work to be done." Only then did the verdict arrive. "Both Terri and I are on board with you," Swedalla said. "We feel like you'll provide the proper home and care for a dog." The anxiety drained out of the room. Daniel and Lee looked, for all the world, like a couple who had just landed their toddler a spot in a tony preschool. "I feel confident you guys can do a fabulous job. You ask good questions. And I always feel that people who take good care of themselves would be good for dogs." They could pick up the dog in a couple of weeks, he said. The cost would be $1,200.

Later, I asked Swedalla why he wouldn't simply sell the dogs to a couple who could obviously afford them. Part of the answer is self-interest: As people with an emotional and financial investment in purebred beagles, they'd see their investment damaged if shady buyers bought Beowulf beagles only to breed and sell them. But the kennel's mandatory neuter policy for pet sales takes care of that concern. Why, then, would he tie his hands by not selling around the Christmas doggie-gift season, or turning down families whose children seem afraid of dogs during their visits, or rejecting those who paid insufficient attention to the questionnaire? "We just really care about this breed," he said. "That's why we do all of this."

The classiest place of all to get a pet may be a Chicago facility known as PAWS. This may seem a bit odd because PAWS, which stands for Pets Are Worth Saving, is an animal shelter. In less euphemistic times, we called them pounds.

PAWS is among the newfangled "adoption centers" that have sprung up around the country over the past decade or so. A pound was once a place where you could count on children—or even their parents—bursting into tears at the sight of the forlorn pets, but the new version is as cheerful as a kindergarten and as consumer-friendly as a Best Buy. In Washington, D.C., a new shelter features waterfalls to create a Zen sense of calm. San Diego's sprawling facility has a coffee shop. San Francisco's SPCA houses dogs in twelve-by-twelve-foot apartments complete with artwork and televisions. The splendor, amid some of America's priciest real estate, once drew pickets from homeless activists.

PAWS Chicago's thirteen-thousand-square-foot facility

may have them all beat. The airy lobby looks like a Pottery Barn showroom. In the morning, the sun dapples the Adirondack chairs. Later in the day, tiny candles help set a mood—and keep the pet-filled building smelling a lot nicer than, say, my house. Executive director Rochelle Michalek gave me a tour not long after PAWS' 2007 grand opening. She touted the cage-free atmosphere in the Marshall Field Family Dog Town, showed off a complex air-filtration system designed to keep animals healthy, and noted the prominent placement given to older cats in an effort to encourage people to adopt them. Still, I wasn't quite prepared to hear Michalek, a woman who has dedicated her professional career to the grim task of ending shelter euthanasia, introduce me to PAWS' canine area by saying, "As you can see, Dog Town's a little more Ralph Lauren–y. It's autumn colors." Like the shade of light green used in PAWS' Kitty City, the color was chosen specifically to flatter the animals—and woo would-be adopters.

The reason facilities like PAWS imitate the look of retail America, of course, is that they're trying to compete with retail America. It works. One afternoon while I was visiting the adoption center, a man named Ken Majewski trotted in to take another look at Sugar, a white bichon mix he'd been thinking about adopting. Eight months earlier, Majewski's West Highland terrier had died. He'd bought that dog at a suburban pet store. He hadn't thought much about it—that's where you get dogs, right? Fancy breeders are expensive, and shelters are grim places in bad parts of town where you can't find the dog you want. As it happened, Majewski's job as a hospital IT guy regularly took him past PAWS' storefront in the tony Lincoln Park neighborhood. The place looked friendly and clean and nice. So he went in. It turned out he could search by dogs' size and energy levels. He could visit their rooms, walk with them, or simply stare through giant panes of glass. The pet boutique where he'd bought his last dog, by contrast, had looked like a hardware store. He was sold.

As he played with Sugar in an Astroturf patch on PAWS' rooftop deck, Majewski explained that he worked across the street. "I would walk by and stop and look and see. And I thought, why not rescue a dog?"

Why not? Getting ordinary, non-humane-activist type people to have that reaction, Michalek said, was exactly the point. "People always say there are too many animals and not enough homes," she told me. "We say there are enough homes, only they're filled with animals that are being bought. So we go after that market." The upscale shelters are hardly alone; adopting animals has never been more consumer-friendly. The wildly popular Web site Petfinder.com allows would-be adopters to cruise pictures and descriptions of animals in nearly every shelter in the country. Visitors can search its 250,000 animals by breed, age, sex, and location. Whereas a trip to your local shelter is a crapshoot unlikely to net any specific type of animal, Petfinder works like the Amazon.com of adoptions. Discovery Network's Animal Planet bought the site as part of a $35-million deal in 2006. Adoption information will remain free, but retailers pay to advertise to a vast audience of people about to jump into the pet industry.

And while Petfinder helps you get to the dogs, an array of new efforts now help the dogs get to you. In a number of northeastern and West Coast cities, two decades of public-interest messages about spaying and neutering pets have led, at long last, to a shortage of stray dogs, leaving shelters increasingly dominated by unadoptable, antisocial pit bulls. In response, shelter operators have started what amounts to a canine underground railroad. PetSmart's charitable arm alone transported fifteen thousand dogs over a hundred thousand miles each year. While many northeastern cities are overrun with unwanted pit bulls, the hounds and working dogs of rural America are easy to find homes for. At Bill Smith's Main Line Animal Rescue, I took a tour shortly after a truck carrying forty dogs from Missouri had pulled in. In a nod to their origins in the home state of Anheuser-Busch, the shelter named them all after beers. "There's Amstel, Natty, and Miller," board member Betsy Legnini said, gesturing to a trio of black corgi mixes. "Budweiser's gone already."

Notwithstanding the horrors of puppy mills, the modern pet market has been shaped by a number of positive changes. Adoptions are more customer-friendly than ever. The campaign against puppy mills and pet stores has gone mainstream. Spay/neuter programs have worked. Drugs and training are available for the behavior problems that lead many to give up their pets; in some places, charitable donations help make such services available to poorer people. The ASPCA's Zawistowski, though, worries about what the consequences will be if humane organizations succeed enough to bring the number of unwanted animals close to zero. In what will remain a largely unregulated marketplace, he worries that the result could be a boon to the very folks activists have spent years demonizing: mass-market breeders. In 2008, he gathered a group of scholars in Austin, Texas, to think about that very subject. If we succeed enough to eliminate those strays we've been encouraging people to adopt, where will people get their pets?

One idea: bring humane organizations into the very business they have fought. An independent nonprofit organization could inspect breeders, certify that they're running a cruelty-free operation—and then conduct unannounced reinspections to make sure they stay that way. "It's a big culture clash," Zawistowski said of the divide between breeders and the humane groups who would have to run such a system. "But otherwise, we could be looking at a train wreck."

Alternatively, for the wealthy, we could be looking at something like Eve Yohalem's $6,000 cat.

In 2007, Yohalem was one of the first customers to take delivery of a much-ballyhooed miracle of modern science: the hypoallergenic cat. Mischief was purchased from a company called Allerca, which claims to have identified the naturally occurring genetic divergence marking cats that don't secrete the allergy-causing protein glycoprotein Fel d 1. Scientists expressed doubts when the firm hit the market, noting that no peer-reviewed study had ever confirmed the company's discovery. It didn't help when the hometown *San Diego Union-Tribune* reported that the company's boss, Simon Brodie, had been sentenced to time for accounting fraud involving a hot-air balloon business in his native England. (He says the media have been unfair to him.)

But none of that stopped Brodie from taking to *The Early Show* and *Good Morning America* to tout the Allerca GD, the amazing, incredible all-natural hypoallergenic kitty. *TIME* magazine named it one of the best inventions of 2006. A year later, Brodie said he had a fifteen-month waiting period for the cats. Yohalem, a writer in Manhattan, grew up with cats but told me her investor husband was rush-to-the-hospital allergic to them. Yohalem considered it a fortieth-birthday treat. "At the time, it was four thousand dollars for everything, plus an additional two thousand dollars if you wanted to be expedited. So we decided to pay the extra money to get the cat quicker."

One fall day, she went out to the airport to take delivery of her new cat. "What came off the plane was the tiniest eight-week-old striped kitten that you've ever seen," she said. "It's now nearly two months later, and nobody's having trouble with this kitten. He is adorable and beautiful." Since Brodie had directed me to Yohalem, it was no surprise that she was a satisfied customer. But I was struck by something she said during our conversation, when the talk turned to the price and whether it was worth it. "In our defense," she said, "now that it's home, we're pretty normal about it."

Brodie, though, is part of a business that aims to make the look and shape of pets an arena for high-end competition. If indeed the pet-sales business follows the old AT&T model of cheap product enabling costly services, he's selling an iPhone— a premium product that also enables costly services. Like, say, the $10,900 Chakan GD (with a "creamy base coat" and "almond shaped bright blue eyes"), or the $31,000 Ashera GD (with "the markings and standing of a leopard" and a size of up to thirty pounds). In 2007, he merged Allerca with his other company, Lifestyle Pets, which sells animals with no hypoallergenic claims whatsoever; they're all about looks. There's the $65,000 White Ashera ("a striking animal that resembles the famed white tigers") and the $125,000 Royal Ashera ("less than four kittens produced each year . . . the rarest domestic cat in the world"). It's the rare place where the usually isolated companion-animal-production business reflects the companion-animal-nurturing business, ever seeking the sweet spot between humanization, animalness, and convenience. Yes, you too can have a rottweiler that fits in a Chihuahua-sized apartment, or a poodle that plays like a Lab, or a cat who gives off dander that's fit for a human.

Brodie's prices may amaze, but the boutique-hybrid phenomenon is growing. Even with enormous populations of free feral kittens in need of a home, several cat breeders will now sell you a Toyger, which is striped like a miniaturized tiger and, at $1,200, is a bargain by Brodie's standards. In the dog world, once-exotic hybrids like the 1970s-vintage Labrador-poodle Labradoodle have become almost run-of-the-puppy-mill. The American Canine Hybrid Club, established in 1969 to register the cross-breeds, now lists four hundred hybrids such as Chugs

(Chihuahua-pugs, little and chubby) and Jack-a-bees (Jack Russell plus beagle, at once sporty and goofy). The number of new litters registered each month grew from 200 in 2000 to between 500 and 700 in 2007. Many of the breeds are designed to solve specific problems, like shedding or allergies. Other hybrids are advertised—with varying degrees of accuracy—as solutions for humans who would rather not choose between one breed's sweet look and another's fun personality.

The hybrid craze represents a rare point of convergence for humane societies and traditional breeders. Never mind their own animals' fairly recent development; the people showing dogs at Westminster regard hybrids as potentially unhealthy products of slipshod breeding who often can't pass the basic test of breedness by producing standard offspring of the same. (Fisher said his cava-chons, for instance, were produced by mating a Cavalier King Charles spaniel and a bichon frise—not by mating two cava-chons; it's unclear what variations would occur after multiple generations of mating cava-chons.) Animal-protection activists fear inhumane commercial production operations geared to ride the hybrid trend. (There are hybrids all over Lancaster County.) Brodie cited "confidentiality agreements" with breeders in declining to say where his animals are produced. "We're so high profile that I wouldn't risk it," he told me. So how do we know it's not a mill? "You don't," Brodie replied, before assuring me that the conditions are perfectly humane.

When Brodie's firm first appeared in the media, he said, its Web site quickly filled up with nasty messages. "I just have to say this is creepy," wrote one visitor. "You are processing and manufacturing kittens like they're pocket radios." Said another, "You should be promoting population control via spay and neuter, NOT pushing animals as a commodity." Brodie was unapologetic. "It's all relative. To them, twenty-two thousand dollars is a lot of money. To our customers, it isn't. Do you tell someone who has a lot of money that they can't spend five thousand dollars on a purse and they have to give it to a cat shelter? Where does it stop? I can't win that argument." By mid-2008, Brodie said, he had five hundred orders. Most of the hypoallergenics were sold to Americans, but he said about 90 percent of the exotics were going to Russia, home to a booming luxury-goods economy. And they'd recently appointed a rep in Beijing. "What I've done is I've made people comfortable with spending many, many thousands of dollars on a cat."

Brodie also said he was consulting for other firms, including a business called FlexPetz, a dog time-share business. With locations in Los Angeles, New York, and London, the firm charges $279.95 a month for membership, which entitles customers to take dogs out for up to four days. Extra days are $45 apiece. Animal-protection activists hate the idea of rent-a-pets, speculating about what might happen when the dogs get old and are less desirable; if you're a frequent traveler who can't keep a pet, they say, why not stop by an animal shelter instead and spend the time walking those dogs? In Massachusetts, where the firm planned to open a branch in 2008, seventeen state legislators cosponsored a bill to ban the leasing of dogs or cats. But more locations are planned; a hundred people signed up for the London branch before it even opened, according to the British press. "A lot of the people here are transients," Chris Haddix, who runs the firm's New York operation, told me when I visited FlexPetz's dogs, housed at an ordinary Manhattan doggie day care whose location I had to promise not to divulge. "But when you're walking along the streets with a dog, you belong here. You're not away from home anymore."

Brodie said he hoped to make his firm synonymous with pricey animals. "What I'd like to see is us getting into what I'd call more standard breeds of the cat, where people are willing to buy from us and pay three, four times the price because they know there's the quality and the backup," he said. "Do you buy a preowned Mercedes from the dealership at twice the price or from the guy next door?" Lifestyle is also getting into dogs. Allergy sufferers might be interested in the small brown Jabari GD, a sniffle-free Westie-like pup that costs $15,000. For those who fear criminals more than allergens, there's the German-bred, German-trained Titan Family Protection Dog, a German shepherd who's been certified in obedience, tracking, and protection. "Even with high-tech surveillance equipment in place, your home or family often requires additional peace of mind," Lifestyle's promotional materials declare. It better deliver a lot of peace; the Titan starts at $85,000 and can be delivered in three to six months. Financing is available.

SEVEN

Legal Beagles

How Much Is Your Pet Worth?

Ben DeLong adopted Freddie the cat back when he was a single guy. That was before his wife moved in with her own cat, Merve, and years before the couple jointly discovered a third kitten under their car in the parking lot of a restaurant named Margarita's, dubbing her Rita in the Mexican eatery's honor. "I went down to the pound," he says a decade later, describing his first encounter with Freddie. "She was the only friendly cat, the only one who came down and rubbed against the bars." He paid the shelter a seventy-five-dollar adoption fee and took her home.

Freddie didn't change as her family grew. "She was probably the ultimate couch cat," recalls DeLong. "You would be sitting on the couch, me or me and the wife, and she would literally just come up and flip over for you and let you rub her stomach. It was just complete trust." Merve and Rita, meanwhile, would take their places on the back of the sofa as the couple watched TV after dinner. "I would think, 'I could not be happier,'" DeLong says.

Here's a story about how much those family pets are worth for this particular family. It was the winter of 2007, and DeLong was moving all of his worldly possessions halfway across the country to the exurbs of Chicago. A few months earlier, DeLong's wife had landed this great new job in Illinois. The plan was for Ben to stay behind in West Virginia until the couple found a home, which they eventually did, a nice place in the town of Wadsworth that they bought for $306,000. DeLong, who by then has quit his pharmaceutical sales job in order to relocate, went back home to Charleston to sell their old house, watch their gear get packed into a moving truck, and hop into his car in the company of the three cats—one tabby, one orange, and one gray with blue eyes.

"I got to the house, pulled up in the driveway, and just put the cats in the house," DeLong says. "Of course, there was no furniture anywhere yet. So I put down some food and some water and drove to the hotel to see the wife." He came back around lunchtime the next day to put down some more food. "And I'm walking around the house, and I can only find two cats. Now, we have a basement and it's two stories and there's no furniture, and I'm like, where the hell's the cat? I'm walking around for forty-five minutes, can't find the cat, and I come up to the second floor. Our second floor is all hardwood floors, and I notice that one of the air-conditioning vents on the floor was moved to the side. And I walk over and I see this little gray butt that's inside the air-conditioning vent." It was Rita. "So I go to grab it, but she scoots forward. And I'm like, oh, this isn't good."

First he called Animal Control, hoping the facility had some cat-specific tool that could yank Rita from the duct. No such luck. But the woman from Animal Control had an uncle who was an HVAC guy and she got on the phone to him. He showed up in about forty-five minutes—"which is unheard-of for a contractor"—and he and DeLong went downstairs and pulled the register off the air-conditioning unit. The cat had by now crawled fourteen feet down the vent and was staring down at the pair, who were unable to get at her. "So I figure, well, it's been about twenty-four hours, hunger is going to get her to move even if we can't. I go and get some tuna fish, and I leave it at the entrance to the vent and figure she'll eventually come out."

By day's end things hadn't improved. "The wife comes over to the house after work, and she calls me and she's like, 'Ben, I don't hear the cat. Are you sure the cat's in the vent?'" he says. "And I'm like, 'If you don't see the cat, the cat's in there.' But she just kept saying she didn't see the cat." Some emotionally charged marital debate ensued about how much longer to wait. Mrs. DeLong won. "I came back over to the house, but I stopped at Home Depot on the way there," DeLong continues. "I purchased a circular saw. And I cut a three-foot-by-one-and-a-half-foot hole in the new hardwood floor of the house that I've owned for twenty-four hours to get the freaking cat out of the vent."

Rita emerged unscathed; it turned out she had gotten herself trapped behind the long screws that held the pipes together. But the punch line landed a few weeks later, when DeLong, having moved into a house that now featured a precarious uncovered manhole on its upper story, tried to find someone to repair the damage he'd done. The final bill: $7,000. "Did I mention I was unemployed at the time?" DeLong says.

Plenty of contemporary pet owners would agree that their animal is more valuable than a new hardwood floor. Most courts, however, would not. At least not yet. In the eyes of the law, even the most beloved pet was until recently regarded as another piece of property—no different than a laptop or a set of golf clubs. Wreck someone's car, and the law offers the aggrieved party little relief beyond the jalopy's market value. Ditto somebody's pet. But that tradition may be changing. To find out why, it's worth listening to another, sadder story that also happens to concern one of Ben DeLong's cats.

A couple of weeks after the air-conditioning vent incident, Freddie got sick. She was lethargic, eating little but drinking up bowl after bowl of water. The couple let this go on for about three days, though something was clearly the matter. "She was being very antisocial, which is completely the opposite of what her demeanor was," DeLong remembers. "Now she would go into another room where no one was at and just lay." Eventually, DeLong took the cat to a local veterinarian. He immediately wanted to admit her.

"A lot of the lab values, like the kidney enzymes, were through the roof," DeLong says. "And she was still dehydrated, even though she was drinking a lot of water. So we ended up admitting her for six days. When we got her out, she was a little perkier than she had been before. But then it was basically a five-day decline." By the next Saturday morning, "she would basically just get up, walk five feet, lay down, and groan. And that's when we knew it was time." The couple drove back to the vet's office. Freddie was euthanized that afternoon.

Neither the DeLongs nor their vet knew it at the time, but their cat had stumbled into what was about to become the biggest news story the pet industry had ever seen. The Wednesday after Freddie's death, a firm called Menu Foods announced a voluntary recall of 60 million packets of pet food following the deaths of nine cats participating in routine taste tests. Based outside Toronto, Menu was not a household name for ordinary pet-owning consumers. In the $16-billion commercial pet-food market, however, it was a titan, manufacturing products for high-end name brands as well as dozens of retailers' no-name generics.

Thus the news about tainted food from Menu, North America's biggest wet-food manufacturer, quickly spread chaos. Ninety different brands were part of the initial recall. The list included budget foods such as Wal-Mart's Ol' Roy and Special Kitty lines as well as premium brands like Iams and Science Diet, owned, respectively, by Procter & Gamble and Colgate-Palmolive. All in all, Menu supplied products to seventeen of North America's twenty top pet-food retailers. Its four production facilities—in Kansas, South Dakota, New Jersey, and Ontario—could produce a thousand cans of food every minute. No wonder the list of recalled products also proved confusing: Menu mainly produced wet food, meaning that only certain "cuts and gravy" lines of each brand were affected by the initial recall. Despite saturation coverage by the news media, including long lists of recalled goods, retailers and consumers reported being confused about exactly what was verboten.

By late March the recall story was earning the twenty-four-hour news coverage ordinarily devoted to trapped miners or missing blonde tourists. "The panic and concern is Manhattan to Mayberry," the *Good Morning America* veterinarian Marty Becker told *USA Today*. The papers were filled with tear-jerker stories of dogs and cats suffering in exactly the same way as DeLong's animal had: lethargy, thirst, kidney failure, death. Some particularly distraught owners mournfully recalled that when their animals had lost their appetites, the owners had force-fed them the food that ultimately killed them. In early April, Congress got in on the act, with Democrats using the recall to make the case that the Bush administration's hostility to government regulation was endangering the public. They also lit into Menu, which declined to send anyone to testify. It turned out the firm had first learned of a possible problem nearly a month before the recall.

"As a pet owner and a dog lover, I have joined with millions of my fellow Americans in anxiously hoping that I had not poisoned my pet, my dog, with a special snack or a serving of food," said West Virginia's Robert Byrd, the Senate's senior member. "I don't have that little dog here with me today, but she's a shih tzu," Byrd continued. "I'll admit she sleeps on my bed, she goes with me to the center, rides in the car with me, she stays in my office. When somebody comes into the office, she rises and comes over and greets them and goes on about her business and gets back on the couch."

Difficult to discern in the fury and the pathos were a couple of key questions: Precisely how many pets had died? And exactly what did them in? The FDA's official death toll was fourteen—the nine cats in the taste test, plus five others whose poisonings had been formally verified. Press accounts, however, projected a death toll in the thousands. By April the respected animal-care Web site petconnection.com was estimating that 3,900 pets had died and another 12,000 had gotten sick from the tainted food.

The search for a culprit, meanwhile, quickly took on a *CSI* flavor. After initial reports of antifreeze and rat poison having been slipped into the food, the blame landed on a more prosaic culprit: wheat gluten. A meat substitute sometimes sold to humans as seitan, gluten is also an ingredient in pet food. Unethical manufacturers have been known to add a chemical called melamine, which can look like protein in chemical tests, in order to goose the protein levels that determine how much manufacturers will pay for the product. When combined with another acid that appeared in the pet food, the melamine turned lethal.

Were it not such an embarrassment to the pet industry, the trail of the poison might serve as a useful illustration of the global reach its leaders so frequently boast about when describing their astounding record of growth. The search quickly led to a Las Vegas firm called ChemNutra, which supplied the tainted gluten to Menu's Emporia, Kansas, plant. ChemNutra, in turn, had imported the gluten from a Chinese supplier called Xuzhou Anying Biologic Technology Development Company. With public hysteria over the dead animals cresting, the name brands blamed Menu, Menu blamed ChemNutra, and ChemNutra blamed Xuzhou Anying, which initially denied any wrongdoing.

The pet-food recall quickly became an international incident. American anger settled on its economically booming Asian rival. China spent much of 2007 embroiled in a series of scandals over exports of allegedly hazardous products, including combustible computer batteries, shoddy automobile tires, and children's toys that turned out to be coated in lead paint. Though adulterating foods with melamine is officially illegal in China, where nearly all of the world's wheat gluten is manufactured, the *New York Times* reported a month after the recall that use of the additive was an "open secret" in the country.

By that point, Ben DeLong was paying very close attention. Freddie's diet had featured Iams wet cat food. She hadn't always eaten that well-regarded brand; DeLong had decided to trade up to the premium product in the name of pet nutrition. Initially, he recalls, he had accepted the cat's death as one of those horrible twists of fate. He'd spent $3,000 on veterinary care as he tried to save Freddie but simply counted it as a part of his job as her guardian. "That's what's normal," he says. "It's what you do." He doesn't like to think of himself as some lawsuit-happy whiner. But the reports of corporate misdeeds started to weigh on him. One night on TV he saw a piece about Dawn Majerczyk, a Chicago woman whose cat was another victim of the recall and who had joined a class-action lawsuit over the poisoning. She mentioned the name of her lawyer, Jay Edelson. DeLong called him the next morning.

It was unclear, though, what DeLong could expect from a

lawsuit. He'd adopted Freddie from the pound back in West Virginia, paying the nominal fee before taking home a theretofore unwanted feline. By traditional dollars-and-cents standards, the cat wasn't worth much more than the multipack of pet food that killed her. Never mind that DeLong's willingness to foot the vet's bill or tear up his hardwood floor suggests a very different conception of his pets' worth. "I don't know what I want," DeLong told the lawyer. "Maybe to recoup my costs. But mostly, I just want them to feel a sting."

Edelson's suit was one in at least ninety class actions filed over the pet-food deaths. Taken together, the cases represented a legal nightmare for Menu. They also represented another minidrama in what has emerged as one of the young century's most dynamic fields of legal scholarship: animal law.

Just like professional dog trainers and full-time cat sitters, the world of animal-focused attorneys has seen a population explosion, with lawyers hashing out tricky questions involving public ethics (anticruelty legislation, dogfighting prosecutions), public safety (dog muzzling laws, bans on allegedly antisocial breeds), and the needs and neuroses of the pet-owning public (liability lawsuits, animal estate law, and custody rulings on pets in divorce). The first animal-law class was taught at Pace University in 1986. By 2007 eighty-nine law schools featured such classes. Since 2001, the animal-loving TV game-show host Bob Barker has donated $1 million apiece to seven prestigious law schools—Harvard, Columbia, Duke, Georgetown, Northwestern, Stanford, and UCLA—to study the subject.

The new animal focus comes at a time when the traditional subjects of animal litigation—service animals—have vanished from most people's lives. Some of the country's earliest examples of humanitarian laws came in campaigns against cruelty to the horses that were then ubiquitous in American cities. An 1866 New York law, for instance, made it a misdemeanor to "maliciously kill, maim, wound, injure, torture, or cruelly beat any horse, mule, ox, cattle, sheep, or other animal, belonging to himself or another." The laws were part of an emerging nineteenth-century ideology of kindness that deemed cruelty to animals a blight on public morality and a bad example for kids.

Before that, laws about animals tended to focus on a more concrete issue: property. The Bible, for instance, is full of parables about farmers and their beasts, not to mention injunctions about how to adjudge the ownership of oxen or asses. But such stories tend to turn primarily on the animals' economic value. Ditto our own national morality tales, which feature bad guys who are horse thieves and cattle rustlers, not parakeet burglars. Common law says almost nothing about the domestic dependents that have fueled the current boom in animal law. For many years, pets weren't even accorded the dignity of being considered property. An 1846 Vermont law titled Offenses Against Private Property, for instance, was notable for what it didn't say. The law made it illegal to steal a horse but not a dog.

As the trade in domestic animals became formalized in the early twentieth century, the law came to consider pets as creatures that are owned rather than wildlife that is simply passing through. States put owners on the hook for carnage their pets might wreak. Cases where pets were the victims of carnage were another story. As property, ordinary pets aren't particularly valuable in the purely financial terms used to assess legal compensation. DeLong might consider his pet worth—at least—the $3,000 cost of veterinary care during her final illness, but the law has seen things in pecuniary terms: What can your animal do for you? Is he a show dog? A seeing-eye dog? Is he the beneficiary of pricey guard-dog training that would have to be purchased anew for his replacement? Absent such factors, the economic figures are small potatoes. And bereaved owners like DeLong have typically not been allowed to ask for the emotional-distress compensation that bring major payouts when a human family member dies. You can't sue for loss of companionship in a property-destruction case: No matter how much you love your comfy old sofa, it's still a couch. Under the law, the same goes for Freddie.

That may be changing. Take the case of *Burgess v. Shampooch*. In 2004, a Kansas woman named Sarah Burgess took her thirteen-year-old Yorkshire terrier to a Kansas City grooming salon for a wash. After paying her thirty-dollar bill, Burgess noticed the dog limping. As it happened, he'd been to the vet two days earlier and received a clean bill of health. X-rays determined he had a dislocated hip and required surgery. Burgess sued for court costs and vet bills: $1,308.89, including a blood workup, anesthesia, pain medications, and the like. A judge agreed.

Sounds fair enough. But to grasp the radical implications, substitute any other piece of property for the Yorkie—say, a digital camera that cost the same $175 that Burgess had paid to adopt her dog. Had the groomers negligently doused that camera with shampoo, she wouldn't have been allowed to sue for the $1,308.89 it may have cost to find an electronics whiz to repair the device; you can't get reimbursed for repairs that cost more than a simple piece of property is worth. The salon tried that argument in court, and again on an appeal, asking judges to limit their liability to $175 and warning that an unfavorable ruling could "open the proverbial 'floodgates' of high dollar litigation" over pets. The Kansas appeals court decided to take that risk, letting Burgess's victory stand.

So much for treating the thirteen-year-old Yorkie as a simple commodity. But at least Burgess asked for a dollar figure calculated via the objectively verifiable method of toting up her veterinary bills. Since the turn of the century, courts in several states have handed out huge payouts to compensate less tangible forms of pain and suffering to owners of killed animals: $39,000 to the owner of a Labrador mix who died after a California veterinarian misdiagnosed his seizures, $56,000 to an Oregon family whose dog was intentionally run over by a neighbor, $126,000 to a Kentucky woman whose two horses—valued at $100, though she testified that she loved them like her "children"—were sold for slaughter by the couple she'd enlisted to board the animal. That last figure consisted of $1,000 for what the couple had received from the slaughterhouse that bought the animals; $50,000 in compensatory damages because the defendants spent months lying about the horses' whereabouts, requiring the frail and ailing plaintiff to hire a private investigator; and another $75,000 in punitive damages to further sting the miscreants.

To be sure, each of the big cases was based on specific allegations about defendants' outrageous conduct, rather than the legally fraught matter of the plaintiff's attachment to an animal. So none of them amounts to a clear-cut precedent about pet financial values or whether pet owners are even eligible for emotional-distress payments. "Think back to the movie *Fatal Attraction,* where Glenn Close's character killed the rabbit," says Phil Goldberg, a Washington, D.C., attorney who has studied the issue. "The killing of the rabbit wasn't the issue there. It was that Glenn Close was trying to inflict emotional distress on Michael Douglas and his family, and the rabbit was the vehicle . . . You're not compensating the person for their attachment to the animal. You're compensating them for the intentional emotional harm done to *them.*"

Despite the headlines, defense lawyers still aren't losing sleep over animal cases. Only five states now formally allow emotional-distress damages to be considered in pet-loss cases, but those states also cap damages at a low level: Tennessee, the first state to legislatively permit the suits, also limits them to

$4,000. Elsewhere, most claims still get tossed out. Courts, even within the same state, are all over the map—embracing Max as a family member one day, relegating him to an economic unit the next. A year after the $126,000 Kentucky horse-death ruling, the same state's courts disallowed emotional-distress claims in the case of a dog that had been shot in the head. Even those few cases—around ten over five years—where vets have been successfully sued for noneconomic damages should not scare ordinary vets. The aforementioned California Labrador owner, for example, spent over $375,000 of his own money to successfully sue his veterinarian for $39,000; few others would press such a case. Defense attorneys note that no big-time pet-companionship payout has withstood the appeals process.

At least one appeals court, though, has backed the principle of such lawsuits. In 2005, Chicago resident Mary Ann Anzalone sued her veterinarian over the death of her cat, Blackie. Anzalone had taken Blackie to the vet for boarding. An employee had taken Blackie out of her cage to get some exercise; at the same time, a rottweiler was exercising in an adjacent area. The dog attacked and killed the cat. In her lawsuit, Anzalone, an unmarried forty-four-year-old with no kids, said that following the cat's death she "suffered extreme distress evidenced by the facts that: She cried constantly following Blackie's violent death and continues to cry every time she thinks about it to this date; has lost sleep and continues to do so to this date; has recurring waking thoughts and nightmares in which she envisions Blackie, a de-clawed cat, ripped apart by a rottweiler; has overwhelming feelings of guilt over the fact of Blackie's death as well as the terror and pain that Blackie suffered"—and so on, down the line to headaches, weight gain, stress, and lost companionship. She asked for $100,000.

Predictably, a lower court tossed the case, saying the damages—based on a calculation of what losing Blackie's companionship meant to Anzalone—exceeded the cat's market value. When Anzalone appealed, though, the appeals court said asking for compensation based on a pet's "value to the owner" was legitimate, but that Anzalone's dollar figure was simply too high. In other words, Blackie was no mere couch. The question remained, though: What was she?

One October afternoon, to help answer that question, I traveled to an auditorium not far from Blackie's old stomping grounds to watch a group of Illinois lawyers attend that mundane ritual of any attorney's schedule: a mandatory continuing legal education session. Such classes ordinarily focus on areas where the law might have changed since the participants were in law school. This session, at DePaul University's law school, was called "How Much Is Fido/Fluffy Worth?"

There was nothing mundane, however, about the cast of characters on the dais. One of the speakers was Jay Edelson, by then a lead plaintiff for the Menu Foods class-action suit. Another was a Harvard-trained animal-law attorney named Chris Green, who has pushed to make it easier to sue over veterinary malpractice. The most noteworthy panelist had flown in from Washington, D.C., to argue the other side. Victor Schwartz is a hugely important figure at the nexus of politics and the law. *National Journal* lists him as among the country's one hundred most influential attorneys; *Washingtonian* magazine calls him one of the city's top lobbyists. Trial lawyers, meanwhile, see him as the charming face of a right-wing campaign to gut people's right to sue. As general counsel of the American Tort Reform Association, Schwartz is regularly called on to provide absurd examples of multimillion-dollar lawsuits over coffee spills or dry-cleaning mishaps. Since 2005, he's also served as a lobbyist for the Animal Health Institute, whose membership includes the veterinary divisions of pharmaceutical giants like

Novartis, Bayer, and Pfizer. National politics has come to the pet world.

If you're looking for examples of over-the-top pet-keeping absurdity, courts are a good place to start. The zany press clippings go way beyond arguments about wrongful-death liability. Take pet custody battles in divorce litigation, where according to one estimate there was a hundredfold increase between 1990 and 2005. Among the most celebrated skirmishes was the case of Stanley and Linda Perkins, a San Diego anesthesiologist and publisher, respectively. When they divorced in 2000, the Perkinses had to divide an estate that included two Porsches, a Ferrari, and a house with an ocean view. But large chunks of the $146,000 legal bill for the split were spent on a battle over custody for a pointer-greyhound mix named Gigi. Evidence on that count included a "Day in the Life" video, submitted by Linda, which showed the pup cuddling and playing with the soon-to-be-ex Mrs. Perkins. She got the dog.

And then there's the frantic development of pet estate law—launched into the headlines by the 2007 death of hotelier Leona Helmsley, who left $12 million to her Maltese while leaving nothing to two of her own grandchildren. The money went to a trustee tasked with ensuring that the eight-year-old animal's lifestyle, which included chef-prepared meals, would remain lavish after the Queen of Mean's death. The story, predictably, became tabloid fodder, spurring wacky headlines ("Heir of the Dog," "Rich Bitch"). Family members later contested the will, saying Helmsley had been "mentally unfit" at the time; in 2008, a New York judge agreed, slashing the dog's haul to $2 million, depositing the rest in a family charitable trust.

But the same phenomenon has taken hold among people without $12 million, or even $2 million, to leave behind. Write-your-own-will CD-ROMs now format documents designed to provide for your pet in the event of your death. The concern over what happens when pets outlive owners has given birth to its own specialty industry. Palm Meow, believed to be the world's first "cat retirement home," opened in 2004 in retiree-rich Broward County, Florida. Working in conjunction with an estate planning attorney, the facility will—for roughly $4,000 to $6,000 a year—board a cat after someone's death. For a $25,000 estate donation, the region's Humane Society will also provide health care and check in on rehoused dogs or cats that belonged to a deceased owner.

As the "Fido" session at DePaul made clear, none of the other pet-law subjects are quite as touchy as liability and valuation. On one side, Chris Green and Edelson painted a menacing picture of above-the-law veterinary and pet-food industries. Vets, Green said, have seen their insurance premiums decline over the past two decades—evidence that the courts remain unwilling to offer payouts for anything other than a dead pet's economic value. Despite that, Green noted, the profession's various state oversight boards are loath to punish alleged malpractice: 98 percent of complaints, for instance, are never even considered by California's Board of Veterinary Examiners. Lawsuits, the implication went, are crucial when it comes to keeping the powerful from getting sloppy. Edelson, meanwhile, estimated that forty thousand pets had been affected by 2007's melamine-tainted food, half of them fatally. "This is a mass slaughter of pets throughout the country," he said. "What Professor Schwartz is really saying is that this is like a toaster recall."

Victor Schwartz, on the other hand, painted a picture of a litigious menace that could bankrupt the beloved neighborhood vet, chasing him out of the business the same way he said malpractice fees had driven obstetricians from their field. Not only would the insurance rates lead to higher prices for consumers, he said, but they would prompt veterinarians to practice "defensive medicine," full of pricey tests ordered up only because doctors were petrified of being sued. Mom-and-pop pet hotels, neighborhood dog walkers, and independent puppy trainers might all be forced out of business by their own rising premiums, or bankrupted by a single lawsuit. "Introducing the concept of noneconomic damages to a new area is something one should think about," Schwartz warned. As for the caps on payouts instituted by states like Tennessee, he warned that they wouldn't last long. Similar caps were once in place for wrongful human death lawsuits, he said, but "all those caps are gone. They do not have a long shelf life once the law is established, once the law is there."

As a guy with one foot in the law and one foot in politics, Schwartz didn't ignore the sea change in how society at large—that is, jurors and voters and even judges—consider their own pets. He talked about his beloved dog, Kylie, whose face would grace his holiday cards that December. But he also talked about the human whom he considers his closest friend. If that friend were to be killed via malice or negligence, he would have no grounds to sue, no matter how devastated he was, or how furious; you can collect when someone has taken your spouse or your child, but not your best friend. Should it be different for Man's Best Friend?

It's one thing for a lawyer to make that argument. It's not so easy for the pet industry, which, as I'd seen at Global Pet Expo, depends on pet owners who call themselves Mommy or Daddy and not just pal. The premise behind shelling out for a veterinary CT scan, or a weekly trip to the groomer, or a diet of top-shelf Iams wet food, is that the animals are part of the family and ought to be fed and housed and nurtured as such. It's a view that has vastly enriched both the veterinary and pet-food industries over the past few decades. And it's been the explicit message used in advertising by some of the very folks most worried about the possibility that courts will adjudge animals to be worthy of emotional-distress claims. Take a peek at the name of the pet-advice Web site run by one of Schwartz's own constituents, Bayer's animal health division: Petparents.com. Or the advertising copy for another Animal Health Institute member, Pfizer Animal Health: "Taking good care of the canine member of the family."

Good marketing, yes indeed. But it sure could complicate matters for an industry lawyer who needs to convince a jury full of people who have seen and agreed with those ads that, really, the late pet was merely the canine property of the family.

The Menu lawsuit never made it to trial. It was settled in May 2008, little more than a year after the recall—lightning fast for a class-action suit, and an indication of how eager pet-food sellers were to avoid more TV coverage of heartbroken pet owners demanding justice. When the various parties gathered in a federal courthouse in New Jersey to present the deal to U.S. district judge Noel L. Hillman, the room contained thirty-one lawyers and no bereaved pet people.

At the hearing, Hillman preliminarily signed off on a final tally that came to $32 million, $8 million of which the various firms had already paid claimants out of court and $24 million that they agreed on in negotiations. Plaintiffs' and defense attorneys still hadn't agreed on how many animals had died or been sickened by the poisoned food, with one lawyer mentioning 1,500 deaths and another citing an estimated 39,000 affected animals—and still another rising to dispute that figure's origins. But for the purposes of the settlement, there would be no cross-examinations about whether a particular pet's sudden kidney failure was due to the melamine or just a freak coincidence. The class of people eligible for damages included everyone who had purchased or used the tainted products, whether or not they'd joined the suit before the settlement. If their collected claims went above the amount of money for the settlement, the payouts would be prorated. If not, anything left over would be given to animal charities.

The settlement did not create any new pet-law precedent. Attorneys in the case said the major hurdle in the deliberations came as defense lawyers struggled to make sure that the agreement didn't contain some implicit acknowledgment that pet owners' simple love for their animals was a legitimate factor in calculating their legal value. "It's watertight," one defense attorney told me. During the hearing, after plaintiffs' attorney Sherrie R. Savett delivered a thirty-minute summary of the settlement's details, the judge asked Menu's lawyer Mary Gately whether she had anything to add. Her only statement: "We've made it very clear throughout the documents to refer to economic damages. A component that's not included in the settlement is emotional damages. I just wanted to make that clear."

All the same, the details of those "economic damages" are ones you'd never find in a suit involving, say, a tainted product that led to the ruination of hundreds of washer-dryers. Beyond veterinary costs and replacement costs for food and animals, bereaved pet owners were entitled to compensation for lost wages at work, transportation expenses related to their pet's illness, reimbursement for any furniture that a sick pet might have damaged, euthanasia costs, autopsy expenses, screenings for pets who turned out to have been healthy, and funeral or memorial service expenses incurred after some of those animals didn't make it. For people who don't keep receipts, the deal permitted $900 in nondocumented expenses. "We tried to be very liberal," Savett said.

The expenses reflect the full range of contemporary pet owning, from basics like food to more recent and unusual developments like formal mourning or long-distance veterinary transport. I also suspect that, whatever the lawyers may insist, it represents emotional compensation by another name; given the way the general public feels about pets, nickel-and-diming their human survivors would have been bad business indeed. For his part, Schwartz said he was not worried about the settlement. "They stuck to the general rule, but in the course of the settlement negotiations it would appear that the way to stick to this rule where both sides are saying no to soft damages—or noneconomic compensatory damages, which is the fancy word for it—was to apply a very liberal concept of economic damages," he said. "All of those things, even if there's a little bit of stretch to what we might think is economic, have an objective measure. We know what it costs to clean a carpet. We know what it costs to bury an animal. There's a market value. When you get into a five-year-old's grief over a kitten who died, there's no measure for that."

Ben DeLong was less happy about the settlement. He claimed he didn't care about his own compensation; by their very nature, class-action suits tend not to enrich any individual plaintiff. But they are supposed to chasten defendants. And in DeLong's opinion, the money—a quarter of which would go to the lawyers—was not enough to sting the firms whose negligence he blamed for Freddie's death. "It's a slap in the face," he said. "In today's legal climate, twenty-four million dollars is a drop in the bucket." He said he still thought of Freddie often, a year after her death, and still raged against those who had taken her from him.

As the case wound down, though, DeLong realized he was ready for at least one form of moving on. He and his wife were planning to get a new cat, a Bengal. "Nothing's ever going to replace Freddie," he said. "But you're going to have different animals at different stages of your life. It's a chain that goes back all the way. Each of them will know someone who knew someone who knew Freddie."

EIGHT

Toy Town

Latchkey Dogs, Prozac, and
the Secret History of the Chew Toy

Watching a dog work on one of Keith Benson's Everlasting Treat Balls feels like watching raw footage for a nature documentary. A couple of hours after leaving the Triple Crown Dog Academy, the Texas ranch where Benson and his team develop the intricate chew toys, I was in a friend's living room in Houston as a tan mutt named Banjo squared off against one of the dark blue contraptions. I hadn't brought my human hosts any particularly interesting treats, but I opened up one of the $24.95 orbs, filled it with food as instructed, and tossed it to their dog.

Banjo, a sort of houndish, cattle-doggy four-year-old who lazes on the living-room dog bed when he's indoors and has a thing for chasing the UPS truck around the block when he's outside, threw his whole body into the challenge. Everlasting Treat Balls aren't designed to be easy. In Benson's world, dogs work for their treats. Tough rubber spheres that can be stuffed with kibble, the balls secret the food behind openings that look like the mouths of man-eating tropical plants, circles blocked by rubber tongues. And before Banjo could even try to squeeze through to the food, he'd have to dispose of the rock-hard, edible disks that can slide securely into grooves atop those openings. Enough licking and gnawing and poking and pawing and the disks might move. But it would take a while.

Banjo grabbed hold as best he could to the sides of the ball with his paws, positioning it so he could use tongue and teeth to lick at the liver-flavored food disk. Occasionally, the ball would scoot out of his grasp. He'd repeat the whole process, inching his way, transfixed, across the carpet. Later, he took to using one paw to steady the ball while he worked at the disk with his teeth. After about twenty minutes, he'd gotten the disk out of the way.

Then it was on to the crunchy food within, another adventure. Squeeze the ball a certain way, and the hidden mouth opens, making access to the inside momentarily easier. Banjo figured that one out fairly quickly, squeezing the ball against the floor as he worked the inside with his tongue in search of the last bits of food. After another twenty or so minutes of wrestling with the ball, Banjo flipped it over again and worked on the second food disk. It was all over in about an hour, with Banjo reveling in a chorus of praise from his family. And, as advertised back at Benson's ranch, he was also good and tired.

The sight of dogs searching out treats isn't the kind of thing National Geographic would ever have to send a film crew up the Amazon to find. But the episode of Banjo and the high-tech Everlasting Treat Ball nonetheless has at least one thing in common with the sorts of scenes you'd find in *The Living Planet*: It depicts an ecosystem often unseen by contemporary human eyes. The treat ball, like dozens of others in the highly competitive field of pet toys, is designed for a world in which people are absent and dogs are left to their own devices, if not their prehistoric instincts: the world of the latchkey pet.

Like latchkey kids, latchkey pets are a relatively recent phenomenon. Single people often didn't have pets; the families that did adopt animals frequently featured a homemaker. Even where the entire family did leave for the day, there were fewer rules and conventions stopping pets from wandering outdoors until suppertime. But today, half of all pet-owning households in the country have two or fewer human members. As pet keeping has become a province of the childless, what to do with all those marooned animals has become a big deal. "A lot of our clients, they are DINKs, Double Income, No Kids," Benson said. "They need more interesting toys, more interactive toys. They can't just go to work at seven a.m. and come back at six and expect the pet to just sit there."

"The idea was, out in the wild, a dog might go hunting, work all morning for his breakfast. And then he'd be tired and take a nap," explained Jessy Gabriel, a Triple Crown trainer who came up with a rough idea for the ball after determining that her German shepherds were bored all day while she was off training other people's dogs. "That's how it's supposed to be. And if you give dogs these, it's the same thing. It works their body and their minds, and exhausts them."

And as they say, a tired dog is a well-behaved dog. Or, more to the point, a tired dog is a dog less likely to chew up your sofa while you're off at work for twelve hours.

Spread across 350 acres of rolling Texas Hill Country northwest of Austin, the Triple Crown Dog Academy is a shining example of modern American petrepreneurialism. Only a decade old, the facility serves as a four-legged version of a boarding school, community theater, and dude ranch, among other things. At any given time, Triple Crown is temporary home to two hundred dogs, including dozens whose owners have sent them away for an intense monthlong behavior course. It hosts dog shows forty-eight weekends a year, with dog-breed fans parking in the RV area. Students from all over the country pay nearly $10,000 for an eight-week course that will turn them into certified trainers. They stay in apartments on the ranch, and the luckiest ones get asked to stay on as interns and buck for a rare chance to join the thirty-five-employee staff.

Benson, the chief operating officer, revved up his Hummer to give me the full tour. Starting in the parking lot outside the thirty-two-thousand-square-foot indoor training area, we rolled down a dirt road to the site where rescue dogs' skills are honed—it has hiding places for humans, to help the animals learn to sniff out bodies—and over to the model drug house used to train police dogs. As it happens, search-and-rescue training has also become a recreational pastime for some ordinary dog owners, making Triple Crown's SearchScape another commercial winner. Passing the academy's indoor dog pool, which has been converted to another training space, we eventually wound up at Benson's own house.

Benson said he was the third employee to join Triple Crown, hired when the firm was nothing more than a handful of kennels in the founder's Tucson, Arizona, backyard. A psychology major at the University of Southern Mississippi, Benson had been training dogs for Mississippi's state highway patrol and had graduated from a St. Louis academy that at the time was one of the country's only schools for dog obedience trainers. Triple Crown wanted to be a competitor. After a few years in Arizona, Benson was tapped to move the operation from Tucson to Texas. While other longtime staffers are still focused on the basics of training dogs and training trainers, Benson is the guy tasked with conquering a world where skilled pet care is in growing demand. "Is Triple Crown going to be a household name?" Benson asked. "I certainly hope so."

These days, though, it appears the company's shot at becoming a marquee player in the pampered-pet imperium has less to do with its two-legged or four-legged students than with something originally intended as a sideline to the main business: chew toys. The Everlasting Treat Ball landed like the PlayStation of the pet products world back in 2004. PetSmart sells it. Petco sells it. Amazon.com sells it. Dog-owner magazines bestowed it with awards. And instead of only focusing on ill-behaved Weimaraners back on County Road 197, Benson now spends weeks at a time in China riding herd on the manufacturers.

The line of toys, now marketed under the brand name StarMark, is an unlikely phenomenon. With its tough-as-nails material and its slightly oblong shape, the ball looks like dozens of other goodies on the market, all of them the bastard offspring of the Kong, a rubber toy that has dominated the category for three decades. Under the surface, though, the Everlasting Treat Ball is a different beast. Developed using a specially created synthetic, it's meant to be the trickiest rubber ball on the market. Of the similar toys out there, Jessy Gabriel said, "They were just too easy. We wanted something that was a real challenge."

After batting around early ideas, Benson's team developed prototypes based on the notion of an enormous, biteproof puzzle for dogs, something like a mashup of a Kong and a Rubik's Cube. Benson said he spent eighteen months working with resin engineers to come up with a suitably indestructible design. They fabricated tools to cast the balls, overcoming a design problem that left the outer edge of the radius too prone to puncture. (Conveniently, the academy had a captive audience of dogs to test out the new toy.) They also injected the toys with a vanilla scent. Though the scent means nothing to dogs, they reckoned that consumers, knowing the toy would wind up on their floor, might react positively to an aroma signifying "clean."

Triple Crown's hometown provides a good example of the market for complex gewgaws designed to distract housebound pets. Empty and rural ten years ago, Hutto, Texas, is in the midst of a suburban boom. New subdivisions seem to march over the hills separating the town from Austin. On a drive to lunch one day, Benson and I passed a half dozen new sites, with names like Lone Star Ranch, the Enclave at Bushy Creek, and Huttoparke. The town's population grew from 630 in 1990 to 1,250 in 2000 to 9,572 in 2006, and will grow even more as buyers flock to the new McMansions, complete with pools and "prairie views."

Watching the clogged traffic in the other direction as I drove back to Austin after each day at Triple Crown, I could easily imagine the guilt-appeasing appeal of an Everlasting Treat Ball for the dog owners stuck on the road home. As much as trainers like Gabriel might talk about crafting toys to mimic the mental and physical exertions of packs of dogs in the wild, the real target here was lonely dogs in the man-made wilderness of empty living rooms.

Well beyond Hutto, the curious condition of the dog in the daytime has turned pet-keeping households into Tomorrowlands of automated care, feeding, and entertainment. There are alarms that clatter the minute a pet enters a forbidden part of the house, and others that automatically shoot a stream of water at the presumably befuddled animal miscreant. One company touts a heated bed as a calming antidote to canine loneliness; another pushes a food bowl embedded with a device that lets humans record soothing messages for the latchkey pet. There are puppy-level nanny-cams to watch marooned animals, collar-mounted cell phones to listen to them, and programmable, refrigerated feeding machines. For those who would like their pets to wander outdoors—but fear the vermin or burglars who might take advantage of the classic swinging pet door—there are devices to mount on collars that can electronically open the door. No device, no entry. "Your pet will think it's on the Starship Enterprise," boasts Power Pet, one automatic-door manufacturer.

Of course, even the most advanced toy isn't enough to help some dogs handle the long commutes and longer hours of their owners. Veterinarians in the United States have diagnosed an estimated 10 million dogs—including mine—with separation anxiety. In Murphy's case, it manifested itself in a propensity to bark at the top of his substantial lungs from the moment my wife and I left home in the morning until the moment we returned. For the first few months, we took turns dashing home from work at lunchtime in a usually fruitless effort to head off his indoor pooping. Our next-door neighbors, a retired couple who were home all day and understandably didn't enjoy the constant soundtrack of canine yapping, were even less happy about this than we were. In less enlightened times, everyone might have chalked up the behavior to canine willfulness, Murphy's untrainability, or perhaps to whatever we were serving for breakfast. But this was the twenty-first century, so we chalked it up to mental chemicals. "You know, there's a drug for this," our neighbor said. Murphy, a dog who, when he's dozing at my feet, has the ability to look more content than I could ever even imagine feeling, was about to go on antidepressants. First introduced in 1998, Clomicalm was never billed as a quick fix for abandoned dogs. The tricyclic medication is a veterinary version of the human antidepressant Anafranil, produced by the pharmaceutical giant Novartis AG. Novartis includes materials with each bottle that encourage training and activity, and advises people to not make a big fuss out of leaving for work or arriving back home, lest the animal pick up on the heightened emotions and convert them into anxiety. Then, while the pet owners are modifying their own behavior, the drug goes to work on the dog's neurochemistry.

Murphy gets a pill every morning, buried in a spoonful of

cream cheese. At first, I worried about what I was doing to him. I imagined myself suppressing his heretofore unknown inner genius, as if he were a precocious young van Gogh whose authoritarian first-grade teacher ordered up a batch of Ritalin. And then I remembered: he was a dog! And now, for about a dollar a day, he was a dog who no longer pooped on the floor. In 2007, one of Novartis's industrial competitors introduced its own line of separation anxiety drugs. The firm was Indianapolis-based Eli Lilly and the drug was called Reconcile. Other than the beef flavor, it's the same medication as Lilly's blockbuster human-medicine drug Prozac.

Unlike chew toys, though, medication doesn't appeal to that other key facet of the modern chew-toy economy: our human urge toward self-improvement, even for our dogs. Thanks in part to Clomicalm, Murphy's latchkey behavior problems had long since disappeared by the time I came back from Hutto bearing a bag full of Benson's chew toys. Somehow, I'd had my own high hopes about the Everlasting Treat Ball engaging the sweet and dopey and bored-looking Saint Bernard in my own living room. It wasn't to be. He took a confused look at the orb, made a couple of desultory licks of the locking food disks, never quite figured out that there was even better stuff inside, and walked off. A couple of minutes later, Murphy was dozing in his regular spot in the vestibule, apparently without a care in the world, and certainly without a clue that his favorite treats were hidden in a ball that sat a few feet away. And for a minute there, I felt a twinge of guilt. Murphy, it seems, is no Banjo. Had I deprived him of the ability to meet his full potential? And was there some product that could change this situation?

The modern market in purportedly educational pet toys began in a Colorado garage in a bad neighborhood sometime during the Gerald Ford administration.

"I had a motorcycle service center, a Yamaha center," recalled Joe Markham. "The police told me that if I didn't have a dog and I wasn't planning on staying over every night, I'd better get a dog. I said, 'You have any ideas?'" The policeman said he had a friend whose dog was "having a rough time." No kidding: Fritz the German shepherd was an obsessive chewer with a taste for rocks. Though German shepherds are sturdy animals, the rocks were, well, rocks. "He was about three years old and had about a third of his teeth already worn off," Markham said. As it was well before recent advances in veterinary dentistry, this was going to be a problem.

Markham eventually sold his stake in the motorcycle shop and started servicing Volkswagens. Seeking to head off the rock chewing, Markham used to offer Fritz alternative chewables from inside the cars' engines. "The thing I settled on for a while was a motorcycle tire and a wheelbarrow tire and a radiator hose," he said. "Those were his toys. He would use 'em for a while, but he would always revert to his favorite rock." Eventually, Fritz appeared transfixed by a tough piece of rubber from the suspension system. "It was a VW suspension part, a rear suspension snub, I think they called it. It kept the suspension from bottoming out against the frame," Markham explained. "He went nuts for it . . . Fritz is really the coinventor of Kong. My dog never went for the rock again unless that Kong was lost."

From such meager stuff are empires born. "People would see my dog with it, and say 'That looks cool,'" Markham remembered. "For a time I was giving away these pieces of suspension." But Markham decided to go one better. Faster than you could say "Horatio Alger," he was mass-producing similar pieces of rubber for canine use. "There was a ball that [Fritz] liked that was made by Gates Rubber Company," he said. "It was a little small. I went to my engineers and said I want to make this configuration out of this kind of material. The first one that we made, Fritz put down the VW part and never went back to it." Today, Markham has ninety staffers and mass-produces the products on what he says is the biggest vertical-injection molding machine in the country.

Markham called it the Kong, an oblong, bouncy ball that was both tough and compelling. The shape ensured the Kong would take odd, unpredictable hops when thrown, forcing Fritz's descendants to work even harder to find it. Its hollow core could accommodate peanut butter or other goodies to further get the pet's attention. But the really novel thing was the language he used to describe it—a scientific vocabulary that spoke of the unmet needs of the domesticated canine. "We were pioneers of really making a new kind of toy," he said. "We satisfy dogs' instinctive and predatory needs in a domesticated way. In other words, they can chase, catch, and kill, if you will, this toy, and it's a thrill. The other beautiful thing is that you put food inside of it. There's the satisfaction of getting a reward for this domesticated predatorial game."

Could any old tennis ball manufacturer credibly make such a boast? The Kong mystique was tailor-made for a nation of strivers. This is more than a toy, it argued. It'll help improve your dogs. Eventually, what had been a toy acquired such a therapeutic, scientific reputation that when Novartis rolled out Clomicalm, the firm approached Kong for some joint marketing to help brand the drug as a part of dog play and training rather than just a canine sedative. Even today, Kong ads boast, as if selling Tylenol or dental products, that the company is the "choice of professionals."

The professionals, for the most part, agree. Kong appeared on the scene at the intersection of two serendipitous trends: On the one hand, the suburban sprawl of places like Hutto meant family dogs weren't playing in packs; on the other, as marketing experts like David Lummis noted, people were becoming newly attentive to enabling the instinctual dogginess of their dogs. "You can say it's ridiculous to spend twenty bucks on a toy you throw to dogs, but your dog will disagree," said *Pet Industry Weekly*'s Mike Dillon. "It's an owner's dream because the dog loves it. That means less time trying to get your dog to play with it; it means more exercise for the dog in a shorter period. And it also has the sense of promoting health . . . It's one of the transformational products in this industry, a game changer."

By the dawn of the twenty-first century, the Kong dynamic had led to a veritable arms race among dog-toy makers. No longer was it enough to roll out a ball or a plush toy. The new dynamic required some promise of improving a buyer's animal. At the trade show where I first met both Markham and the Everlasting Treat Ball crew, educational toys were all the rage. In booth after booth, vendors pushed projectiles made from ever-tougher materials. Here, a Frisbee-type disk made from the same material as the tires of an 18-wheeler. There, Mammoth Pet's TireBiters, donut-sized replicas of actual 18-wheeler tires. For cats, there's the five-in-one "laser pet toy and exerciser" from Muse Ments. An adapted laser pointer, it projects a tiny red mouse, among other things. Cats see them and give chase. Exercise ensues. And, from a company called Ruff Dawg, there's a toy that Fritz might particularly have appreciated: the Rock, a bouncy yellow rock whose—wait for it—unpredictable zigs and zags promise entertainment and improvement for canines of all sizes.

Markham, though, was still moving the market. In 2007, his Kong Wubba, a squeaky, easy-to-throw toy with a tail, won Global Pet Expo's award for best new product. A year later, the company was out with Kong Senior, a toy for geriatric dogs that featured the very quality Fritz long ago rejected: softer rubber.

As for what's next for latchkey dogs, marketing consultant

Dillon is betting that the dog-toy future belongs to automation. Already, Kong has led the way. In 2005, it licensed an innovation called Kong Time, an automatic dispenser that, several times a day, emits a beep and then tosses out a treat-filled Kong ball to a presumably unwatched dog. Thus the chew-toy wars may wind up as the robot wars. "You could see some sort of digital light and noise system, where the dog would have to figure something out to get a treat, and then the treat itself would constitute a challenge," Dillon said. "And you'd sell it based on the idea that this will keep your dog from getting bored and this will make him smarter. People really want to think they're doing well by their dogs, and they really want to believe their own dogs are the best they can be."

Benson is also focused on a dog-toy future involving more and more interactivity. A new design was in the planning stages when I visited the ranch. Citing the competitive marketplace, he wouldn't so much as describe it to me. "We can't really talk about that until it's out," he said, sounding less like a pet trainer than like one of Steve Jobs's designers. About a year later, when I checked in once more, he was in China visiting the factory. He'd said he might be able to give me a glimpse, since this book wasn't on a schedule that would scoop his marketing plans. A week later, he told me there'd been a hitch that would delay production. "We're testing those solutions now," he said. I'd have to wait. Still later, he said his engineers were adding features that allowed the dog owner to raise the toy's difficulty level as the dog learned. But no, I couldn't see it.

Whatever the new toy may look like, the firm had already followed its success with chews of increasing complexity: the Everlasting Fun Ball, the Everlasting Treat Ball, the Everlasting Beanie Ball. All followed the same basic model of projectile plus food plus tough material plus a design that makes it difficult to get to the good stuff. And, of course, purpose-built refills for all of them. A couple of years later came the Everlocking Treat Ball ("the toughest chewing challenge yet!"), where the food was actually molded into the shape of a screw through the middle of the ball and two nuts clamped to it at each end. So far, in a crowded field, it remains the Baby Einstein of the fur-baby era.

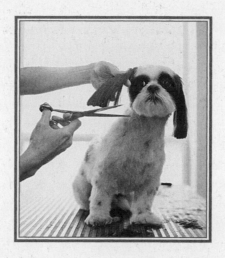

NINE

The $100,000-a-Year Dog Walker?

Pet Care in a Service-Industry Country

Frankie the beagle mix is a slightly undersized, slightly graying dog with a sweet disposition and a generally beaglish lack of pretension. But make no mistake: Frankie the beagle's social life is as logistically complex as anyone's. As it was described to me, the story of one of his recent playdates involved at least seven people, not counting the dog's owner. There was Frankie's owner's personal assistant, who called to arrange the transportation. There was Frankie's owner's doorman, who rang up to the apartment, wherefrom Frankie's owner's housekeeper descended with the pup. A few miles to the south, there was another doorman, who phoned another maid, who emerged to take the dog up to visit his playmate. At some point, apparently, a dog walker was going to show up and take the pair of pals out for a stroll. That makes six. I spent the better part of an afternoon riding around with number seven. That would be a pet chauffeur.

Back in 1996, David Lang bought a beat-up Pontiac Grand Marquis station wagon to work as a delivery guy for New York veterinarians, dropping off prescription dog foods for clients around the automotively challenged city. He gave the operation a sober, essential-sounding name: Veterinary Food Delivery, the sort of service you wouldn't feel absurdly self-indulgent in hiring. VFD was good business. But it was especially sweet on those occasions when he was asked to deliver veterinary patients back home along with veterinary medicines. Grateful owners would throw nice tips Lang's way, along with stories about how hard it is to hail a cab when you're standing at the curb with, say, Frankie the beagle. This was during the height of the Internet bubble: Wall Street was booming; Manhattan was awash in dollars—and, Lang noticed, well-tended animals. "People just had more money than they knew what to do with," Lang said. "So people started all these services for them: Why should I walk my dog? Why should I let my dog be dirty? I can make more money while someone else is picking up their shit. It's a niche. It's a huge niche."

Sensing an opportunity for a niche within that niche, he turned VFD into the Pet Chauffeur, delivering pets to medical appointments, playdates, training sessions, the dog swimming pool in Chelsea, airports in Queens, beaches in New Jersey and the Hamptons, even, on one occasion, to Atlanta, a $2,000 trip. ("We get all kinds of people who've had horror stories with the airlines," Lang told me.) The original Pontiac has been replaced by a fleet of six bright orange minivans, specially equipped with adjustable pet seat belts. He also has a half dozen newer competitors; the market is big enough that when Pet Chauffeur is all booked up—a fairly frequent occurrence—Lang will refer callers to one of the other firms. He said his business takes in about $1 million annually.

It is not easy money. While Manhattan's cats and dogs relax in his minivans, the thirty-eight-year-old New Jersey–bred Lang spends most of his days in a small office next to the Pet Chauffeur parking lot, on the Queens side of the East River. He shares the space with a dog, a cat, a bank of phones and radios, and several walls' worth of giant regional maps. The task of dispatching pet rides resembles a humanitarian mission to some distant republic. When I visited the office, Lang was sitting in front of a wall-sized whiteboard listing the day's appointments. The runs shifted from column to column as new calls came in. Which happened constantly. "I got one going to Petco, Thirtieth and Lex," he called into the radio. "Thirty, cash. Go get 'em." On the whiteboard, a few things switched places. "Okay, 401 West Eighty-ninth to East Side Vet. Let's go! That's seventy-two-dollars, a round-trip." On to another driver out in the field: "So, you're going to pick up a client, take her to 220 West Seventy-second and bring her back to 67 Wall, okay?" And then another: "James, what's your twenty? Good, good. Go to the AMC. I got a client ready to go." And another: "55 Wall Street, going to Clifton, New Jersey. Bring your GPS!" And another: "Hey, Maria the housekeeper is waiting outside. You don't have to go up."

Adding to the complexity are the clients, who have a way of not being ready on time, throwing the whole operation off schedule. Watching Lang react to such events, I worried for his health. He was raging after I arrived, as he fielded a call from someone wondering where his dog's ride was. Lang insisted that two of his vans had been there. "I called you six times," Lang fumed. "Our drivers have been waiting in front of City Vet on West Seventy-second for twenty minutes." A pause. "We were there for twenty minutes! No: thirty, actually! Look, you want us to come back, we're going to have to double up." He clicked off. "She's absolutely retarded," he said to no one in particular. "There's been two cars waiting outside there for twenty minutes. She's a moron! She's too dumb to see two orange vans out there that say Pet Chauffeur."

During a rare quiet moment, Lang explained one source of pressure. "We're dealing with some of the wealthiest people in the world," he said. "You can't get to them without a referral. And once you're gone, you're gone."

Occupied with the business end, Lang doesn't get behind the wheel anymore. So on a sunny Friday, I hopped in a van with a thirty-year-old driver named Andy Rodriguez. Rodriguez was among the newest of Pet Chauffeur's twenty employees. A GPS device—and occasional bursts of anxious radio communication from Lang—helped him navigate his way through the day. Of all the jobs in New York City that require being stuck in traffic, Rodriguez's may be the best. Taking the leash of another client, a mixed-breed, recently rescued dog named Fred en route home from the vet, he leans down to deliver an energetic pat as the dog's tail wags happily to and fro; when they arrive at Fred's apartment near Wall Street, the pup's new owner greets Rodriguez like he's a guardian angel. How many cabbies can say that? But what does it feel like for a guy to watch people spend almost as much on a round-trip to the dog gym as he makes all day? Rodriguez shrugged. "Modern times, I guess. Some people take better care of their dogs than they do themselves."

Modern times indeed, and also like the Victorian era— *Upstairs, Downstairs,* with the doghouse in between. Ordinary New Yorkers may opt for the occasional hired ride to the vet, but many Pet Chauffeur regulars live in a world of dog walkers and pet sitters and animal trainers and canine swim therapists and pet Reiki masseuses and veterinary acupuncturists, personal chefs and personal assistants and personal trainers, the baroque and endlessly subspecialized array of service providers— to humans, to pets, to anyone who can afford it—here in the capital of capitalism. "It's all servants," Lang said of the firm's most wealthy and famous clients, with whom he rarely speaks. "It's butlers, personal assistants, whatever. We coordinate with them."

In a contemporary adaptation of *The Graduate,* the hero might be counseled away from plastics and straight toward the real wave of the future: services! Federal projections for the thirty fastest-growing professions for the decade ahead include home health aides, personal financial advisers, skin-care specialists, and marriage and family therapists. Veterinarians and veterinary technicians also made the list.

America's transformation into a service economy coincided with its transformation into a land of fur babies and pet parents. This has been an irresistible combination. Between 1998 and 2006, the number of workers employed in the nonfarm animal-service field had doubled from 100,000 to 200,000 (add in vets and their assistants, and the figure doubles once more, to nearly 400,000). And customers spent $4 billion on services, double what they had in 2000. In 2007, for the first time, the federal Bureau of Labor Statistics issued a report on pet services. Predicting 19 percent growth over the ensuing decade, the statisticians forecast a bright future indeed for those who clean, walk, and train dogs. "Pet owners—including a large number of baby boomers, whose disposable income is expected to increase as they age—are expected to increasingly purchase grooming services, daily and overnight boarding services, training services, and veterinary services, resulting in more jobs for animal care and service workers," it concluded. "As more pet owners consider their pets part of the family, demand for luxury animal services and the willingness to spend greater amounts of money on pets should continue to grow."

Uncle Sam's statisticians didn't address by name the blueberry facial for dogs. The facial is one of several grooming

services available at Wag Hotel, an especially swanky new kennel in San Francisco. I visited Wag more or less on a lark. I had
scheduled a visit to the city's enormous SPCA building a few
blocks away and figured I'd pop over to Wag while in the
neighborhood. On other research jaunts, I'd toured all sorts of
lavish doggie day cares. In Hollywood, there was L.A. Dog
Works, with a bamboo-and-slate-accented "Zen Den" room
where diffusing machines release Dog Appeasing Pheromones
designed to calm anxious pups. (I couldn't smell a thing.) In
Houston, there was Rover Oaks, housed in a purpose-built
limestone building that could be the home of a tony East Coast
prep school. In Silicon Valley, I didn't even have to go to A
Dog's Life, the fancy local pet hotel. The attorney I was inter-
viewing pulled up an electronic copy of the local dog spa's most
recent report card for her boxer, Ralph. It revealed that Ralph
had played most recently with Stella, Murphy, Cali, and Norris,
and that his favorite activities were "romping, chasing, and
playing with Stella." Under additional comments, the card
noted that Ralph had also "worked on high-distraction recalls,"
that is, coming when called even in a cacophonous space. And
to think his owner had worried that Ralph would botch the
kennel's admissions.

Still, most other kennels—or day spas, or pet hotels—look
like a Motel Six compared to Wag, which fashions itself the W
Hotel of the canine world. I should have known it would be different when I first phoned. "You'll need to call our publicist," a
manager informed me. The publicist made an appointment for
me to see the hotel founder, Ritu Raj, but when I arrived Raj was
showing around a potential investor, an Internet heavyweight. So
I walked the thirty-five-thousand-square-foot, 239-room facility
with the manager, Jose Gonzalez. From a bay window in the
lobby, we looked into a vast room with several separate play
areas. In front of us, a boxer relieved himself. A staffer in a San
Francisco Giants jersey ran out to clean up the urine. (Wag's

floors are coated with a special epoxy to keep liquids from soaking into the surface.) As we watched, Gonzalez explained the intricacies of something called the Wag-care system—basically, a way of screening dogs for play styles in order to maximize romper-room fun. "It's not just about keeping them safe," he said. "It's about them being more doglike rather than sitting on the couch at home watching TV and being more peoplelike."

Which was funny, because a couple of minutes later—after wandering through the spotless kitchen, with its airline-style food carts imprinted with the Wag logo; after inspecting the antibacterial rooftop Astroturf on which dogs can have a special after-dinner walk for fifteen dollars; after learning about the online room service system that lets traveling owners order up pigs' ears or peanut butter–stuffed Kongs—Gonzalez's tour arrived at one of the eleven eighty-five-dollar-a-night luxury suites, where dogs can . . . sit on the couch and watch TV. Matsi, a lanky, serene-looking black mixed-breed, didn't actually seem to be paying much attention to the afternoon's showing of *101 Dalmatians* on her suite's flat-screen TV. Perhaps she was transfixed by the art—depicting dogs, of course—on the wall. Anyway, the real technological marvel of the room isn't what Matsi can watch, but who can watch Matsi. Via a camera mounted not far from the television, Matsi's family can check in on her online, watch her sleep or snack or hop on the luxe bed. Should something seem amiss, the traveling pet owners can get on the phone to fix it. "We get calls all the time," Gonzalez said. "The dog looks hungry. Can you bring him something?" Matsi, for now, looks supremely content.

Back downstairs, Raj was tied up again—a meeting with architects about plans for new Wag establishments. I poked around an office whose walls were festooned with mock-ups of new kennel designs that aimed to move beyond the standard paradigm of cages, however luxurious, stacked upon one another. As with any kennel, the goal is to minimize sight lines from room to room, which minimizes barking. The Wag project was being run by a team of trendy industrial designers, and the proposals seemed appropriately unusual. One of the two leading prototypes looked like a giant Rubik's snake, twisting at awkward angles down the hallway. Somehow I expected it when Raj begged off our chat once again. Could we do it later? No problem, I said. A few minutes later I got a meeting scheduling notice from his BlackBerry.

When we finally chatted, Raj said it was numbers that drew him into the pet industry. A former partner at the consulting giant Accenture, he said he had spent two decades in California's high-tech economy. But he started thinking about the pet sector when he heard about a former colleague who'd taken a job selling kitty litter to Wal-Mart—$1.8 billion of it, he said. "That was just shocking." More impressive, though, were the things his colleagues were doing for their own pets. "Being part of Accenture, some of the people I know live a certain lifestyle. And the lifestyle we live involves having a pet. Since dot-com, since 9/11, the pets were getting closer to the owners. But the services, the products, everything for them was obsolete. It was twenty years old. It wasn't keeping up with the trading-up luxury lifestyle in America . . . How many people have Starbucks coffee? Is it basic, or a luxury? It becomes, like, it's my coffee, it's my Starbucks, it's my lifestyle."

Kennels once meant gloomy facilities full of cages. No more. Nationally, chains like Central Bark and Best Friends Pet Resorts care for tens of thousands of dogs; retailers like PetSmart, whose annual report identifies services as its major growth area for the decade ahead, aren't far behind. Total spending on pet boarding was over $2 billion in 2005—almost $500 million more than it had been in 2001. But Wag, with a new coffee-table magazine and ludicrously high prices and over-the-top extras—did I mention that the gift shop sells nonalcoholic doggie beer?—was aiming higher. And with his jargon-laden talk about high earners who "will not settle for second best," Raj, an earring-clad onetime mathematics grad student, sure seems to have thought through the implications of canine cuteness.

When we met, Raj pulled out a personal notebook bearing details, including sketches, of nine distinct "psychographics" among Wag's clients or potential clients. One is a thirtysome-thing professional woman who treats her dog as a "sentinel." "They're attorneys, accountants, professional designers, archi-tects. They love their dogs, they spend a lot of time with their dogs . . . If they want to get married, guess what? [The prospec-tive husband] has to pass the test" of getting along with the pet. Another psychographic is a member of a two-earner gay couple. "They actually really treat their dogs like their kids," Raj said. "Rituals you'd have for their kids, they'd actually do them." This group, he added, has strong "brand loyalty." A third group is made up of young couples in what Raj calls the "testing" phase, starting with a dog before going on to a baby. "This is another relationship where the dog comes first," he said. A fourth group, one with less tendency to spoil their pet, fits into the "white picket fence" psychographic. But, according to Raj, they're good customers because "the thing about them is that they all go on vacations, and when they go, their friends and family also go on vacation," leaving no one to take in the dog. His list also included aging empty nesters (their dogs, he said, will be as well behaved, or as unruly, as their grown chil-dren were) and single men with dogs ("they're hard to find, but good"). In fact, he wrote off only three groups: the single women of the "pets-as-accessories Paris Hilton syndrome" psy-chographic (they don't leave home without their Chihuahuas), the "macho" psychographic (they don't leave home without their pit bulls), and the exurban hunting dog guys ("their dog isn't getting anything special").

Raj opened the first Wag in Sacramento in 2005. The San

Francisco facility came a year and a half later. When we chatted, he was planning a new location in Las Vegas. Within three years, he said, he wanted forty or fifty locations. "Wherever there's a Neiman Marcus," he noted, "the market is there." (There are thirty-eight Neiman's stores around the country.) At least two competing chains have proclaimed equally grand ambitions. And both Paradise 4 Paws and Pet Paradise are also aiming for the ultimate killer app in dog boarding: locations adjacent to the airports—in some cases with free parking and shuttle service—in cities like Chicago and Houston. Whether it's Raj or someone else who finally triumphs, upscale shelter is coming to a well-lit facility near you.

But is the market for the blueberry facial there, too? It costs only $40, a small chunk when you think that the average bill for a Wag Hotel stay runs upwards of $300. Yet none were being performed when I visited. For the record, Raj's dog, an English bulldog named Zoebe, has had one. It involves a blue cream that turns foamy white before being washed off. "What happens is her face becomes softer and her hair becomes silkier," Raj said. Another thing that happens is this: People write articles about the luxe new hotel whose services include blueberry facials for dogs (or, like me, they write it up in a book). And then other people talk around the water cooler about the absurd forms of pampering rampant in modern pet-owning society. Somewhere along the line, the plan goes, the name of the chain will stick in some people's minds. In a competitive marketplace, a blueberry facial can make a big difference.

Pet grooming, the business of haircuts, baths, and pedicures—and, yeah, the occasional blueberry facial—pulled in $1.2 billion in 2005, roughly 50 percent above what it had in 2001. Pet aesthetics is the most visible of the services that have become growth drivers for the big pet chains now that they've figured out how to sell expensive chew toys in every corner of the country. Services posted annual sales gains of over 20 percent at PetSmart and Petco in the first years of the twenty-first century, outstripping same-store sales.

Why do we care how beautifully coiffed our pets are? More than perhaps any other chunk of the pet economy, grooming hints at the changed place—literally—of animals in domestic life. You're not liable to notice or care how the dog in the backyard lean-to smells. It's a different story once that animal moves inside, as America's pets have done over the past few decades. In 2006, only 13 percent of dogs and 8 percent of cats spent their nights outdoors; in 1998 those numbers stood at 24 and 16 percent. And even the 1998 figures represented a major change. One academic study of animal depictions in women's-magazine advertisements depicts a kind of canine manifest destiny, with the animals losing their leashes and moving inside, to the hearth and beyond. Ads from the 1920s almost invariably showed dogs outside and on leashes. Things gradually changed, with the biggest shift taking place between the 1960s and the 1980s. By late in the century, the archetypal image was a Bayer ad that showed a boy lying sick in bed next to his dog as his mother gave him aspirin.

Animals and night once went together in our imagination. Nowadays, the old echo of the hound baying at the full moon is a lot less familiar than the sound of the pup snoring in front of the TV. But don't take my word for it. Think of that iconic TV cartoon, set in prehistoric times but profoundly reflecting America's Eisenhower era, *The Flintstones*. The program's closing credits show Fred putting empty milk bottles outside the front door for the milkman—and then depositing the cat outside as well. "Someday maybe Fred will win the fight / And the cat will stay out for the night" went the theme song. Try to rest in peace, Fred; by 2003, 47 percent of pet owners reported that the pets sleep in their masters' beds at night.

Clearly, that's 47 percent of pet owners who would care deeply about any stench emanating from their four-legged bedmate. In 2004 alone, 326 new grooming products came into what was by then a $165-million market for shampoos, conditioners, and other animal beauty products. The market has lured executives from luxury human brands like Paul Mitchell into the pet aisle. And, given that washing your dog's hair remains more cumbersome than washing your own, it also prompted a spike in the market for professional pet groomers—8 percent a year so far through the century's first decade, according to one study. Still other businesses have gotten in on the action without even needing to hire the skilled labor. In Phoenix, I visited a self-service dog bathing store that provided custom bathtubs, flexible hoses, and strong-enough-for-a-husky air dryers for customers to use on their own dogs at an hourly rate.

Thus there was no small amount of self-confidence on display on the sunny fall weekend I spent at Groom Expo 2007, the budding industry's big annual gathering in Hershey, Pennsylvania. Make that *one of* the industry's big annual gatherings. *Groomer to Groomer* magazine lists a calendar brimming with contests, symposia, and trade shows aimed at the nation's population of professional groomers. In addition to sales staffs touting a variety of new shears, dog-fur removers, or mobile grooming trucks, the event featured a $30,000 grooming contest, billed as the largest purse in industry history. As chains like PetSmart get into grooming, folks who were trimming dogs when trimming dogs wasn't cool need a way to differentiate their own ostensibly higher level of expertise. The contest was one stop on what has become a global circuit of such shows, from the SuperGroom Super Model Dog contest in Las Vegas to the US PetPro classic in Dallas to Intergroom in New Jersey to the international battles featuring Groom Team USA against foreign stylists at shows like Groomania in Brussels.

By the time the final face-off began, on Sunday morning,

the Groom Expo had already been under way for two days. Preliminary rounds had whittled a field of dozens of groomers down to twelve. Now, on a stage flanked by Ionic columns and decorated with a faux-Roman dog bust, the dozen contestants got down to work, clipping and buzzing and combing a dozen poodles borrowed specially for the occasion. Judges circled, taking notes. The competitors worked furiously: intense Veronica Frosch, wrestling with the mountains of hair on her gray poodle; tall, quiet Julie Wilkins, casually pushing aside her nonchalant model's scrotum so she could trim some nearby fur; impassive Jackie Boulton removing the tape from yet another poodle's ears before brushing them out until they looked like the ear flaps of an old-fashioned winter hat. By the time the three hours of grooming had finished, the dogs all looked like billowing cotton balls.

Most ordinary pet owners wouldn't choose such a look for their own animals. But the spectacle of brand-name groomers pushing the stylistic envelope in front of their peers underscored a trend that crosses the entire pet-service world: professionalization. The National Association of Professional Pet Sitters, founded in 1989, now boasts 2,400 members who abide by its Pledge of Professional Conduct. Its rival, Pet Sitters International, founded in 1994, has 7,900. The American Boarding Kennel Association, established in 1977, now offers accreditations attesting to the high standards of its 3,000 members. The International Association of Canine Professionals, established in 1999, represents 1,200 members ranging from groomers and pet first-aid instructors to boundary fence installers and dog walkers, the latter being newly prevalent since IACP's 2007 merger with the eleven-year-old Professional Dog Walkers Association International.

Once you've got a professional organization, and once that organization starts handing out certifications, of course, the next logical step is attempting to give those certifications the force of law. One of the hot subjects in grooming is licensing: Should pet groomers, like cosmeticians, need to get a government certificate to do their job? For career groomers, a permitting process separates wheat from chaff: professionals in command of specialized skills on one side, the nice neighbor who will wash your dog for twenty dollars on the other. But the nature of the pet economy is such that even if older services become enshrined in the celestial world of bureaucratic licensing, newer ones arise out on the unregulated frontier. Since 2005, the Association of Professional Animal Waste Specialists has represented two hundred members who clean animal droppings from clients' laws. The group's annual convention features a "turd-herding" contest, said Deb Levy, the association's president as well as the owner of Saint Louis–based Yucko's Poop-Scooping Service, which charges eighteen dollars for weekly cleanings of a yard used by one or two dogs.

As the grooming contest in Hershey approached its first intermission, my mind started to wander. However popular the field might get, professional grooming will never give pro wrestling a run for its money in the spectator-excitement department. I strolled around the show floor for a while, drawn to an enormous truck parked near the back of the room, which stood out among the shampoo sales booths and clipper demonstrations. This turned out to be the Wag N' Tails Pet Stylist Elite, custom-built by a company that tricks out Ford F-450s into mobile grooming trucks better equipped than your average ambulance. Complete with built-in bathroom, refrigerator, microwave, 20,000-BTU furnace, floor-to-ceiling stainless-steel bathtub with multiple hoses and nozzles, odor-resistant floors, fifty-gallon onboard water supply, and 360-degree rotating grooming table, the PSE is the Air Force One of mobile grooming, available for $82,000. "A lot of people get the flat-screen TV option, too," said Chuck Perry, who has been building the vehicles for a decade.

Perry's wife opened a grooming salon in the 1970s, moving into mobile grooming several years later. The couple have been involved in the field, one way or another, ever since. He says things really took off in 2001. While some say the age of terrorism prompted a new focus on nurturing pets, Perry offered a more prosaic explanation: real estate. "Rents were just huge," he said. "We're very strong in Florida, California, and the Northeast," the country's high-rent districts. "The other part of our clients are people who have had shops" but tired of paying the bills. And the concept of mobile grooming fit in with other trends. "Nowadays, there's a lot of people who come to your house to do this or that for you. Look at landscaping and how that has boomed in twenty years. It's the same thing. The keys are in the flowerpot, the dog's in the bedroom, the check's on the table, book me again in four weeks." He estimated that the firm sells twenty new vans a month.

By the time I made my way out of the PSE, the contest was about to end. After some final trims and clips, the referee ordered the contestants to lay down their scissors. It took a team of judges about a half hour to decide who had done the best job grooming their dogs to the desired degree of balance and texture, based on the degree of difficulty presented by the dogs before the contest began. Confetti fell as the $30,000 prize was awarded to Boulton, a forty-two-year-old groomer who operates a salon called Mucky Pups from her Calgary home. If the local press picked up on the award, she told me, it would do wonders for her business, which was already booked solid for the next two months. "When they hear about the money, they know it's big," she said. "You're not just clipping toenails." Though canine-grooming awareness among her fellow Canadians was "so far behind the Americans, it's scary," Boulton noted that at the very least her clientele has raised its ambitions over her twenty-one years in the business. "It used to be just shave-downs and dematting. But we've come a long way educating clients that they need to do this regularly. They used to think we just wanted the money."

Thirty grand still represents a very big deal to most of the people who care for America's pets. According to federal statistics, median earnings for nonfarm-animal caretakers was $8.72 an hour in May 2006, which would work out to about $18,000 a year. It's a paradox noted by more than a few kennel owners, dog trainers, and even veterinarians: If this business is so great, how come we're not making more money? But even as many providers told of tight finances, I heard tell in interviews all over the country about a fabled creature of modern pet culture: the six-figure dog walker.

Few people could actually point me to one, of course. Some said they existed in Hollywood, providing exclusive private walks to celebrity pups. Others placed them in Manhattan, whose dense residential patterns might let an enterprising soul walk dozens of dogs each day. As I asked around, though, most doors slammed shut. Sure, owners of the burgeoning number of dog-walking chains did nicely, pocketing a cut while sending underlings out to actually pound the pavement. But what about that legendary scrapper, the Paul Bunyan of pets, who racks up the dollars while personally doing the walking? Did my fruitless search reflect some fear of the IRS in an informal, cash-driven industry? Or could it be that the $100,000-a-year dog walker was an urban myth, a piece of pet-mania hype?

Then, one rainy autumn morning, I was visiting a Labradoodle breeder in northern New Jersey. She was telling me about all the different people she had met at "Doodle romps," regular gatherings for enthusiasts of the breed. One of them, she said, was about to come over. She also sometimes works as my dog sitter, she added.

Lauren Huston graduated from Lehigh University and has

a master's in social work from Rutgers. She began walking dogs to help put herself through graduate school. In the process, she learned that there's good money in it for someone willing to rustle up the clients. Of course, once she was armed with a diploma as a licensed social worker, she left that stuff behind for grown-up work. There was an apartment and a paycheck and a job—a very stressful, very serious, very professional job—as a family and child therapist in Hoboken. Eventually, she got a dog of her own and went looking for someone to walk it while she was busy working with troubled kids. "I told all of them, you know, I've done this before, so I knew exactly what I wanted in a dog walker," she said. She wound up with one of the city's busiest dog walkers, a woman who did thirty or so runs a day. They became friends. "And, I guess a year or two after hiring my dog walker, she said, 'Why don't you get back into this and do this instead of what you were doing?'" Huston demurred. "It's kind of a risky jump because I don't have any clientele . . . and I don't know that it can pay me what I'm making in my current job." At the time, Huston said, she was earning $75,000 a year. "And she said, basically, that she was making close to $200,000 a year. And I said, okay, I'm going to give it a try."

Her friend, who was so busy that she was turning away clients, threw her a couple of names. Huston started walking their dogs at lunch or after work, which was fairly easy because her day-job hours were seven to three. "It would be an extra, oh, four hundred dollars a week," she said.

In 2007, between jobs, freshly out of a relationship, and having moved back home to the affluent suburb of Morristown, Huston decided to make dog care a full-time job. She christened her business Camp Fido by Lauren and began passing out business cards at local veterinary offices and pet-supply stores. "My goal was about two thousand dollars a week," she told me. Which, a little back-of-the-envelope calculation determines, represents about—

ka-ching!—$100,000 a year. "Can I come shadow you for a day sometime?" I asked. I wanted to see this gold mine at work.

Huston was not an easy person to catch up with—despite the fact that she is always in touch with her perpetually buzzing BlackBerry. First, there was Thanksgiving week ("I was working from six, seven in the morning until after midnight"). Then, Christmas (dog walkers tend to take their own vacations at less traditional times, like the most unpleasant part of February). A couple of times the weather got in our way: A bunch of Huston's clients are teachers, and if they have snow days, their dogs don't need walking. It wasn't until March that I finally joined her for her daily rounds. By this point, Huston had renamed the business Petcetera, the better to reflect the things she offers besides walking dogs, like boarding, adoption counseling, youth education, and bereavement services. As business grew, she still hadn't reached consistent $2,000 weeks that would bring her into the six-figure annual salary range, but she was getting closer. "I should be there by summer," she said.

I met her in the courtyard of her apartment building as she was finishing up her first walk of the morning: her own dog, Raegan, named (though not spelled) after the former president. "Busy day ahead," she said.

First stop: Jeff Brandes's apartment. A tennis coach, Brandes was about to go to Florida with the school team he leads. Which meant he was leaving behind his cat, Booboo Kitty. He had asked Huston to look in on Booboo twice a day. Each of the twenty-minute visits would set Brandes back twenty dollars. Today's visit, though, was a "consultation," a chance for Huston to get the lay of the land. The apartment's decor was high bachelor pad: guitar against wall, paintings of hockey players, TV tuned to ESPN. But the occupant acted like anything but the carefree young male. When we arrived, he had his grooming gear all laid out on the leather sofa. He demonstrated how he'd like the cat to be brushed. The fluffy

Booboo was impassive for a while but then gave Brandes a look that prompted him to put the brush down. "The problem is, he likes to be brushed, but then he likes to bite the brush," Brandes explained. "It'll be fine," Huston said, reaching out for the cat. "Don't worry. I'll send pictures." The cash was handed over, along with a long list of emergency contact numbers.

Next stop: a ramshackle house and its four pugs, Finnegan, Maddox, Elsa, and Emmett. Huston parked far down the driveway. "The minute these dogs see my car, they like to go pee on it," she said. We popped into the house, where the dogs were in the bedroom listening to NPR. The arrival set off a happy frenzy. Once the excitement ebbed, Huston ordered the dogs outside—Maddox wouldn't come at first, so she carried him—and they strolled around the yard while they relieved themselves. Then it was back inside to play and serve treats. The kitchen showed signs of a hasty postbreakfast evacuation; there was still jam on the knife that never quite made it into the dishwasher. The owner had left a note for Huston. She was trying to train the dogs and wanted her to say the words "do your business" when they went out to the bathroom, and to then offer them a treat as a reward. "Too late for that," Huston said. In a corner, Elsa was having diarrhea on the kitchen floor. Taking out a piece of Petcetera stationery, Huston left a note about the mess along with her receipt: seventy dollars, for that visit as well as a return engagement later that day.

Back in the car, Huston worked the BlackBerry with one hand and drove with the other. A couple of new appointments had come in—she prefers e-mail so she can have everything in writing—and she juggled the midday schedule around to accommodate them. Before lunchtime, she made stops with Chester the golden retriever, Roxy the corgi, Shadow the Lab, Orla the King Charles spaniel, and Cassidy and Cooper the cockapoos. Walking the dogs along the suburban street made for a surreal experience. No one was home. The only people in sight were contractors, mail carriers, and the occasional police car. I started to feel like Huston and I were suspects: Why weren't we at work like all the upstanding citizens? Except that Huston was walking Chester, which was a perfect way to fit in.

Huston had recently been through her own funny experience with the police. She had been booked to make twice-a-day visits to the home of a family that was away for the holidays. Their two cats, Buttons and Bows, both needed daily medication. But the family locked the storm door when they went out of town; Huston only had the main door key. When she arrived, Huston could hear the animals whining. Through a window, she could see her check sitting on the kitchen table. The family wasn't picking up their cell phone. After trying windows and a back door, she called the cops. "I said, the animals need their meds. You can check—there's a check for me right there," she said. "They said they can't do it." No wonder; the home also housed a collection of Ferraris. Huston sat in the driveway and waited. Hours later, they returned her call and gave her the secret pass code to the car-collection garage, from where they helped her navigate passage back into the main house. Once they were back, Huston got a very nice reference. And a few days later, she got a call from the woman asking whether she could set Huston up on a date.

Huston has wound her way into the lives of many of her clients. Conversations about dogs tend to segue into conversations about life. "People just spill their guts to me," Huston said. Thus late in the day, as we made our final stop to visit a pair of skittish Manchester terriers named Mocha and Roman, Huston was able to tell me all about both the dogs and their humans. The pups were owned by a woman who had fallen in love with a man in North Carolina. She flew off to see him every weekend, leaving the terriers alone save four daily visits—twenty-five bucks a pop—from Huston. After letting the dogs out for a pee on the lawn of their modest row-house development, she tossed toys to them in the kitchen. The dogs rambunctiously clamored after them, a small bit of exercise in a lonely day. I sat and played with her key chain, a massive collection of dangling metal that might make her look like a Manhattan super, if the apartments were occupied by the likes of Brooklynne, Yogi, Jackson, and Agatha. "There's a story for every one of them," she said.

You can credit all sorts of things for the growth of dog walking as a business: the rise of two-career couples (homemakers, by and large, don't need to pay someone to let the dog out), the elongation of the American workday (a dog might be able to last eight or nine hours without a bathroom break, but modern commuting times take a lot longer), the evolution of public-safety standards (the old practice of simply letting the dog out to bound around the neighborhood was a victim of leash laws and liability fears), and even public awareness about canine needs (these days, most experts will tell you a dog has to have a serious walk rather than the mere option of playing alone in the backyard).

Mostly, the driving force is the simple, sweet truth that people want to have pets. And, what with all the other things they want or need—jobs, vacations, nights out on the town—service providers like Huston make it possible to have those pets. Like dog groomers, animal chauffeurs, and pet hoteliers, she enables pet ownership for the single, the globe-trotting, the overbooked. The very folks who might have been told, in another decade, not to get a pet at all. Perhaps the plethora of pet-servants-for-hire indicates a troubling national reversion to nineteenth-century inequality. All the same, the four-legged subjects of all that spending—the dogs and cats whose care we're now willing to shell out for—demonstrate that the citizens of what during two decades of economic bubbles was sometimes called a new gilded age have some very different, twenty-first-century sorts of priorities.

TEN

Trick or Treat

What Dueling Pet Trainers Can Tell Us About the Culture Wars

Jade was a mess. Taken into Mike and Michelle Monreal's house as a rescue dog—she'd been found tied to a tree—the lean young rottweiler had in a few short weeks taken on the role of guerrilla insurgent in the young couple's new suburban home. She'd snap at the Monreals. She'd snarl at visitors. And her anxiety-based aggression was starting to infect the pair's other dog, a Bernese mountain dog that, like my own pet, is named Murphy. When Michelle was trying to corral Jade into the kitchen one day, the dog managed to nip her hand. It didn't require medical attention, but the incident was scary all the same.

At this point, a lot of people might have decided to give up on Jade, concluding that whatever happened before her rescue had left her unable to live with a human family. Not the Monreals. They'd brought Jade into their house, and they were going to stick with her, even if it meant a bunch of hard work. "You have a problem with something you love, you fix it," Michelle said. So it was that on a chilly, early winter evening, Wendy Whiting visited a Bucks County, Pennsylvania, subdivision at the rate of a hundred dollars an hour to teach a twenty-four-year-old union carpenter and a twenty-four-year-old bank employee how to walk their dogs.

The goal was to have the two dogs saunter calmly alongside their owners, following the humans' instructions rather than pulling the couple all over the cul-de-sac as they chased smells, squirrels, and strangers. To watch the Monreals struggle at the far end of the two dogs' leashes was like watching a pair of teenagers try to drag race the very first time they got behind the wheel of their dads' cars. If, that is, their fathers drove forty-year-old clunkers imported from the former Soviet Union. And if those clunkers had flat tires, too. The couple lurched and jerked along the cul-de-sac as their pets alternatively raced forward, hung back, and tried to play with each other. It was about halfway between Election Day and Christmas, but it was easy to imagine that completing the simple loop that Whiting had asked the couple and their dogs to walk—from the tattered campaign placard on one neighbor's lawn to the inflatable Santa Claus snow globe on another's—might take until Valentine's Day.

Nevertheless, it was progress. Whiting had first visited a few weeks earlier, after the biting incident. She had landed in the couple's house like a leash-wielding Mary Poppins. Her injunctions were aimed more at Mike and Michelle than at Jade and Murphy. No more letting the dogs go through doors in front of you! Let them know you're the boss by going first. No more leaving the kibble out all day! Make them eat on your schedule and not like the patrons at a twenty-four-hour buffet. When they come up to you for a pat, ignore them! They'll get love only when you call them over. And that goes double for when you first walk in the door! It was all right there in Whiting's fourteen-item "Alpha Rules," a photocopied list that serves as the constitution of her benign monarchy. The document's bottom line: This ain't no democracy, poochie.

Whether it was a result of implementing the Alpha Rules or more a matter of the sessions making the couple more comfortable with their animals, things improved rapidly. No more biting. No more intimidation. A certain amount of frenetic barking and circling ensued when Whiting first rang the doorbell, but even that was far less than the growls and jumps she'd experienced on previous arrivals. The Monreals were delighted. Whiting, though, seemed a bit let down. She'd brought me along to show off her lion-tamer skills, and now it looked like the final three installments of this $600, six-session package would be about basics like how to walk calmly on the leash, or sit quietly when there's a knock at the door, or chill out when company visits.

I'd first met Whiting a couple of years earlier. My wife and I had hired her to work on those same placid basics with our own Murphy. Things went well. And where they didn't—the big guy still howls at every single visitor—we've tended to blame our own laziness, rather than Whiting's training tactics, for the breakdown. Indeed, as ordinary consumers, we had only the vaguest inkling that her method was dramatically different from that of other trainers. We'd hired her one-woman business, Proper Paws, mainly because she had a smart-looking Web site, seemed nice, and returned our phone calls. Since then, her business had grown. By the time I called her in order to research a newspaper article about the booming, unregulated market for dog training, she was talking about turning Proper Paws into a national chain. She'd become, in other words, an example of the phenomenon I wanted to write about.

Come on along, she said. Proper Paws was adding staff, so she was used to having new hires shadow her training sessions anyway. We visited a piano teacher with a skittish new puppy and a newly pregnant yuppie couple anxious to drill some basics into a mutt that would soon cease to be the household's center of attention. The most interesting stop, she promised, would be the Monreals. In the previous session, Whiting had needed to stare down a snarling, threatening Jade in the couple's kitchen.

Notwithstanding Whiting's disappointment at the lack of *Crocodile Hunter* theatrics, the lesser challenge of getting the dogs to walk on leash was exactly what I'd wanted to see. Though the booming field has been dramatized by crisis interventions on TV shows like Animal Planet's *It's Me or the Dog* and National Geographic's *Dog Whisperer,* starring the charismatic cultural sensation Cesar Millan, the phenomenon that has caused Whiting's business to grow like a three-month-old Labrador isn't a new glut of nasty dogs in need of miraculous behavioral cures. Rather, it's the fact that millions of ordinary working Americans have over the past decade or so decided it's perfectly appropriate to hire an expensive professional to help them live with their pets.

Back on the cul-de-sac, even a simple walk continued to seem like a complex logistical procedure. Once upon a time, pre-Jade and pre-cul-de-sac, walking the dog was a regular thing for the couple. Their recent move to a suburban house, with a fenced-in backyard and no front sidewalks, had changed that. For the most part, the dogs now flounced around out back, peeing and pooping and playing as they pleased—and growing unused to trotting calmly alongside their humans. Whiting's Alpha Rule philosophy, though, applies to mundane endeavors and dangerous situations alike. Eventually, she had Mike and Michelle each take one of the dogs to a different part of the street. Mike and Murphy were down near the cul-de-sac, Michelle and Jade in front of the house with the jiggling snow globe. Separated by forty or fifty yards, they did a little better.

Whiting, in football-coach mode, kept on the couple. *Hold your head up! Stick that chin out!* (In doggie-speak, she said, a drooping head conveys submission.) *Hold that leash close—like a lady with her purse!* (The dogs have to know to walk with you, not to pull you.) *And when the dogs do pull, for heaven's sake, jerk the leash and go the other way!* (That'll show 'em who's boss.)

After fifteen or so minutes, the dogs were exhausted, panting in the middle of the street. With the workout, even Jade's hard face had morphed from forbidding to welcoming, her tongue lolling out on the pavement. We headed inside to practice some door greetings. According to Whiting, people mustn't pat the dogs upon arriving. In canine language, she said, that leads dogs to view people as supplicants instead of leaders. Ignoring your excited dogs when they seem to be welcoming you home runs counter to nearly every instinct of pet ownership. But to Whiting, it's an example of the self-discipline that will make life easier for dog and human alike.

When the hour was up, Whiting finally offered the dogs a big, loving pat—and then whipped out her PDA to schedule the next appointment. She headed off with a command: *Take those dogs out for a walk. Every day.* "You guys have to practice this stuff," she said. "Five, ten minutes a day. Every day. No excuses."

There is more than one way to walk a dog.

Just a few suburbs away from Whiting, Leigh Siegfried, proprietor of Opportunity Barks, is equally as certain about the theory and practice of dog walking. But in her version, there's little attention to head posture or authoritative leash grip, and none whatsoever to who gets to walk through a doorway before whom. Instead, the focus is on a sandwich baggie full of chopped-up hot dog pieces. When the dog trots alongside you in the desired manner, she tells clients, follow up with a treat. "You want to make it so he wants to walk with you," she says.

Whiting and Siegfried represent opposite sides of an acrimonious, and recently very public, pedagogical debate. On popular TV shows, in the op-ed pages of the *New York Times,* and in the forest of books published each year about how to train a dog, proponents of Whiting's and Siegfried's respective methods go at it like members of rival psychiatric schools—or dueling street gangs. Chat up a random trainer, and you may find arguments over the seemingly innocuous question of how to keep the puppy from jumping on strangers quickly eliding into angry accusations about coddling or cruelty, academic myopia and anti-intellectual backlash.

Wendy Whiting adheres to the "pack theory" notion of dog training. The basic idea is that dogs respond to countless subtle markers of leader-of-the-pack "alpha" status, markers like going through the door first or choosing the direction when the pack is on the move. Become the alpha, goes the theory, and discipline is easy. Siegfried, meanwhile, comes from the "positive-reinforcement" school. She teaches by rewarding good behavior—and views alpha tactics like leash jerking or door-order fetishizing as usually pointless and occasionally cruel. Her model, adherents say, leads to both better-behaved pets and better relations with their human housemates.

Siegfried has the vast majority of outspoken scholars, trainers, and behaviorists on her side. Whiting has Cesar Millan. I'd say it's a fair fight.

Despite their different stances on the particulars of what they do, Whiting and Siegfried have remarkably similar biographies. Both are affable, educated thirtysomething refugees from corporate America. Siegfried worked in advertising for a department store chain. Whiting worked for a big advertising agency. Both of them loved dogs. Both of them were bored with their jobs. Each of them started looking into ways to combine loving pets with making a living. They did so at the right time. Their field, professional dog training, is in the middle of a boom. According to the Bureau of Labor Statistics, there were forty-three thousand animal trainers in the country in 2006, at least half of whom worked with dogs. That represented a threefold jump over six years. The boom has turned chains like Bark Busters—four hundred thousand dogs served—into global brands.

Back on the ground, the growth has meant that the bulletin boards at dog parks and veterinarians' offices where folks like Whiting and Siegfried post their brochures are crowded with flyers from newcomers offering to teach you how to keep the dogs off the couch, on the sidewalk, and out of trouble. For a price: Siegfried charges $250 for two private sessions, with $100 for each follow-up. Whiting's six-session basic package ranges from $450 to $600, depending on the dog's history.

"It's become one of those basic, normal, good-citizen things that people just do," Whiting told me. "Get a dog, get some training. And if you have a problem with your dog, you hire someone instead of just giving up or getting rid of it." Even in her five years in the business, she said she'd noticed subtle changes in the popular view of her job. When she started out, clients used to go to great lengths at their first meetings to explain that their animals were not bad dogs, the same way psychotherapy rookies might need to explain to a new shrink that just because they're sitting on his couch doesn't mean they're, like, crazy. Nowadays, more people dispense with the initial awkward explanations. The service is sufficiently ordinary that no rationalization is necessary.

But becoming common doesn't mean pet training has become standardized. One winter Saturday, I tagged along as Siegfried paid a call on another pair of newlyweds. Their dog's problems were similar to Jade's, but the training advice they got could hardly have been more different.

Rich Cousins and Susan O'Brien had recently adopted Norman, a brown pit bull with a scraggly build and a round, puppyish face. The shelter said the dog was perfectly social. For the first two weeks he was. Then things changed: He began growling at anyone who came near his food bowl and jumping up on anyone who walked through the door. Jogging with Rich became impossible because the sight of another dog would send Norman into a howling panic. "He's mouthing, jumping, barking, lunging," reported Cousins, an artist. "He chews my foot," said O'Brien, an Internet advertising manager. "Any attention gets him all riled up. We don't know what to do." Siegfried's working theory was that the dog had been sick when he was found wandering the inner-city streets of North Philadelphia. Perhaps shelter personnel interpreted his sluggishness as docility. Now, after a couple weeks of regular meals, his true style was showing through.

Siegfried, whose day-to-day routine is as nondramatic as Whiting's, tagged it as one of her more challenging current jobs. Unlike Whiting, however, Siegfried didn't make anyone feel like there was a new governess on duty. On arrival, she crouched down to give Norman a great big pat. The food bowl left out on the kitchen floor? No problem—work on his "resource guarding" by offering treats when a human hangs out close to his food. That way, the dog sees human company not as a dangerous challenge but as a sign of good things. Same goes for Norman's disturbing tendency to snarl when touched anywhere near his collar, something the couple feared was a legacy of abuse suffered earlier in life. Siegfried put them through an exercise where they offered treats while reaching, slowly, for that same collar. "This is the order he needs to understand," she said. "I touch you near your collar, good things happen."

Eventually, we prepared to head outside, where Norman had lately been staring and growling and acting as if the leash was the only thing keeping him from disemboweling any passing dog. Siegfried planned to work through a similar treat routine with Norman and a stuffed model of a dog she keeps in her car for such eventualities. O'Brien asked whether she ought to make Norman go through the door after her, a trick she'd heard about somewhere. "How many doorways are there in the wild?" Siegfried scoffed. When Cousins followed, holding Norman's leash tight, she suggested he give the dog a bit more lead as they approached the stuffed model, which, as she had accurately predicted, sent Norman into a raised-hackles, teeth-bared fury. Over the course of a half hour with the stuffed dummy, and a lot of doggie biscuits, the real dog went from a snarling menace to something a little more manageable, without so much as a jerk of his leash.

Teaching dogs new tricks is an old trick. But the market for professional pet training dates back only as far as the Reagan administration. In 1982, a Berkeley-based veterinarian and behaviorist named Ian Dunbar started offering what he called "puppy classes." The idea was to teach ordinary, newly adopted dogs—and their owners—some basic lessons in obedience and socialization. In the pedagogically up-to-date college town, the classes were a smash hit. "This was pet dog training, so it was geared to all owners, even children, and all dogs," Dunbar recalled. "I taught the first one. We had twelve families, twelve puppies. Pretty soon I was teaching nine classes." By mid-decade, Dunbar said, he had turned his classes into a company with twenty locations.

Before Dunbar, organized dog training was for the most part limited to service animals—seeing-eye dogs, Hollywood animals, and hunting dogs. Trainers regularly published books aimed at ordinary pet owners, but their methods were based on work with nonpets. For these dogs, basic training was still cast in the stern Teutonic image of Colonel Konrad Most of the Royal Prussian Police, author of *Abrichtung des Hundes,* a hugely influential 1910 manual emphasizing techniques he'd perfected on military dogs, where "agreeable experiences" like pats were balanced by "compulsions" like sharp jerks on the choke collar. The German book wasn't translated for nearly fifty years. But during World War I, thousands of German soldiers were trained in Most's style to command service dogs. After the armistice, a number of them made their way to the United States, opening up dog-training clubs and publishing manuals. The most successful émigré trainer may have been a man named Carl Spitz, founder of the Hollywood Dog Training School, whose alums included Buck, the Saint Bernard who starred with Clark Gable in *Call of the Wild*. Spitz's most celebrated trainee was his own cairn terrier, hired in 1939 to play Toto in *The Wizard of Oz*.

Toto's harmless looks shouldn't fool you; he'd been trained like a marine. After the attack on Pearl Harbor, Spitz was put in charge of the U.S. military dog-training program. By 1945 thousands of American GIs had picked up his methods. And while the Allied victory led to the demobilization of America's dog trainers, it did not mean the demilitarization of their methods. The most influential trainer of the postwar years was probably William Koehler, a veteran of wartime military dog training who went on to work for Disney for twenty years. For the general public, *The Koehler Method of Dog Training* was the best-selling training manual of the 1960s, full of injunctions to correct bad behavior before it was too late. Among his suggestions: To teach a dog to heel, attach a fifteen-foot leash to the animal and then open the gate. If he dashes off without permission, run the other way. "He'll come with you," Koehler writes, "if only to be near his head."

In those days, most of the people who had their dogs trained were those who wanted to take part in canine obedience competitions. "If you want to find masses of people jerking on leashes, go to one of those clubs," said Jean Donaldson, the director of the San Francisco SPCA's academy for dog trainers and an author of several training books. The situation made it tough for Donaldson to establish herself professionally when she started out in the 1970s. As she recalled, "The idea was, once you amassed enough ribbons and trophies, you had credibility, and you proceeded to counsel people on house-training or aggression. When you think about it, [competitive obedience is] not the same thing at all as pet training."

Even as Donaldson was discovering that punitive disciplinarians still ruled the animal-training scene, the top-down approach was being questioned almost everywhere else in American life. In classrooms, rote memorization was out, critical thinking was in. In the wake of the upheavals of the 1960s, educators and psychologists—not to mention parents—increasingly came to believe that sparing the rod could actually help the child. It was only a matter of time before the era's advances in learning theory were applied to four-legged creatures, too. Ian Dunbar, from his post in Berkeley's psychology department, began applying that new critical framework to pets. Influenced by B. F. Skinner's behaviorism, the new trainers saw positive reinforcement as a better way to shape an animal. Punishment, Dunbar argued, was inefficient because the dogs might not even know what the yank on the choke collar was supposed to be correcting. And aversive conditioning, the polite euphemism for indignities like shocks to the collar, was especially unsuited to an animal whose only job was supposed to be living with a family. "What's the point of winning the battle, losing the war?" he asked in one lecture. "Dog jumps up. Boom! Knee him in the chest, tread on his hind paws, flip him over backward. Won't do that again. But he doesn't like you now."

Serendipitously, Dunbar came up with the idea of classes for ordinary dogs just as the demand for dog training was being boosted by major changes in American life during the 1950s, 1960s, and 1970s. With suburbanization and women's entry into the workplace, the newly enlarged population of dogs was spending large chunks of time alone. Even the time they spent socializing with their humans had changed: less walking on the sidewalk and becoming accustomed to new sights, more trotting out to the enclosed backyard. To this day, Dunbar insists that the best-behaved dogs in the country live in Manhattan. "Suburban dogs just don't get walked," he says. "People get a puppy there, but they aren't going to walk him and they aren't going to take him to the dog park if there even is one. He has to be better trained because he's never going to leave the house and garden in Concord, California."

To the uninitiated, Dunbar's first classes in the 1980s must have seemed like a holdover from Berkeley's hippie era. Many of the students were Dunbar's academic colleagues. In class, their dogs were off leash, sometimes simply passed around the room from person to person, offered copious treats for jobs well done—and neither yanked nor spanked when they botched tasks. "Puppy training was, you bring your pet to class, you let him off leash, and you teach him off leash," he recalled. "The rationale was, he's off leash at home . . . And it was fun. It was so different from having the dog on a leash, pulling and pushing." To Dunbar, the goal was teaching manners, not drills. Not that results were any less important. Subjects included using rewards to teach a dog not to snap at a child stealing its food or jumping on its back.

Far more influential than the classes, Dunbar said, were the videos, which began circulating soon afterward. Ditch those shock collars and quit pretending to be a prehistoric alpha wolf, they argued; training is simply a matter of associating good deeds with swift rewards. "It was just such a revolution," declared Donaldson, who quit her work with the competing clubs in 1986 to set up her own pet-training school. "Positive training is just such a juggernaut now, you don't realize how new it was." In 1993, Dunbar sought to turn his fledgling circle of influence into an institution, establishing the Association of Pet Dog Trainers, its name intentionally designed to telegraph its difference from those who would mold seeing-eye dogs or Hollywood movie pets. Its first conference, in Orlando in 1994, drew 307 people. A year later, in Chicago, there were 1,100. Today, membership tops 6,000. It's the largest pet-training association in the world.

One thing APDT didn't do, however, was discriminate based on philosophical approach. So even as Dunbar legitimized the idea of professionally training an ordinary, nonproblematic puppy, he didn't ensure that practitioners whose methods he disapproved of could be kept out of the club. Siegfried, who idolizes Dunbar, is a member of the organization. So is Whiting, who does not. Its growth helped provide an institutional infrastructure, with its training courses and apprenticeships, to help both women follow their puppy-loving hearts out of desk jobs and into the training business.

Siegfried began by volunteering at an animal shelter, walking dogs and helping socialize newcomers. She took some weekend shifts at a dog-walking business. Eventually, she quit her advertising gig in order to manage a doggie day care. After taking a correspondence dog-training class and apprenticing with a local colleague, she started teaching some pet classes of her own. Eventually, she turned those classes into a business, Opportunity Barks. She started passing out cards at veterinarians' offices and pet-supply stores and never looked back. "I think my parents must have been kind of freaked out," she said. "But eventually everyone knew this was a good business."

Whiting also started out by moonlighting from an advertising job. She'd had a problem dog of her own, a Shiba Inu, a husky-type dog that had been euthanized after several biting incidents. Whiting eventually got back in touch with the trainer who had worked with the dog and started apprenticing with her. "I wanted to help people with the same problem," she recalled. She planned to go to veterinary school and to eventually study animal behavior. But as she contemplated the year of science classes she'd need to take before starting vet school, Whiting realized she disagreed with most of what any academic animal-behavior program would teach. Her issue boiled down to pack theory. Watching her new dog, Sonoma, play in the park, she'd come to believe in the alpha-dog approach that scholars shun. "I was getting the opportunity to see how dogs really do interact with one another," she said. "When Sonoma would come into the dog park . . . the dogs would come and she would turn her head away. It was the alpha dismissal, and Sonoma's a classic alpha." Whiting came to believe that communicating via this language was much more effective than the treats preferred by many academic behaviorists.

So, putting her MBA to use, she decided to turn Proper Paws into a full-time business. A few months later, Cesar Millan's TV show hit television screens. "A lot of Cesar followers started working with Proper Paws," Whiting said. "It was a much harder sell before Cesar Millan came on the air."

Before 2004, Cesar Millan was a self-taught, Los Angeles–based dog trainer whose uncanny ability to communicate with both people and dogs had helped his Dog Psychology Center win a following among Hollywood celebrities like Jada Pinkett Smith, Ridley Scott, and Rebecca Romijn—and their dogs. Eventually, in 2002, the *Los Angeles Times* wrote him up: the twenty-seven-year-old wunderkind who could save even the meanest dog. *People* magazine followed suit, among other publications, and before long TV producers were showing up at the gritty industrial lot that served as Millan's canine boot camp.

Launched in 2004, *The Dog Whisperer* became a surprise hit for the National Geographic Channel. It also became an hour-long weekly advertisement, complete with an immensely sympathetic and compelling hero, for Dunbar's idea that hiring a pet trainer is something ordinary people ought to do. Each episode features Millan parachuting in to help an out-of-control dog and out-of-their-heads family. He doesn't come bearing treats. Rather, he brings his own personal alpha status and a seemingly supernatural ability to communicate that status to dogs. His diagnosis of most canine behavior problems is that the dog has somehow become convinced that it is the boss of the humans. Over the highly edited hour—an unedited dog-training show would be like an unwatchable art project—Millan sets out to change that dynamic by communicating to the animals in their own language. Some of that communication is the same stuff Whiting shared with the Monreals, a matter of posture and gestures and timing. But he also gets more physical, calmly grabbing a bulldog that snarls whenever someone touches its harness, flipping the dog on its side, and holding it down. "This is what dogs do among each other," he says, tightening his grip. "My hand becomes a mouth and my fingers become the teeth. But I'm not angry. I'm calm." He warns the owner not to get on top of the dog to hold him down. "If you get on top of him, he knows you don't know how to dominate."

On TV, Millan never claims to be an animal behavior scholar. But the field's professional establishment still saw something threatening in his sudden success: the resurgence of everything they had spent a quarter century fighting. Millan advocated a top-down, discipline-heavy, and occasionally physical way of dominating a dog; he derided reward training as a bribe to animals for doing what pack obedience should make them do anyway. It was a painful irony. The positive-reinforcement revolutionaries had ascended to the pinnacles of dog-advice power. And now the man who had become the face of their profession for mainstream America was advocating a course of training that people like Ian Dunbar absolutely despised.

The establishmentarian backlash was ferocious. The American College of Veterinary Behaviorists denounced Millan's physical techniques as "dangerous." The Humane Society of the United States demanded that the network take his show off the air, specifically criticizing his tactic of "flooding," or exercising a problem dog to the point of exhaustion. Writing in the *New York Times,* Mark Derr, author of *A Dog's History of America,* described Millan as a "one-man wrecking ball directed at 40 years of progress in understanding and shaping dog behavior." Claudia Kawczynska, editor of the popular dog-owners' magazine *The Bark,* called him "a poseur" and noted, "He doesn't have credentials. And it is shocking to me how easily people are ready to fall for it." Donaldson and Dunbar, two of the pet-training business's biggest names, released a training DVD designed to rebut his tactics. Its title: *Fighting Dominance in a Dog Whispering World.*

The attacks have done little to dent Millan's popularity. When I met him, at the 2008 Global Pet Expo, the silver-haired trainer was traveling with a group that included his wife, a publicist, and two hulking bodyguards who towered over Millan's minuscule, muscular frame. He was there to launch several new products bearing his name. Millan's entourage also included a pair of dogs from his training center, the younger one's leash tied to the older one's collar, an alpha-learning technique he explained to bystanders would help calm the skittish puppy. Were the bodyguards there because he was afraid of being set upon by some irate positive-reinforcement theorist? Hardly. A publicist explained that Millan is regularly deluged with people telling him, in great detail, of their dog-care woes. Sweetheart that he is, he usually obliges, which at the big trade show could have delayed an already frantic schedule of autograph signings.

Born into rural Mexican poverty, Millan has an improbable life story. Raised on his grandfather's farm in Mexico, Millan became known as *el perrero*, "the dog boy." As a youngster, he was fascinated with the dogs that ambled about the rural spread. "Their daily patterns and rhythms formed a culture unto itself," he writes in his best-selling autobiography, *Cesar's Way*. "These dogs seemed completely in tune with Mother Nature, and that's what amazed me and drew me back to observe them, day after day." Millan cites his grandfather as the greatest example of how humans should behave toward their dogs—an example that modern urban gringos have lost touch with. "My grandfather never had any training manuals or self-help books or scientific techniques to rely on, yet he could always elicit that perfectly calm, submissive, and cooperative response from his dogs." How so? Millan describes the scene in language used every week on his show. The old man's "calm-assertive" posture engendered "calm submission" from the farm's dogs, exactly as an alpha dog would. "Never work against Mother Nature," Millan quotes his grandfather as saying. "You only succeed when you work *with* her." The farm's dogs were well balanced, he says, "because the humans knew they were humans and the dogs knew they were dogs. Who was in charge and who wasn't was crystal clear."

In this version of the classic log-cabin tale, Millan's family eventually moved to the big city, Mazatlán. Before too long, the sour economy had Millan paying his only hundred dollars to a *coyote* who sneaked him across the American border. He arrived in San Diego "dripping wet, filthy, thirsty, hungry, my boots covered with mud . . . the happiest man in the world." He found work in a dog-grooming salon, amazed that the dogs were a damn sight cleaner than he was. Of course, all was not well in the earthly paradise, despite the astounding sums its residents spent tending to their pets. "During my time at the groomers, I saw the most beautiful dogs I ever imagined—stunning examples of their breeds, with clear eyes, gleaming coats, and healthy, well-fed bodies," he writes. "Yet I could tell

just by looking at them that their minds weren't healthy."
Pampered by owners who indulge Hollywood fantasies about
canine humanity and treat their dogs as junior people, the pets
had fallen victim to owners who give "nothing but affection,
affection, affection!"

Millan diagnosed the dogs with a malady unknown back on
the farm: status anxiety. Uncertain about where they stood
in the pack, the dogs would be prone to acting out unless and
until they were reminded of who was the boss. They were victims of both modern anomie, as their humans left them alone
for hours on end, and modern coddling, as the owners plied
them with guilt-induced treats. The only breaks in the pampering were the owners' occasional temper tantrums, which followed when the dog, predictably, did something wrong. But in
dog language, he says, temper tantrums convey insecurity, rein-
forcing pack uncertainty instead of clearing it up. "My fulfillment formula is simple," Millan concludes. "For a balanced,
healthy dog a human must share exercise, discipline, and affection, in that order."

Millan's autobiography spent fifteen weeks atop the *New
York Times* best-seller list. The popularity is partly due to his
charm and his unarguable communion with dogs. But I think it
also says a lot about some of our current national neuroses—a
twenty-first-century fear that the pace of modern life is wound-
ing us, that we've gotten on the wrong side of Mother Nature,
and that the institutions and elites of society don't even seem to
notice that something's wrong. Millan, alien but not *too* alien,
cool but not *too* cool, new agey and authoritarian all at once, is a
perfect character to offer a solution. Millan became a celebrity
at about the same time that low-carb diets became a national
passion. Like Millan vis-à-vis the behaviorists, the cardiologists
behind the South Beach and Atkins diets came from outside the
nutrition-advice establishment. Like Millan, they offered a
method that more or less flew in the face of everything

that establishment had been saying for decades. Like Millan, they capitalized on a hunch that the old ways hadn't worked—we were still getting fat, right?—and tapped a deep vein of suspicion of white-coated professional authority. Maybe it was time to go back to a more traditional culinary approach. Real meat for the dinner table, real discipline for the dog. Like Millan, the low-carb-diet doctors achieved popular success without winning over establishmentarian skeptics. But the attacks from the ivory tower weren't a problem; they probably even helped their reputations.

"In our culture there's always been this mystical attachment to people like him," Donaldson explained to me. "It was, 'He didn't have any book learning to corrupt him. He just grew up on a farm and has this native ability.' People find that very romantic." She views the show's popularity as a backlash against modernity itself. "It's the urge to dominate at least something."

By the time I interviewed them, a couple of years after the initial furor over Millan's show, Donaldson and Dunbar had lowered the volume on their criticism. Millan's show, they allowed, was good television—even if it had little to do with what actual pet trainers actually do. Donaldson—who once wrote that "notions like dogs rushing through doors ahead of their owners or pulling on leash to exert dominance over their owners are just too stupid for words"—told me that "a lot of what he says makes good sense," especially his advocacy of exercise and lots of human-dog social interaction, two things sorely missing from the lives of America's latchkey pups. Reward training, Dunbar said, was simply easier and faster than rewiring human behavior to suit an unverifiable notion about how dogs communicate. "It could be that [dogs are] really hung up about alpha dog stuff," he said. "I don't know and I don't care . . . I think people are overthinking it. You see a lot of dog classes where the owners are sitting in chairs and listening to the trainer's theories on why the dog misbehaves, and not working with the dogs. The fact is, in the past twenty-five years we have applied scientific methods to the age-old problems. What used to take forever now takes minutes. I just don't get into why."

Spend time with workaday trainers like Wendy Whiting and Leigh Siegfried and the big philosophical arguments quickly fade. Both of their businesses skew heavily to normal people with normal problems that they'd like some normal help on. In many of those cases, either method would suffice. For Siegfried this was fine. She slowly grew her business over the years, tricking out a garage behind her house for classes, making an arrangement with a new local doggie day care to teach some sessions there, letting word of mouth carry her name around the region. She didn't have to spend a lot of time on theory; Dunbar and the gang had paved the way already.

Whiting worked with less methodological infrastructure, and also had loftier goals. Millan had helped usher in a new generation of celebrity trainers, as bookstore shelves filled with tomes by would-be rivals like Los Angeles–based Tamar Geller, who stresses positive training and casts herself as the anti-Cesar. Could Whiting grow her business via the burgeoning pet-care media market? It was a good time to do so, with pet people finding advice and community in all sorts of media outlets, from Internet must-reads like petconnection.com to the expanding roster of cable shows on Discovery's Animal Planet, home to *Groomer Has It, Pet Star,* and *Animal Cops*. After my initial story on Whiting, I checked in every few months. And every time, there were different dreams on display. At first, she talked about turning Proper Paws into a national chain, complete with franchisees. A few months later, the plan was to set up a training academy. Still later, she came to me with grand ideas about a Web site that might centralize pet-care information. Millan's show is fine and all, but even a fan like Whiting knows it is highly edited and bears little relation to what she does. She did a few bits on local TV. And later on she had the notion of setting up her own trade group, the Association of Dog Behavior Consultants, a pack-theory counterweight to Dunbar's APDT.

In each case, the demands of actually running a small business—dispatching trainers hither and yon, dealing with clients, handling a few cases herself—got in the way. And even that had started to feel a lot like the corporate work she had quit. With a glut of trainers, prices for the Google advertisements that led to our first meeting had tripled. As Dunbar had said, pack-theory training is harder than basic treat training; she found herself frustrated at clients who didn't want to put in the work it took to rewire their behavior around their dogs. Despite her exhortations, the dogs were still being invited onto beds and let out doorways before their humans. "It just burns you out," she said. If Millan had been on hand to deliver a diagnosis, he might have said Whiting was out of balance.

So Whiting did something altogether nonalpha. She quit. The last time we spoke, she was talking about going back to graduate school to study another newly popular field held in low esteem by established authorities: herbal medicine. Maybe, eventually, she'd come back to dogs—but not to her business and media ambitions. "I'll reemerge as a solo practitioner down the road," she said. "I'm just not going to be running a business. I still think I have techniques that are valuable. At least I think they are."

ELEVEN

From Alpo to Omega-3 Fatty Acids

Inside the Pet-Food Wars

Bogner Meats is a small business with two locations around Hartford, Connecticut, the newer of which was built in 1966. Insofar as Bogner is known to the world beyond the seventy-five employees who grind, cut, and package its lamb chops, pork butts, and hamburger patties, it is through newspaper circulars aimed at luring bargain hunters to the firm's walk-up window. The fall morning I visited, specials included 85 percent lean ground beef for $2.69 a pound, whole corned beef brisket for $2.89 a pound, and a twenty-pack of Bogner kielbasa dogs for $16.95 each. A bunch of construction workers on a morning break were also lining up for lunch meats from the deli counter.

The scene was a flashback to the unpretentious years before America became a land of arugula-loving gourmands—a time when few people would feed themselves meals of "grilled tuna, wild rice, broccoli, and dill," much less buy such things for their cats. Which makes it a bit surprising that Bogner is a home base for the hottest trend in upscale pet food, a trend that banks on consumers becoming as natural and healthy and conscientious about what they feed their animals as they are about what they feed their kids. Though this isn't advertised at the deli counter, Bogner is also the manufacturing facility for the Bravo! Raw Diet, one of a handful of uncooked pet-food brands that feature meat good enough for humans to eat, prices high enough to make venture capitalists wince, and customers enthusiastic enough to seem almost evangelical. To raw-pet-food devotees, such as the folks who post to rival Internet groups like Raw Paws and Raw Cat and Raw Pup and Raw Chat, the logic behind spending as much on a two-pound tube of ground raw ostrich meat as you might on a twenty-pound bag of ordinary pet food is simple: This is what nature intended.

Back in the wild, the argument goes, a dog might hunt all morning for his prey; when he caught it, he'd dig in and maybe wind up with some bone and intestine and undigested stomach content as part of the bargain. Or something to that effect. But whatever he ate, it wasn't some crunchy tan kibble cranked out by a multinational and featuring twenty-nine ingredients that sound like automotive lubricants. "A raw diet recreates the way our pet's ancestors have eaten in the wild for thousands of years" is how the Bravo! promotional materials put it. Many fans of raw diets are less polite about anyone who would dare feed an animal mainstream pet food. The Raw Feeding listserv, for instance, warns new members that certain conversations will be squelched at once. "This list was started to promote appropriate feeding methods, not ways to harm your pet," says a message to newly enrolled members. The deadly subject? Kibble, the dry, crunchy food that most dogs still dine on.

David Bogner—one of three heirs to the family-owned business and the facility's point man on all things Bravo!—is not a guy who typically visits such sites. "I have two dogs and I love 'em, but they're not my life," he told me. "I'm not crazy." Bogner said his grandfather, who founded the company, would be flummoxed by the idea of making dog food from people food. "And my father would've rolled over in his grave. He wouldn't understand it at all." But like a lot of smaller-scale meatpackers, Bogner began the twenty-first century looking for ways to diversify as corporate meat giants squeezed regional manufacturers. It proved a good time to get into the business. Not long before I visited, lots of ordinary members of the dog-owning general public, folks who wouldn't meet Bogner's definition of pet crazy, had their interest in raw foods piqued by the tainted pet food scandal. A mere 1 percent of the total pet-food market before the scandal, raw-food sales briefly soared, with some manufacturers reporting sales bumps of up to 30 percent and market analysts predicting years of double-digit growth in the "alternative" pet-food sector. Bravo! increased production by a fifth.

Bogner began my tour of the facility by telling me I'd have to wait awhile. Publicity-conscious businessmen don't usually like saying that to a visiting journalist, but in this case it reinforced Bravo!'s major sales pitch: that the food it makes for pets is good enough for kids. Literally. "We're still doing the hamburger meat," Bogner said. The plant grinds up roughly forty thousand pounds of the stuff each week, shipping it out to restaurants, stores, and school cafeterias. And the meat is chopped, ground, and boxed up on the exact same equipment used for the week's approximately one hundred thousand pounds of raw pet food. Bogner suggested I just watch the hamburger process. It was essentially identical, he said, to the Bravo! production: a succession of conveyor belts between spotlessly menacing machines that reduce sixty-pound chunks of frozen flesh into minuscule morsels with the ruthless efficiency of the big blond villain from the film *Fargo*. But after shivering through a tour of the thirty-seven-degree room—the mandatory hairnets do little for one's core temperature—I said I'd still like to see the staff making the pet food, which after all was why I'd come. Suit yourself, Bogner said. So I retreated to the business office and waited at a desk, listening in as a bookkeeper chatted up customers, most of whom she seemed to know quite well, about payments.

By and by, Bogner reappeared to announce it was time to make the Bravo! True to his word, it did look much like the hamburger process. About the only initial difference was the addition of a man-sized block of frozen green veggies. "Up to this point, you can eat it, too," he told me, pointing to the second grinder. That's when the bones, amid great dissonant sound, got added in. The result, said to promote dental health, looked like grains of sand in the strands of ground pink meat that rode a final stretch of conveyor belt that took them to the tubing machine, where they were shot into neat packages of Bravo! By the time the product got to my local store, the two-pound tubes of beef blend would sell for $6.99—or about a dollar more per pound than the ground chuck advertised for humans at Bogner's consumer window. (Bravo!'s raw ostrich, elk, duck, quail, and rabbit cost more.)

As a lifelong meat guy, Bogner was accustomed to how astonished civilians like me can be when they watch the spectacle of where their meat comes from, what with the two-thousand-pound boxes of chicken frames and the giant containers of pork shinbones. But he shared a bit of the wonder at the industry he joined in 2002, sixty years after his company was founded as a strictly-for-humans firm. "I just never thought about it," Bogner said. "But I guess it makes sense—if you get a fifty-pound bag of kibble and it costs you ten dollars, what do you think is in it? No wonder people want this stuff."

Back home, Murphy seemed to agree. I dropped a piece of lamb blend in his bowl and it was gone in an instant; he tossed his head back to consume the whole chunk. Murphy stared up at me for more, not quite an ancient wolf but a happy pup all the same. I had other plans, though. I tossed some into a sauté pan and cooked it through. Then I ate a bit myself. It tasted like bland lamb. What's good enough for Murphy is good enough for me. I let him finish off the rest.

The U.S. pet-food industry, valued at $16.2 billion in 2007, was the first piece of the modern pet economy to establish itself as a truly big business. As early as 1941, though most pets still ate human leftovers, pet-food sales amounted to $50 million—$731 million in 2008 dollars.

By most accounts, the history of the industry begins with a man named James Spratt. An electrician from Cincinnati, Spratt had patented a new type of lightning conductor in 1850. Later in the decade, he traveled to England to sell it. According to industry lore, he had a quayside epiphany in London when he saw a group of dogs eating discarded hardtack, the cheap, tough biscuits carried on ships and known to sailors as "molar breakers." The first major chunk of today's pet industry was born.

In 1860, still in England, Spratt unveiled Spratt's Patent Meat Fibrine Dog Cakes, a combination of wheat, beetroot, vegetables, and beef blood. Before long, he had competitors with names like Dr. A. C. Daniels' Medicated Dog Bread and F. H. Bennett's Malatoid Dog Biscuits. The products embraced the dubious science and the lightly regulated hucksterism of their era. Spratt, for instance, counseled that meat could "overheat the dog's blood," apparently ignoring that the animals are traditionally carnivores. He established a pattern that holds true today: pet food as a perfect reflection of an era's vogues in human food.

Thus, during the 1890s period of especially quackish medicine and discredited health-food fads memorably captured in *The Road to Wellville,* an impresario named Webster Edgerly founded a social movement called Ralstonism, claiming it would lead to the establishment of a new race free of impurities. Over the years, Edgerly pseudonymously published some dozens of self-help books—sample titles: *Instantaneous Personal Magnetism* and *Operations of the Other Mind: Making Known the Unseen Powers of the Universe in Their Control over Human Life*— including a number of tomes on diet and health. Though some of his books were published under the name Everett Ralston, Edgerly elsewhere claimed that the name stood for the essential principles of his philosophy: Regime, Activity, Light, Strength, Temperation, Oxygen, and Nature. Utopia never quite arrived, and human interest in Ralstonism faded. But pets still experience it, if only in name. One particularly eager Ralstonite was a feed distributor named William Danforth, whose alliance with Edgerly led to an endorsement of his brand by "Dr. Ralston" and the subsequent renaming of his company, Ralston Purina.

Pet food's subsequent evolutions were also representative. In the TV-dinner era after World War II, the selling point shifted to housewifely convenience. "It is unnecessary to cook special foods, measure this and that—why bother when it takes less than a minute to prepare a Kasco meal for your dog?" went one advertisement. Even the can opener became obsolete. In 1957, Ralston Purina released the first kibble: Dog Chow, the result of experiments in which ingredients like liver, buttermilk, and soy meal were fed through an extruding machine ordinarily used to make breakfast cereal. The dry food could now be sold in bulk and stored almost indefinitely. In an indication of how pet food had become a middle-class staple, it also became the first dog food sold in supermarkets rather than pet specialty stores.

And what's for dinner in our own era, with its yawning gaps in taste, wealth, and priorities? Over the past two decades, pet food became a front in the new diet wars—and, in the implicit message carried by their advertising and their packaging, a vehicle for social differentiation among pet owners. Out went appeals to convenience; in came promises of pure ingredients and specific wellness. Since the 1970s, when pet-food firms began offering brands targeted at specific ages, conditions, sizes, and breeds, they have carved out progressively tinier slivers of four-legged demographics ranging from Purina's Puppy Chow brand through Eukanuba's Weight Control line to Royal Canin's Mini Dachshund 28 recipe. In 2006, 664 new pet-food products were introduced in the United States, up from 282 in 2002.

Beginning with the rise of the Iams and Hill's Science Diet brands in the 1970s, befuddled pet-food consumers also found themselves sorting through an ever-more-upscale array of "premium" lines that offered an increasingly lavish array of promises, from veterinary approval to "hormone-free" ingredients to "human-grade" meat. The firms also marketed in ways designed to stress their superior nutritional credentials. Then-independent Iams, for instance, sold through veterinarians and breeders, recognizing it would have a hard time battling major multinationals for supermarket shelf space.

Though much of the innovation came from smaller firms, the industry's major players followed suit, establishing brands like Purina's ProPlan and Mars's Goodlife recipe or buying premium players outright, as Procter & Gamble did in its $2-billion 1999 acquisition of Iams and Mars did with its 2007 purchase of the Nutro brand. Old standbys like Alpo, meantime, had become the dog food of dog food. In 2007, even that down-market brand tried to gentrify its reputation, launching a line called Chop House Originals that touted "Angus beef" and "restaurant-inspired" recipes.

In one way, the variety is an illusion. Whatever the brand names may be, the vast majority of the business is controlled by a handful of multinationals. In 2006, five companies accounted for 66 percent of pet-food sales globally; in the United States, the five controlled 81 percent of the market. And yet, as anyone who's gotten lost in the rows and rows of pet food at even a small local store can tell you, new and mostly independent brands continue to push the top of the market ever higher. These days, an eleven-pound bag of air-dried raw lamb-and-fish from a brand called Ziwipeak will cost you $105. That's American dollars, not the currency of Ziwipeak's native New Zealand. By contrast, a thirty-five-pound sack of Iams Healthy Naturals costs around $35. But people who buy Ziwipeak tend to look with suspicion on even well-regarded brands like Iams, now owned by a multinational and sold in, God forbid, grocery stores. By 2006 Packaged Facts reported that over half of the new pet-food products coming onto the market were tagged as "upscale."

And all the while, the best-selling brand in the country is Ol' Roy, the generic house brand of Wal-Mart. For anyone who would declare that the creativity of the modern pet-food industry means a change in the diets of all American pets, its continued dominance serves as a useful corrective. It's also a perfect parallel to the consumer history of a country that went from being a society of Safeway shoppers to a nation where the market is diverse enough to encompass the astounding bargains and bulk brands of Sam's Club and the pricey artisanal lines of Whole Foods—and where still others abandon the entire corporate sector, snapping up cook-your-own-pet-food books and creating a new economy of homemade pet-food delivery businesses. "Rachael Ray just did a one-hour show on feeding your pet," notes industry analyst Mike Dillon. "And PetSmart or the pet-food companies are watching that and just going, no, no, no!" (Ray launched her own line of pet food several months after Dillon and I spoke.)

The uncertainty around what to feed your animal also creates opportunities. It's one thing to delegitimize Spratt's mass-marketing heirs in the public mind. It's quite another to find a commercially convenient way to replace it. In 1993, an Australian veterinarian began promoting a home-prepared feeding philosophy then known as the Bones and Raw Food—BARF—diet. One major limitation on its commercial success was that it's awfully inconvenient to make daily runs to the butcher to feed the family dog. That is, unless firms like Bravo! figure out a way to bring the flesh and bones straight to your freezer. Enter the commercial raw feeders.

A guy who runs a small meatpacking plant in New England doesn't jump on a whim into an industry viewed with suspicion by large chunks of the public, not to mention the federal Food and Drug Administration. In Bogner's case, for most of the five years he'd been doing Bravo! he worked with a woman named Melinda Miller. Miller was also the person who hipped me to what Bravo!'s promotional material calls the "raw diet revolution." I originally met her the first time I went to a Global Pet Expo. She was busy staffing the Bravo! booth, but when I bounded up bearing a notebook and an inquisitive look, she took the time to talk me through the culinary politics of the show. Or, rather, to tell me, with great wit and an impressive command of detail, about how nearly all of the big-time vendors in the convention center were in the business of feeding trash to dogs. "Most dog food is complete, complete garbage," she said. "This isn't."

If Bogner seems an improbable candidate to take raw pet food into the mainstream, Miller looks straight out of central casting. Driving an SUV whose innards are littered with dog effects, she is at once effusive about how much she loves dogs and brutal about the industry that feeds them. Though she and Bogner amicably parted ways at the end of 2007, she continued to run the trade organization that represents Bravo! and its three competitors in the budding commercial raw-pet-food industry. Before entering the four-legged economy, Miller spent years as a mergers and acquisitions consultant in the telecommunications industry. On the side, she bred Portuguese water dogs and did some dog training. After one of her pets got sick, she went looking for answers and came upon the more or less underground community of raw feeders and the equally obscure world of holistic veterinary medicine (she now manages a holistic veterinary practice). They both fit with her values and a generally skeptical worldview. "I had two passions," she said. "One was business. One was dogs. I figured I'd put them together."

One autumn Sunday, at a daylong symposium on pet nutrition held on a suburban New York college campus, I listened to Miller explain what pet food was really all about. To hear her tell it, that entire history had been about greedy people trying to beat back nature, both human and canine. From Spratt's warnings about meat to the postwar ads in which white-coated veterinarians importune housewives against serving pets that filthy-sounding substance derided as "table scraps," she claimed, it was a steady progression away from the carnivorous animals' wolfish past, all in the name of human profit. "There's a lot about pet food that has to do with trying to reverse-engineer nature," she said. "We just got it in our heads that somebody was opening bags of Science Diet in the woods for wolves." And even though some brands may have grasped for healthier ingredients in recent years, she thinks the implicit message of the advertising remains that pet lovers aren't smart enough to figure out what their animal needs. "You had women who were trusted to feed their kids, their families, but now you tell them, oh, no, you can't be trusted to figure out what's right for your dog," she said.

The debates over pet food, predating the scandal, display a deeper unease about science, chemicals, corporations, and health—an anxious modern-day equivalent of the self-confident pet-food engineering of the postwar years. The symposium where Miller spoke about pet-food history featured as its scheduled speakers a pair of veterinarians who were supposed to make sense of the recent news, and how pet owners could avoid a repeat. Their presentations turned into a debate that showcased vastly different postures toward both human tampering and the nature of evidence. One of the speakers was a man named Daniel Carey, who at various times had been a staff veterinarian at both Purina and Iams. The other was Martin Goldstein, "Dr. Marty," a holistic vet who founded the Smith Ridge Veterinary Clinic—the practice Miller manages—and is more or less the Andrew Weil of the veterinary world. (He's gone on the *Today* show to question the need for frequent pet vaccinations and has treated Oprah Winfrey's dog.)

Carey, who spoke first, walked the audience through a wonky, scientific presentation about ingredients and nutrition. He sounded like the scientist he is, explaining the chemical makeup of arachidonic acid, the meaning of low-glycemic grains, the ideal ratios of omega-6 to omega-3, the convoluted history of pet-food standards as maintained by the Association of American Feed Control Officials, and so on. And whatever pronouncements he made about the good and the bad of pet food came couched in the language of research. Rather than simply declaring something—like, say, "grains aren't bad"—he would explain that research hasn't necessarily shown that grains, a raw-feeding bête noire, are bad.

Goldstein, by contrast, offered a presentation heavy on anecdotes. Though he graduated in 1973 from Cornell, one of the nation's finest veterinary schools, and maintains a practice that features cutting-edge diagnostic technology even as it dispenses unconventional advice for some stricken animals, he opened his address by announcing, "I have an issue with the basic foundation of science." Rates of canine cancer, he said, had shot up since the 1970s—what had been a disease of old dogs was now common in the young. Over the ensuing two hours, he spoke of detoxification, fasting, acupuncture, a case where a brown rice diet helped roll back arthritis. "This [reaction to nontraditional treatment] is the kind of experience I have seen multiple times over the years," he said. "Will it happen again? I don't know." He also showed a picture of wild dogs eating meat, then an ingredient list for Hill's Science Diet. "I've got a question for you: What more replicates what you see [in the picture]?" he asked. "Is this contributing in some way to the quadrupling of canine cancer?"

Yes, scientists—albeit some of whose research is underwritten by food manufacturers—may vouch for commercial pet food. But Goldstein said an ominous question lingered around the entire industry: "What happens if they're wrong?"

Given the big news of 2007, it should have been a banner year for Bravo! After the recall, its obscure corner of the pet-care universe was the subject of glowing media attention. Packed into frozen tubes of prepared meat, raw food suddenly didn't look so inconvenient or dangerous or alien. But in September of that year, the company received a nasty surprise: a recall order from the FDA. Salmonella had been found in some of Bravo!'s chicken formula. Earlier in the year, the same fate befell Wild Kitty, a raw-cat-food line produced by Maine lobstermen.

Miller was furious. She saw dark forces at work—the feds were too close to the major pet-food firms to which her product served as an implicit rebuke. Bravo! began sending its raw chicken tubes on a cumbersome journey from Bogner's Connecticut plant to a facility in Wisconsin that offers a service called high-pressure treatment, a way of killing salmonella without cooking the meat. Miller said the disruption ate up her profits from the year's final quarter.

On the political side, Miller sprang into action. She got her firm together with the three other retail raw-food manufacturers— Bravo! is believed to be the second-biggest in the industry, after Nebraska-based Nature's Variety—to form the North American Raw Petfood Association. They hired a lawyer and started badgering the FDA to change its rules. Miller traveled to a meeting in Washington, D.C., with a 450-page book full of studies purporting to show that salmonella doesn't pose the same danger to dogs that it does to humans. But so soon after the feds had been accused of negligence in the melamine scandal, Washington was in no mood to ease off its watchdog role. "Their bottom line was, there's a regulation on the books, it's our job to enforce it, and the bottom line is, it's your problem," Miller said.

According to Miller, "some of the big boys have been interested" in buying into raw-food firms in the past. But she believes that fear of the feds is the main thing keeping the raw-food business from going mainstream. If Bravo! and its rivals eventually became subsidiaries of Colgate or Mars or Nestlé, though, the corporate blessing of raw feeding wouldn't put an end to the cycle of insurgents pushing the pet-food envelope. In the raw-feeding world, a sizable population actually thinks Miller's preferred type of food already represents a corporate sellout. By chopping and grinding the meat and bones and packaging them into a convenient tube that required pet owners to do nothing more than yank it from the freezer and wait a few hours for it to defrost—or, worse still, by selling the product in convenient "medallions," as Nature's Variety does— aren't the raw manufacturers guilty of the same effort to counterprogram nature? So say advocates of the "prey model" of feeding, which suggests that animals be given whole chunks of flesh and left to gnaw meat from bone, chew through tendon, and otherwise act as their ancestors have.

"I mean to say, how hard is it to take one chicken leg and give [it] to your poodle?" asks Jane Anderson of *Raw Learning*. "Simple is how it needs to be. Feeding a dog does not need to be a process of overengineering a solution. Unfortunately pet-food companies, both raw and commercial, have used slick marketing techniques to convince people that it is necessary. And, of course, nice packaging seems to convince people that an item is better. All we need to feed our dogs is a quick trip to the butcher's."

Thus if the foot soldiers of Bravo!'s "Raw Diet Revolution" ever make their way to the corner office of some raw-food multinational of the future, and ride a cascade of TV ads and pet-show sponsorships to make their brand of prepared raw food a household name, I'll bet you the full contents of James Spratt's estate that they can look forward to being disdained as pet-hating monsters by the antiestablishmentarian leader of something that will doubtless dub itself the "Prey-Model Revolution." Revolutions always eat their young, raw or otherwise.

Whether the blame lies with malicious corporations, Uncle Sam, or the simpler fact that it remains relatively cumbersome to prepare, package, ship, and store raw pet food, Bravo! and its competitors had not yet turned into the Next Big Thing a year after the recall. They were doing a decent business, and at the 2008 expo their sales folks reported far fewer instances of buyers asking them what on earth raw food was all about. Instead, the big new splash in pet food was something called WholeMeals, made by one of the oldest, biggest names in the business: the Mars corporation, makers of Pedigree, Whiskas, and countless other brands.

Any multinational worth its stock options can gin up a high-profile product launch, but Mars's new offering was truly different from the rest of the items in the pet-food aisle. Rather than kibble from a bag, or morsels and gravy from a can—or even raw food from a tube—a WholeMeals meal looks a lot like a bone from an actual animal, with three angled sides, a tough outer layer, and a meatlike inner core. The promotional materials show an array of dogs clutching the meals in their paws, eagerly chomping down on the edges like the wolves of yore. The point was: no bowl required, ever. Just like in the wild! Promotional materials boasted that this new way of eating was "more closely aligned with his natural feeding patterns. . . . WholeMeals allows your dog to carry his meal to his favorite spot and consume it in a natural, relaxed 'tummy-feed' position."

As part of the media rollout for its big new product, Mars invited a handful of reporters to lunch. As we nibbled on sandwiches, Dr. Tiffany Bierer, the firm's director of nutrition, walked us through the multiyear process of developing it—from conception through patents for aspects of its shape and contents through biometric research on the shape of dogs' mouths through studies by the Spokane, Washington, Center for Non-Verbal Studies that examined whether the pups enjoyed eating the food (conclusion: "much greater feeding satisfaction than ordinary food," as evidenced by a tendency to parade around with their WholeMeals, as if showing them off before tucking in). The bonelike objects were indeed a marvel of science, with multiangled edges to allow paw grips, a variety of widths to serve as a toothbrush for different parts of the mouth, and a dual texture to keep things interesting. There were four sizes of boneoids for different sizes of dogs; the largest size had six hundred calories of protein, omega-6 fatty acids, vitamins E and C, chondroitin, glucosamine, calcium, and phosphorus, among other things, crammed into scarcely six inches.

On a video screen, Bierer showed footage of a dog named Flex grabbing, playing, and chowing down on the floor. Flex looked transfixed, working the phony bone like a piece of freshly hunted prey. It was a brief reminder that canines didn't begin their evolutionary careers nibbling from imported feed bowls before napping on fluffy dog beds. On the other hand—unlike his wild ancestors—Flex wasn't leaving a mess of blood and entrails on the kitchen floor: WholeMeals boneoids had been formulated to minimize crumbs on the owner's carpet. "It's official," Bierer concluded. "The revolution in feeding has begun." Where had I heard that before?

As I listened to Bierer describe the food's raison d'être, it sounded like the raw feeders' obsession with naturalness had made its way into the mainstream. "It's kind of a little bit left over from dogs having to hunt for their food," Bierer said. "It's part of what made dogs dogs, and what made us like them. We're really trying to feed on that." Miller, who'd actually drawn my attention to the impending arrival of WholeMeals well before the big roll-out, agreed. For a moment, she seemed impressed by the pictures of dogs gnawing while lying down, by the promises of decreased plaque and slower eating times, the attention to natural habits, and the willingness to think outside the box, the bag, and the food bowl. "The whole thing is a result of raw," she said.

WholeMeals' contents, though, are not at all revolutionary. Like other mainstream premium brands, its list of twenty-six ingredients includes items like chicken by-product meal and wheat gluten—components unlikely to win Bierer a spot on Miller's holiday list. "Leave it to corporate America to take what could be a very good concept and make it out of the most horrible ingredients ever," she said.

I'm not so sure most consumers will see it that way. Commercially, the new food seemed to hit that sweet spot between atavism, solipsism, and anthropomorphism. It mirrored how wild dogs ate, it was convenient for pet owners, it was good for the dog's bones and teeth—didn't you owe your sweet special fur baby that much? I'd actually consumed the ingredients, too. They're not officially "human grade," though Bierer said I could go ahead and take a bite. The result, to the human palate, is a bit like a cardboard, Elmer's glue, and chicken jerky sandwich. But it was no worse than the other pet victuals I'd sampled on my rounds: the pigs-in-blanket snacks, the $105-a-bag freeze-dried fish-fed raw New Zealand lamb, the beef ice cream, the mineral water. But, of course, I wasn't the audience. Flex was, and, up on the screen, he was taking to it like, well, a dog with a bone.

TWELVE

It Takes a Village to Raise a Puppy

Spreading the Gospel of Modern Pet Care

R ed the pit bull is, to use the polite term for it, altered. This is not a novel condition among pets in the United States, and especially not among pets in New York City. But for Arturo Ortiz, Red's twenty-year-old owner, the procedure still took some getting used to. Red is a tough-looking dog, and Ortiz likes it that way. Neutering the dog, Ortiz feared, would snip off his strength right along with his testicles. Many of the dogs he knew around 132nd Street and Madison Avenue were intact, and their owners were often proud of it. Would Red still be able to hold his own? When I first met Ortiz, on a beautiful fall afternoon, he was learning that the answer was yes, absolutely. A mere thirty pounds, Red had yanked more than his entire body weight to win the year's final weight-pulling contest in Morningside Park. He'd accomplished that feat before—"one time he pulled, like, a hundred and fifty pounds,"

Ortiz said—but today his owner was going home with eighty dollars, twice the usual winnings. Why? Under the contest's rules, designed to encourage positive treatment of pets, prizes are doubled for altered animals. Or, as Ortiz put it, "Because he's got no balls, man."

Much of Manhattan seemed an island of glittering wealth back in 2007, but it still has neighborhoods, like Ortiz's, where pet chauffeurs and doggie masseuses rarely visit. Those were also the neighborhoods sought out by the organizers of Lug-Nuts, the series of weight-pulling contests that Red had just won. The events work like a tractor pull, only with pit bulls instead of John Deeres, and a cheap plastic sled piled with bags of bulk kibble in place of the trailer loaded with dead weight. For weeks, flyers around the park had advertised the contest, geared toward young men like Ortiz and tough dogs like Red. "How Strong Is Your Dog?" the flyers asked. "Cash prizes!" The contest drew several dozen newcomers, along with veterans like Trevor Smalls, whose pit bull, Miss Thang, sported a Harley-Davidson collar; Ray Perez, there with Diamond, another young pit bull; and eighth-grader Alec Bowen, who brought a Norwegian Duck Toller, Cujo, and a Great Pyrenees, Isis. They didn't exactly engage in an Olympian struggle. While a small handful of people took the competition seriously, the disorganized, everyone's-a-winner vibe made it feel more like the three-legged race at a county fair than a definitive bragging-rights showdown.

And yet, in addition to the pet parents who brought their dogs and the animal-shelter volunteers who ran the contest, the onlookers included an ESPN camera crew. The sports network does not make a habit of covering friendly neighborhood park dog contests. Rather, the crew was there because the contests had been touted as a way to combat dogfighting in disadvantaged neighborhoods—a cruelty-free way to combine canines, machismo, and competition. NFL star Michael Vick, who would begin his scheduled twenty-three-month federal prison stay less than a month later, was very much on the media's mind. "Talk about this kind of event versus what kids might get from dogfighting," the ESPN reporter asked Bowen. Alec, a clean-cut kid, replied that he'd never been anywhere near a dogfight, but his construction-worker dad turned out to have a decent perspective. Growing up nearby during the 1980s, he said, he had a couple of pit bulls and used to fight them with his friends around the neighborhood, which in those pregentrification days was a far tougher place. They wouldn't fight to the death, and it wasn't really about money, either. "A man thing," he said.

Which is, in a way, what the Lug-Nuts contest is supposed to be as well. Part of a broader series of outreach efforts known as the Training Wheels program, it's the creation of Sue Sternberg and Jane Kopelman, a pair of upstate shelter operators who have spent the past decade teaching a sort of humane work that not so long ago would have been hard to fathom: the pet-care intervention. Since the first Lug-Nuts event, in New Haven in 2002, Sternberg has staged the contests in inner cities and rustic towns from Philadelphia to Dothan, Alabama. They stage several events in poorer areas in and around New York City each year. The goal, according to Sternberg, is to demonstrate a way for pet owners to show off their dogs' muscles without resorting to dogfights. Vick's big-money, well-organized criminality obscures the real story in the neighborhoods where she takes her program. "I think the majority of the damage is done by informal, street-corner dogfighting, one kid taking his pit bull and sparring it with another," she says. "That's the population we hope to target with Lug-Nuts, with weight-pulling events to take the place of dogfighting."

At the weight-pull events, the rules seem to have been designed by a social scientist with a keen eye for how people respond to incentives. As Ortiz discovered, the grand prize is doubled for dogs that have been spayed or neutered. Anyone can enter, but dogs with visible facial scars are ineligible for any of the money; it's a way of trying to bring the fighters into the program's orbit without seeming to reward them. Winners get cash, but everyone gets to take home healthful dog food. And so on: a checklist of contemporary ideas about good canine care—ideas that are not always honored, even by dog lovers, everywhere in the American pet kingdom.

It's also fun, even if unlikely to give other violent sports—either the legal or illegal kind—a run for their money when it comes to pure adrenaline. As the afternoon unfolded, Sternberg and Kopelman coached contestants on how to motivate the animals to pull their food-laden sleds: hot dogs held a few feet from their noses, good; threats and pushing, bad. A lot of the pups couldn't make one thirty-yard length, let alone the round-trip. But no one seemed especially fazed by this; nor did the organizers evince any particular hurry. Many of the participants headed home for dinner as the contest stretched past sunset. As for those cash prizes, the standard purse of forty dollars is less than half the cost of an eleven-pound bag of Ziwipeak premium raw dog food. Still, the repeat contestants demonstrate that dogs can really scoot once they figure out what all these hot-dog-wielding humans want them to do. Early in the contest, Bowen proved adept at exhorting Cujo, and luring him with enough treats to keep him charging forward, but not so many that he stopped. But the sixty-pound dog topped out at pulling slightly under forty pounds of weight, or a thirty-five-pound bag of kibble and a five-pound bag; by his second try, Cujo grew distracted and didn't finish. Perez, a hulking, goateed truck driver, started to get the hang of it with Diamond, a dog that earlier had been lunging and pulling at bystanders on her leash. She crossed the forty-pound threshold, and Perez said he'd be back another time to show what the seventeen-month-old could really do.

But in a contest where the winner is determined by heaviest weight pulled as a percentage of body weight, Cujo and Diamond had nothing on Red. Ortiz, hair pulled back into a ponytail, showed up late, clad in a Pittsburgh Steelers jacket. By this point in the contest, he knew roughly how much the dog would have to pull to win. Instead of treats, he had his girlfriend serve as the lure, scampering a few steps ahead of the pit bull as Red lunged along with the sled connected to his harness. On the first run, the dog pulled thirty-seven pounds. It was enough. After Sternberg toted up the results for the handful of remaining spectators under a streetlight, Ortiz said Red would be getting a steak for dinner, a meal fit for a still manly dog.

The uptick in pet spending and pet-care standards over the past few decades masks a fair amount of contradiction. For one thing, as vegetarians often point out, our society has proved very able to compartmentalize when it comes to nonhumans. We embrace dogs and cats and a few other species as pets, while global warming and industrial agriculture make life more miserable than ever for other beasts. But even within the realm of pets, the pet-owning largesse that has turned Petco and PetSmart into household names is not universal.

Even the industry's own statistics, with their endless upward trajectory, suggest that not every pet lives like the designer Bjorn Gärdsby's, or even mine. Forty-three billion dollars in projected total pet spending seems like a lot of money. But the figure is less overpowering when divided by the number of households with pets: 71 million, including 45 million with dogs and 38 million with cats. That works out to a little over $600 a household, which doesn't buy too many nights at Wag Hotel. It grows a bit when you exclude birds and rodents. The pet trade association asked a group of 580 dog owners and 402 cat owners to record their spending on a list of pet-related expenses over a twelve-month period. Cat owners clocked about $1,200; dog owners, $2,000. That's still a third of what I watched Ben the beagle's

owner spend on experimental chemotherapy. That new purvey-
ors of pet goods and services are appearing in unpretentious
spots all over the country—as I write this, my Google Alert
popped up with news of a new doggie day spa in Saginaw,
Michigan—and that the APPMA number has doubled over a
decade suggests which side history is on. But that's not to say it's
the only way of living with dogs, or even the only way of living
with a dog you love.

What makes some people embrace the fur-baby notion of
pets while others stay in the loyal-servant or man's-best-friend
eras? Why do some people invite a dog onto the bed while
others remain part of that dwindling minority who keep the
animal out in the yard? It's tough to find a hard-and-fast rule.
Several of the veterinarians I visited with told me that lower-
income clients were often even more keen to choose expensive
animal-saving procedures, and just as devastated when their
pets died as wealthier ones. And yet much of the discourse
about proper pet treatment winds up, after you pick through
layers of euphemism, to be about class. Vick's 2007 arrest laid
bare all sorts of anxieties about what poor people allegedly do
with dogs. Never mind that he was a multimillionaire football
star; the minute his dog ring was exposed, he went right back to
being a southern Virginia hoodlum. "Doubly frightening is the
realization that a culture of dogfighting exists in America's
underclass that has gone unnoticed by the mainstream," edito-
rialized the *Pittsburgh Post-Gazette*. "As this once-impoverished
athlete became wealthy, he didn't necessarily shed his fondness
for the blood sport he apparently knew from an earlier day."

In 1990, the sociologist Elijah Anderson captured this phenomenon, from both sides, in a study of life in an unidentified
gentrifying urban neighborhood he calls the Village. A passage
in the book looks at the contrasting takes on dogs. "When I see a
strange dog, I am very careful," he quotes a young black resident
of the area as saying. "But white people have a whole different

attitude. Some of them want to go up and pet the dog." Anderson wonders whether the phenomenon isn't so much racial as a reflection of class—which, in modern America, represents a significant overlap. "Many black working-class people I interviewed failed to understand" how the newcomers could give their dogs the run of the house. "When they see a white adult on his knees kissing a dog, the sight may turn their stomach . . . within the black community, dogs are used mainly as a means of protection, whereas the middle-class whites and blacks of the Village generally see them as pets as well."

You don't need a famous sociologist tagging along to see the same thing if you take a stroll someday with me and my Saint Bernard. Pop culture provides two major references for that particular breed, and I know precisely where to go to hear either of them. Trot south or east from my house, and Murphy is the subject of oohs and aahs, patted like a giant teddy bear: "Beethoven!" Hike a few blocks the other way, and fewer people assume he's the big cuddly lug I know. "Uh-oh, it's Cujo!" Guess which one is the poorer neighborhood?

Violence against pets is one thing, but even the most dedicated pet lover would probably not go to the trouble of butting into the lives of perfect strangers when the contrasts in pet culture are simply a matter of someone being grossed out by kisses. Kopelman herself notes that many dogfighters "love their dogs" and don't grasp that they're devastating them. The same is even more likely to be true of owners whose sole divergence from mainstream pet keeping consists of, say, housing the animal in the backyard, or declining to have it spayed, or wanting it to be intimidating. Yet the slew of research on the human-animal bond over the past two decades has also taught people a lot about how and when that bond breaks down. The data point to the sorts of things that Training Wheels volunteers go out to change.

For shelter administrators like Kopelman and Sternberg, the motivation is simple: Fewer people giving up their dogs means fewer dogs that face the unhappy prospect of euthanasia. Though some surveys have found that low income is closely tied to whether someone will abandon his or her animal, others show that people who give up their pets share a set of recurring issues. Volunteers aren't in a position to do much about some of those issues, like losing a house. But other factors can be changed. Not having a pet altered, or not fixing its troubling behavior, or ignorance about health, behavior, and nutrition all increase the chances an animal will wind up languishing in one of their facilities. People giving up their pets displayed a degree of ignorance about animal brains, like believing they misbehaved out of spite, that might have actually hurt the owners' ability to improve matters. With Lug-Nuts, which is only the most public part of the broader program Sternberg markets under the name Training Wheels, they're out to change those things.

"Training Wheels began in 1999, and it began basically because there was a study done at Tufts University that showed people deliberated eight months before relinquishing a dog," Kopelman says. "If you've been deliberating for eight months, it's not a spur-of-the-moment decision; you've kind of already broken an emotional tie by the time you come into the shelter. The idea was to go out and find people before they reach that point, to go out when the puppy was two or three months old. The vast majority of people, really, they love their animals. They just don't have the financial wherewithal to deal with their issues, or the knowledge."

Just like the marketing in the pet industry's top tax bracket, the outreach efforts by the teams Training Wheels has trained all over the country are aimed straight at humans. Rather than hitting the streets in search of stray cats or rabid dogs, the program reaches out to people who haven't quite gotten the message about how to handle a pet. Volunteers cruise neighborhoods local authorities say are responsible for the largest portion of relinquishments to nearby shelters—that is to say, "the poor part of town"—in search of people with pets. Offering treats and toys, they strike up conversations to find out how it's going. "Doing it in a nonjudgmental way is the whole philosophy of Training Wheels," explains Kopelman. "It's not to say, 'Hey, why is your dog tied up outside?' or 'Why isn't your dog spayed or neutered?' You see a pet and a person, and you stop and offer things for the pets and you start a relationship."

Over the years since they started their drive-arounds in the upstate New York counties near their Rondout Valley shelter, the efforts have led to some awkward moments in unfamiliar neighborhoods. "It's all pet people, so of course they're really keen on talking to everyone," Kopelman says of volunteers. Once, early on, she remembers preparing to offer treats to a man standing on a corner with a fairly tough-looking dog; she realized, belatedly, that she was interrupting a drug deal. Other times, though, she says people who initially seemed taken aback by strangers bearing rawhides came in search of help much later. "You never want to imply you're a better dog person than anyone else," Kopelman says. On spotting, for instance, an animal tied to a backyard tree, she won't knock on a door to correct the owner. Rather, she'll make a note of it and pass by the house hoping to see the person and start an informal chat about how tying up a dog is liable to promote aggression. "After a while, people know to call us," she says.

It's a slow process, trying to salvage endangered human-animal bonds. When I spoke to her several months after the Lug-Nuts contest, Kopelman told me of someone they'd randomly reached out to on the street months earlier. They hadn't seen her again, but a friend later turned up in search of low-cost training for her own troubled pet. The animal, Kopelman suspected, might have wound up getting killed in a shelter had it been surrendered because the owner was too frustrated and didn't know where to find help. "Why should the people in animal service capacity make the assumption that people should automatically know what to do with their pets?" she said. "As people, we don't get vaccinated every year for all these diseases, and yet we assume that pet owners know to do it."

Like human babies, fur babies can be a lot of trouble. Unlike human babies, fur babies can legally be abandoned by owners who are too logistically overwhelmed, or too financially strapped, or, for that matter, simply bored with the animal. For all the dog-friendly hotels and pet-industrial titans the past few decades have created, that still happens enough to be deeply disturbing.

Statistics on pet shelters are notoriously erratic. The most comprehensive study took place during the mid-1990s and included only shelters that housed more than a hundred animals. Those facilities alone took in just over 2 million dogs and just under 2 million cats each year. About half of the dogs and 70 percent of the cats wound up euthanized, an annual death toll that runs into the millions of the animals we supposedly love most, dogs and cats that get trucked off to the crematorium in garbage bags, not taken to the groomer in a specially designed van. Even the 1990s numbers, though, likely represented a decline from earlier decades. As the campaign to spay and neuter pets took hold in the 1960s and 1970s—think of *The Price Is Right* host Bob Barker imploring viewers, in his daily sign-off, to spay or neuter their animals—the number of strays in some places declined dramatically.

Over the past two decades, a vocal group of agitators has been pushing for a policy shift that would reduce the number much more: an end to shelter euthanasia. Once marginalized as a bunch of hopeless utopians, the movement was galvanized by a 1989 essay by activist Ed Duvin, who took aim at the paradox of shelter workers—people who got into their profession because they loved animals—killing untold numbers of them each year. "It borders on the obscene to describe the killing of many millions of innocent and healthy beings as a merciful act," he wrote. In the years since then, cities including Richmond and Phoenix have embraced the principle of "no-kill" shelters, guaranteeing that healthy and treatable animals at their shelters will be adopted. The San Francisco SPCA, one of the nation's oldest, ended its contract to provide city animal-care services and declared itself no-kill. Maddie's Fund, a charity endowed by $300 million from the founder of the software firm PeopleSoft, helped turned the idea into a mass movement.

Euthanasia remains a hugely divisive topic among humane activists. Like the Victorian anticruelty campaigners who first instituted euthanasia, contemporary critics of no-kill say a pain-free death may not be the worst fate for some animals. An entirely no-kill country, they say, would be one where miserable, unwanted animals languish in dank dungeons until the end of their unhappy lives.

Other activists think purportedly no-kill facilities aren't humane enough, saying such places boast about being cruelty-free only because they can take the most adoptable animals from municipal facilities where lesser pets would be put down. "'No-kill' animal shelters should really be called 'leave-the-killing-to-someone-else' shelters," declared People for the Ethical Treatment of Animals in 2005. Yet society seems, slowly, to be moving in this direction, aided by enthusiastic no-kill champions like Nathan Winograd, the Stanford-trained attorney whose book, *Redemption,* serves as a gospel for the movement. Winograd may be a former San Francisco SPCA director, but his campaign is no left-coast anomaly. Even in Philadelphia, a city with one of the most dismal euthanasia rates in the country, a veteran Republican city councilman helped himself squeak to reelection in 2007 by embracing no-kill.

The statistics further suggest the number of deaths can be drastically reduced in a lot of ways. A study of annual animal euthanasias per 100,000 humans shows that municipalities are all over the map: In San Francisco, the number is 2.5; in Baltimore, it's 9.2; in Dallas, 23.0; and in Augusta, Georgia, it's 45.3. Some of those numbers reflect the no-kill stance of facilities in San Francisco, but others reflect how effective the various places have been at controlling the unwanted pet population through less heroic sorts of intervention. That's something Duvin's original essay advocated, and it's something that the Training Wheels team, who don't come from the no-kill movement, also work at: reducing euthanasia by slowing the influx of pets into shelters while at the same time improved adoption facilities and pet-search Web sites are speeding more animals out the door.

Watching Lug-Nuts's incentive-laden rules quietly push the pet-care gospel, I got to wondering about how culture changes. It's tempting to imagine outreach workers tracking down the country's last tied-up dog in some Idaho backyard a few decades from now, spaying it, grooming it, and tarting it up in a couture vest before plunking it down onto its befuddled owner's living-room couch with a complimentary package of organic dog food and a list of positive-reinforcement local trainers. It brings to mind the World Health Organization investigators who hunted down the planet's final case of small-pox in Africa in 1977.

I suspect that the message is ultimately transmitted better by capitalists than by humanitarians. The implicit argument in the well-financed advertising for everything from corporate pet food to big-box pet-supply chains is that your animal, a member of the family, deserves to be nurtured as such. For a lot of people, that remains debatable—and expensive. And yet the chains continue to grow, and the culture continues to change.

The process—and the pet-keeping contradictions—don't necessarily stop at the water's edge. Japan and much of Europe are home to pet-keeping cultures that at times seem even more smitten than ours—Bjorn Gärdsby has also had an opening in

Tokyo, where canine couture is a much bigger deal than even in Manhattan; Swedish rates of pet insurance are far higher than our own, in part because Swedish humans have far more experience with collective health care than we do. And as Western-style capitalism, complete with Western-style consumerism, has spread to new lands over the past couple of decades, pet ownership has spread along with it. In 2007, India hosted its first pet fair, with manufacturers displaying the standard array of shampoos, sweaters, snacks, and nonskid pet bowls. China, which got a free-market head start on its erstwhile rival, was a few steps ahead. Though Chairman Mao had once clamped down on pet ownership as a bourgeois affectation, Beijing, Shanghai, and Guangzhou are in the midst of a pet-pampering craze as the new century dawns. Chinese spending on pet food and care rose from $463 million in 2004 to $757 million in 2007; by the end of 2009 the number will have doubled since 2004. The bulk of the growth comes from dogs and cats. In the capital, the number of registered dogs tripled between 2003 and 2006, to 534,000. And the service jobs recently added to the state Labor Ministry's list of 1,979 officially recognized jobs included "pet tutor," Chinese bureaucratese for dog trainer. ("Wok repairman," fading fast, had been removed from the list.)

China, where dogs were celebrated long before the Maoist interruption and the twenty-first-century economic boom, is as deep in pet contradictions as we are. In Beijing, an estimated 120 restaurants serve dog meat. Does the contemporary pet craze portend better days for dogs beyond a thin slice of the Chinese upper crust? It can't hurt. The breathless tones in which the state-run Xinhua news service reports on the advent of high-end pet boarding in Beijing or the popularity of pet tutoring in Shanghai are much like those used by boosterish locals when middling U.S. cities get their own doggie day spas or canine couture salons. In both cases, pet pampering is presented as an advanced state of economic development, something for provincial American municipalities and rising world powers alike to aspire to.

Back home, where our pet economy still dwarfs China's, the many places where we fall short of that advanced status still attract the occasional push from both activist citizens and the government they elect. Puppy mills will likely survive whatever new regulations are imposed on them, but a host of new legislation shows they'll also likely face a future filled with minor legal harassment. The push against unethical breeding may eventually help achieve some other pet-protection goals in the process. In Los Angeles, the campaign was partly responsible for a law mandating that dogs be spayed or neutered. Likewise, a slew of municipalities have new laws against tying up animals outdoors, yet another way of declaring that an animal's rightful place is inside the house, with the humans.

In Florida, state lawmakers recently expanded the dog's domain a bit further. Until 2006, restaurants had been forbidden to allow patrons to bring their pets. With the passage of the "Doggie Dining Bill," dogs were now allowed, if the restaurant chose, to dine alfresco. Then-governor Jeb Bush signed the bill a day after his own black Lab had succumbed to cancer; a state legislator's dog sat in at the signing ceremony, affixing its pawprint to the document. As supportive restaurant industry lobbyists looked on, the governor said citizens and dogs could now "have a brewski together, have a hot dog together or whatever they want outdoors." For all the doggie-love trappings, the bill was a classic response to an industry—hospitality—that wanted greater access to a burgeoning market: pet owners who go everywhere with their animals. But in terms of cultural history, it was also an implicit rebuke to those Floridians who might not want someone's dog at dinner with them. History, for now, is on the pooch's side. And the pooch is at the side of its human.

THIRTEEN

SHANA TENNENBAUM
TO MY PRECIOUS
AND LOYAL FRIEND
I LOVE YOU SO DEEPLY
& MISS YOU TERRIBLY

TISH TENNENBAUM
TO MY BELOVED FRIEND,
NO ONE COULD EVER
IMAGINE HOW DEEPLY
I LOVED YOU,
I MISS YOU BEYOND WORDS

The American Way of Pet Death

About two hundred yards from where Drs. Weisse and Berent perform regular miracles with the fluoroscope at the University of Pennsylvania's veterinary hospital, there's a small room whose light blue walls are adorned by a painting of a rainbow. As with most other spaces in the hospital, the corridor outside could easily be part of a human-focused facility: gurneys whiz past, doctors confer, walkie-talkies squawk, a hushed, antiseptic air of technical competence prevails. The Rainbow Room, as it's known, is a place without any parallel in human medicine. But one glance at its gentle decor lets the uninitiated know that they pretty much never want to enter. It's where owners say good-bye to pets that are about to be euthanized.

Merry Klimek visited the Rainbow Room one horrible fall night in 2007 in the company of a ten-year-old border collie named Lad. A few hours earlier, Lad had collided with one of the horses on Klimek's spread at the countrified edge of the suburbs. Thinking the dog had broken its leg, she put him in the car and raced to a nearby veterinary clinic. The staff there took one look at the dog and decided its problems were beyond their abilities. So Klimek jumped back in the car and hightailed it to Penn's hospital. "He was screaming and he struggled, and I had to raise my voice a couple of times," she said. "I feel so terrible about that. I think he was nervous. I just told him to calm down." The news didn't get any better at the hospital. The collision had broken the dog's back. After examining Lad, doctors told Klimek there was a less than 10 percent chance that a surgery would do any good. The procedure would also be long and involved for the doctors, difficult for Lad, and, alas, expensive for Klimek.

Not that Klimek needed to be reminded about the price. When Lad had his accident, she had already maxed out her credit cards caring for Holly, a second border collie, whom she had put to sleep seven weeks earlier following a long and increasingly futile battle with pancreatitis, epilepsy, and a host of related ailments. "It was probably thirteen or fourteen thousand dollars over four years," Klimek said. "I hate, I hate that money is a factor. But someone said that if you'd had unlimited funds, you might have just put her through too much pain. We had enough fighting. I just felt that the quality of her life, this year, was not what it should have been." So Holly, too, was given an injection that quietly, painlessly ended her life. "Two in two months," she said, sighing. "I just feel trampled myself, feeling like I let my babies down."

Try as it might, the American pet industry has never managed to cure that saddest fact of pet ownership: They die, 9 million dogs and cats each year, succumbing to old age or disease or accident. We stretch out their lives via healthy eating and miraculous surgeries, ease their pains with pneumatic beds and potent narcotics, max out our credit cards to help them along. But still they leave us. It's the great big hole in the middle of any argument that pets are surrogate children. No one ever expects to outlive their kid.

And yet even in the face of this most unassailable of scientific facts—the global death rate, for human and animal alike, is and always will be 100 percent—the new world of American pet ownership bends old rituals and creates new ones to reflect that the dearly departed is a lot dearer than he might once have been. How do you bid farewell to the dog that has everything? With more sadness—and more goods and services. Today's dead pets have access not only to holes in the backyard but to their own sections of human cemeteries. Their bodies can be tended by pet-specific mortuary scientists and blessed by specially trained pet chaplains. Where medical-waste incinerators once sufficed, the likes of Klimek now can opt for guaranteed individual cremations. And as they mourn, they can also lean upon a hefty network of professional assistance—grief counselors, pet-death advice handbooks, twenty-four-hour support hotlines.

The first time I met Klimek was about a week after Lad died. She was standing in that same first-floor hallway, staring through the Rainbow Room's open door. With one hand on each side of the doorway, she looked almost cruciform, her blond head cocked to one side. Yet she wasn't there to visit the scene of her dog's demise. It was a Tuesday night, which meant the real drama was across the hall in another small cinder-block room. The hospital's pet bereavement support group had a new member.

Anthropologists like ritual and transition. Birth, marriage, and death tend to explain a great deal about a society, whether it's tribesmen from the highlands of New Guinea or the pet people of twenty-first-century America. But animals' births usually occur before ordinary people have adopted them as pets. And— Ada Nieves's parties notwithstanding—marriage is not quite in the cards, either. That leaves death. To get a sense of how we now grapple with that grim tradition, it seemed wise for me to stop in at the Tuesday group sessions led by Christina Bach.

Bach has a master's degree in social work and a specialty in end-of-life and bereavement counseling. Until recently, she was employed as a counselor in a human hospital's oncology division, working with terminally ill patients and their families. In 2007, she came over to the veterinary hospital, joining a nationwide roster of only about two dozen full-time veterinary social workers. But the move from dying humans to dead pets did not necessarily mean a transition to less fraught subject matter. Bach should know; she introduces herself to new members of the group as "mom to Gus and Maggie, my two crazy beagles," and notes that she went through the deaths of Gus and Maggie's two predecessors. "It was devastating," she says. "The literature says the hardest thing is losing a child, and I see this as a parallel."

Each of Bach's meetings begins with new members telling their stories. To call these tales depressing is like saying the end of *Old Yeller* was "a little bit of a letdown." The group sits in a circle in an ordinary-looking veterinary examining room. There's a swiveling medical lamp on the ceiling. There are diagrams of dog and cat innards affixed to the white cinder-block walls. There's a sink for conscientious doctors to wash their hands. The only hint at the room's designated purpose on a Tuesday night comes from the box of tissues strategically perched atop the X-ray lightbox. The box is emptied by the time the meeting ends ninety minutes later.

The first time I visited, the newcomer was a woman named Marlena Schmid, who'd driven two hours from her home in the suburbs of New York. Two weeks earlier, Schmid had come to the hospital to euthanize a perfectly healthy Shiba Inu named

Foxy. She wept as she told her story. Adopted from a shelter, Foxy had been a difficult dog. Sweet around the house, Foxy— as her name suggested, she looked a bit like a fox, tan and brown—was aggressive around others. She barked and snarled and lunged and once bit a neighbor who was walking toward her carrying a pair of gardening clippers. Schmid tried to help. She took the dog to an obedience class at her local PetSmart and eventually started working with a team of behaviorists at VHUP, even though it was two hours away. But whatever demons controlled Foxy's behavior were not appeased. On Labor Day, Schmid accidentally left the garage door open and Foxy got out. Wandering the streets unleashed, she came upon a woman who was walking another dog. Snarling and barking ensued. The other dog, petrified, wrapped its leash around its owner's legs. Foxy lunged and bit the woman, tearing a chunk of flesh from her leg. Police were called. An ambulance carted the victim off to the hospital. And Schmid, consulting with the team back at Penn, started tiptoeing toward what she called the most difficult decision of her life.

"It was Rosh Hashanah, the Jewish holidays," she told the group. "And there were all these children at home, running around the neighborhood. I was thinking about it. It's a terrible thing when an animal bites, but I don't know if I could have lived with myself if she had maimed a child." After agonizing until the end of the month, Schmid drove her dog back to the hospital. After taking Foxy on a final walk through the tree-lined neighborhood, she had the four-year-old euthanized. Foxy's ashes were sent back to Schmid's house by FedEx. "She trusted me when I brought her here," Schmid said, breaking down. "And I left without her." She still hadn't been able to open the FedEx box, which sat right by the door, exactly where she had put it when it arrived.

Schmid's hell this night is a particularly excruciating one. The dog hadn't died of old age. It had been killed. And, right or wrong, she'd made the choice. But while the decision to euthanize a dangerous dog may be among the hardest a pet owner faces—Bach has since started a group specifically for people in Schmid's situation—there was a touch of Schmid in nearly everyone who visited the group over the three months I sat in on meetings. Whether it's the obvious case of euthanasia, or some lingering jitter about whether a family pet should have been fed that down-market brand of pet food, animal death has a way of implicating human caretakers in its web of guilt. The common denominator in the grief group is a sense that somehow the pets didn't deserve this.

There was the woman named Denise, whose poodle had flown out the window in a car accident on the New Jersey Turnpike. Denise herself was badly hurt in the wreck. Now she was in the group wondering whether she could have shaken off her own injuries and driven the dog, Coco, to a veterinary ward. There was a retiree named Mary, whose cat, Callie, had died after eating what Mary believes was melamine-tainted pet food. Should she have paid more attention to ingredients? Or Amy, the state trooper whose tiny white schipperke had to be euthanized after being mauled by her daughter's pit bull. The attack was the last straw in a troubled family relationship and left Amy wondering why she hadn't put her foot down sooner. "She was my best friend, my soul mate," Amy said. "I know it sounds silly. I have a lot of pets. I've had to put them down before. But this was just so terrible." And there was Rene, a graduate student whose dog had simply died of old age but who still couldn't seem to shake his blues. "I feel bad because I don't feel worse," he said.

The room grew very quiet as each story wound to its end. The low thrumming sound of the fluorescent lights punctuated the stillness. Participants mumbled sympathy, let one another off the hook. Bach intoned empathetically in the language of counseling: guilt, bad; grief, appropriate; euthanasia for the dangerous and the dying, not something to feel ashamed about. She was nimble enough that no one noticed that she actually kept the meetings on a clockwork schedule. After about an hour, she started to steer the conversation from abject misery toward something approaching acceptance. She asked people to tell a happy story about their animals. She invited everyone to show pictures. "She has a beautiful smile," she said on seeing Schmid's photo of Foxy. After ninety minutes, everyone was ready to go, slightly more able to face the week ahead.

The novel thing about Bach's bereavement group isn't so much the grief, which has long been a part of the human-animal bond, but the nature of its display and management: professionalized, therapeutic, emotionally expressive, aiming to manage sadness rather than "cure" it. It is to the early twenty-first century what the Hartsdale Animal Cemetery might have been to the turn of the past century.

America's first pet cemetery dates to the 1890s. Soon after a Manhattan veterinarian named Samuel Johnson let a friend bury her dog on a corner of his Westchester County orchard, the place had bloomed into a prototypical Victorian cemetery, with frilly headstones and poetic inscriptions, flowing fountains and ornate mausoleums for the likes of Honeybunch ("A faithful and loving companion"), Dot ("She lived to love"), and Bum ("My dear old pal"). Hartsdale is still active today, sixty thousand burials and some fairly significant real estate acquisitions later. In its way, the pet historian Katherine Grier has written, the century of headstone inscriptions demonstrates society's evolving take on pets, from noble servants to steadfast friends to innocent children. One autumn Sunday, the crowd at the cemetery included tourists bearing cameras as well as mourners carrying flowers. A plaque hints at why this space might draw more attention than the average graveyard: it

proclaims Hartsdale as AMERICA'S FIRST AND MOST PRESTI-
GIOUS PET CEMETERY. Its permanent residents include the for-
mer animal companions of such luminaries as Elizabeth Arden,
Kate Smith, Evelyn Nesbit, and Mariah Carey.

Hartsdale wasn't alone for long in the pet-cemetery business. And over the years animal burials reflected the country
outside the cemetery gates. Posted to Washington, D.C., during
World War II, the African American scholar and diplomat
Ralph Bunche was horrified when his family dog died and he
had to tell his children that even the local pet cemetery was seg-
regated, with one area for white people's pets and another area
for African Americans'. Over time, as the country prospered,
the redoubts were transformed from exclusive upper-crust gardens to basic resting places for ordinary people's pets. In the
process, the facilities acquired a slightly wacky, slightly seedy
reputation—not quite the stuff of Stephen King's *Pet Sematary,*
maybe, but not quite in the bosom of middle-class suburbia,
either. The filmmaker Errol Morris memorably captured their
world with his 1978 documentary *Gates of Heaven,* which
focused on a scandal involving a pet cemetery that had closed
and, following a slew of news reports, was forced to exhume
and move 450 animals before selling the property. You can find
nonscandalous, if still eerie, down-market cemeteries in exurbs
all over the country. I visited one in Pflugerville, Texas, where
many of the flimsy grave markers had lost the plastic tiling that
identified the animals buried underneath. No tourists were
on hand.

The truest twenty-first-century heir to the Hartsdale graves
may be on the Internet. With more room than even the fanciest
Hartsdale headstone, sites like ilovedmypets.com and Heaven's
Playground offer mourners a chance to permanently eulogize
their pets in cyberspace, for a small annual fee. The tributes are
heartfelt and heartbreaking, no less so because they're often
hokey in the way that shows off the uncalculated nature of pet

affection. Thus we know that Bandaid (1983–1986) "will always be our baby girl (you little pizza thief)!" And that Sasha (1990–2005) "was so much more than 'just a pet.' She was my angel . . . Mommy misses you." And that Jordan (2002–2005) "had the cutest facial expressions and loved to talk, either by telling me you wanted to go out, or fussing at me if I told you that you did something wrong." A tour of the inscriptions says a lot about the qualities we attribute to our pets, and the holes they leave behind.

Offline, the pet death industry has also changed in recent years. Entirely new fields like veterinary hospice care have appeared on the scene to aid a glut of geriatric pets; many vets now make housecalls so that animals can be put to sleep in their own beds. One example of where things are headed on the mourning front can be found in a strip mall in the upscale Phoenix suburb of Scottsdale. Fairwinds Pet Memorial Services, opened in 2007, is one of only about a dozen pets-only funeral homes in the country. With its oriental rugs and cherrywood furniture, the decor reflects its owner's background in the human funeral industry. There's a tastefully appointed arrangements office, where owners come—often before their pet's death—to schedule services and cremations. There's a somber viewing room, complete with two different sizes of doggie bed, where the deceased are laid out. A staffer grooms dogs before they are displayed. "Sometimes you have to work to keep their eyes closed," says the groomer, a retired nurse named Mary Rauchwarter. And whether their eyes are open or shut, no human funeral home could offer patrons a pawprint of the dearly departed.

The manager of Fairwinds, Elizabeth Vaughan, says the home's main business is cremations. In Arizona, it's illegal to bury an animal. And a dirty little secret of the veterinary facilities that handle most pet deaths is that although they'll give you ashes, the ashes might not be entirely those of *your pet*;

industrial crematories can incinerate multiple animal cadavers at a time. "You wouldn't put your aunt Rose with a bunch of other people, would you?" Vaughan says. Instead, for $495, Fairwinds offers what it calls the Safe Journey system, which guarantees a private cremation. Rauchwarter says many of the clients also ask to have some of their pets' toys wait with them in the cooler. "They don't want them to be all alone," she explains. Afterward, customers can keep the ashes in a 24-karat gold-plated keepsake ($220), or memorialize their animal with a silver pendant ($75) or woven photograph ($130). Those who want more might turn to the Illinois firm LifeGem, which uses a patented process to capture carbon from the ashes and turn it into a diamond—$24,999 for 1.5 carats.

The cremations may keep the doors open, but it's the full-on funerals that make Fairwinds—which boasts its own animal chaplain—stand out. Donna Rae Yuritic has been a professional tennis player for much of her adult life. A minister in the United Church of Religious Science ("It's metaphysical," she says), Yuritic three years ago also attended a lecture and took an online course to become certified as one of about fifty animal chaplains in the country. She hung out a shingle, performing adoption blessings, offering prayers for sick animals, and performing services for those that have passed. "I have magnetic signs on my vehicle that say COMPASSION FOR CREATURES ANIMAL MINISTRY and have had people drive up and say all kinds of things. Mostly, they say, 'I need to call you,' or 'I need to get your number and give it to so-and-so.' [The ministry is] really growing." Yuritic says she's planning a telephone prayer hotline.

As for the funerals, she's nothing if not flexible about which owners—not that she uses that term; she prefers *companions*—she'll serve. "I find out if they want a traditional service, if they want God, Jesus, higher father, Allah, infinite spirit, whatever pertains to them," she says. Some have a large gathering. Some include only the animal's human companion. "It's basically just being there when the person is first viewing the body, to offer them support. What I do is talk to them before the service, so when I write up a blessing it's as individual as possible."

When I visited Fairwinds, Yuritic had been working with the facility for about five months, doing a service every few weeks. The most dramatic event of her tenure—it was even covered on local television—had been the funeral for a border collie named Tashi. Tashi's family and friends, including the family's surviving dogs, gathered at Fairwinds for the ceremony. Each family member read a remembrance. There were tears all around: Mom, Dad, even the two teenage boys. But a moment of relief happened during Yuritic's benediction. One of the remaining dogs, a Jack Russell terrier, spied his old playmate up on the altar. He jumped up into her bed to lie down next to her. This was not, in the end, your aunt Rose's funeral. And no one seemed to mind. "People who've had an animal as a companion, they know," Yuritic said later. "No matter what anyone says, you look into their eyes and you know they have a soul."

From an inscription on one of the urns at Fairwinds to a mural on the wall of the veterinary hospital's Rainbow Room to an out-loud reading in one of Bach's bereavement sessions, it's hard to think about pet death without encountering "The Rainbow Bridge." The poem has since the 1980s become a standard prop of pet mourning, imprinted on sympathy cards and quoted on pet-grief hotlines.

The basic gist of the poem is this: Especially beloved animals that die go to a place called the Rainbow Bridge. The spot features "meadows and hills for all of our special friends so they can run and play together." Not to mention "food, water, and sunshine." Grievous wounds are cured, old-age infirmities wiped away. "The animals are happy and content, except for one small thing; they each miss someone very special to them who had to be left behind." The crux of the story, speaking directly to the sadness of those same people, describes how the separation between human and animal will eventually be overcome.

> They all run and play together, but the day comes when one suddenly stops and looks into the distance. His bright eyes are intent; his eager body quivers. Suddenly he begins to run from the group, flying over the green grass, his legs carrying him faster and faster.
>
> You have been spotted, and when you and your special friend finally meet, you cling together in joyous reunion, never to be parted again . . .
>
> Then you cross the Rainbow Bridge together.

"The Rainbow Bridge" has been published online some thirty-five thousand times. That's about twice as many as Edgar Allan Poe's American classic, "The Raven." Photocopies of the fable are handed out freely to the newly bereaved; Klimek told me a local pet-supply store had sent copies along with a condolence letter—and a coupon for future purchases—following the deaths of both Lad and Holly. It's been reprinted in books such as *The Complete Idiot's Guide to Getting and Owning a Dog, How to Start a Home-Based Pet-Care Business, Boston Terriers for Dummies,* and *Hope for Healing Liver Disease in Your Dog.* As poetry, it will never secure a place in the canon of American literature. And yet, year after year, its words prove hugely affecting, and deeply comforting, to pet owners at their most vulnerable. The cornball sappiness is part of its appeal. Rather than seriously contemplating the bleak reality of death, it tells mourners that they'll see their animal again. In other words, it offers them precisely what they want to hear, in the least subtle, most unpretentious way possible. Which, if you think about it, is a lot like what a pet does, too.

No one quite agrees about the provenance of the poem, which is often attributed to "Unknown." In one version, it is a variation on a poem written by a Brooklyn psychologist named Wallace Sife. Back in 1987, Sife wrote one of the first books about pet death following the demise of his beloved miniature dachshund. "It completely turned my life upside down," he recalled. "There were three pet bereavement counselors in the world at the time. All we could do was give each other warm fuzzies, because there was nothing available . . . We were taking books on human loss and bereavement and . . . extrapolating from them." But Sife, who went on to found the Association for Pet Loss and Bereavement, told me his feelings on the subject predated his own brush with canine death. A few years earlier, he said, "I wrote a little essay for a friend of mine in California whose dog died. And he belonged to a dog club, and they printed it and it was called 'All Pets Go to Heaven.'" In Sife's telling, years later he was playing around on the Internet and discovered his old poem, slightly altered and attributed to "Anonymous."

Sife says he doesn't mind not getting credit. The same can't necessarily be said for several others. A Web site for animal-rescue activist William N. Britton's book, *The Legend of Rainbow Bridge,* includes a link to a form authorizing noncommercial users to post the poem, so long as they attribute it correctly. "We know that this sounds very legal and official," the document reads. "If you've looked around the web you might understand why. Mr. Britton's work has been used illegally and stolen repeatedly." Another purported author of the poem, who actually holds a copyright for a book called *The Rainbow*

Bridge, is an Oregonian named Paul Dahm. In 2000, Dahm announced plans to sue Universal Press Syndicate after the poem ran in the "Dear Abby" column. He claimed to have written it in 1981 and sold it as a pamphlet for two dollars. But, he told reporters at the time, he hadn't bothered to put his name on it. He copyrighted a book with that name only in 1998, well after the advice maven had reprinted a version as the product of an unknown author, and well after it began its voyage into the pet-owning canon. The lawyers for "Dear Abby" asserted that there was a "cloud" over the authorship. The case was settled confidentially, according to the attorney who represented "Dear Abby"—meaning the syndicate didn't publicly acknowledge anything one way or the other about who, if anyone, owned "The Rainbow Bridge." At any rate, the poem has been reprinted—still attributed to "Anonymous"—thousands of times since.

I tried to reach Dahm at his Oregon home in the spring of 2008. The man who answered the phone identified himself as the nearly eighty-year-old poet's younger brother, Jerry. He said Dahm was in ill health and unavailable, but that he knew what I was going to ask. "You're probably the tenth person to call about it in the last eighteen months," he said. Jerry Dahm said his brother had written a draft of the poem as early as 1958, but finished it only in 1981. As for trying to claim his fair share of the proceeds from the trinkets, cards, and books that contain the poem, Jerry Dahm said, "He gave up. He was going to sue all those people. He says it just wasn't worth the time and effort. Everyone who uses the poem is in violation of his copyright. I don't think it's right that people can do that."

But by now ownership of the poem—whatever the legal technicalities—has long since passed to society as a whole. In bookstores and on Web sites, there are dozens of new interpretations. One version aims to rectify Dahm/Sife/Anonymous's alleged exclusion of unowned, untamed feral animals from paradise. Another provides a more explicitly Christian vision. I suppose it's the truest indication of philosophical success in a heterogeneous land like ours: "The Rainbow Bridge" can be appropriated by one and all.

Airports and workplaces may be pet-friendly, but the hereafter is not. At least not in most major religions, which don't simply ignore the old chestnut that all dogs go to heaven, but go one step farther, declaring paradise off-limits to animals. People who work with pet grief say religious teaching that animals lack souls, and thus a means of accessing the afterlife, is the biggest stumbling block a lot of people face when dealing with their animal's death. "I met with a woman within the last year, and one of the things that was keeping her in her grief was the fear that she would never be able to be with her dog in heaven," says Betty Carmack, who twenty-five years ago began leading one of the country's first pet-loss groups, in San Francisco. "Her priest had told her animals don't have souls and won't go to heaven. And she kept saying, 'Betty, if I thought I could see him again I could sleep better.'"

If that changes, it will undoubtedly happen at a glacial pace. Venerable though the Park Avenue institution may be, the Regency Hotel has far more capacity to respond rapidly to an evolving culture than even the least traditional of the religions based on ancient scripture. The vacuum is one reason poems like "The Rainbow Bridge" and memorial sites like ilovedmypets.com or nontraditional funerals by nontraditional officiants like Yuritic are so popular: For bereaved pet people, the institutions that would support them at other moments of grief are unavailable.

Even the oldest religions, though, morph from time to time in ways that reflect their parishioners. For decades, New York's Cathedral of Saint John the Divine has celebrated the legacy of the animal-loving Saint Francis each fall at a service that features an animal blessing. Manhattan being Manhattan, the first service I attended featured a procession of llamas and camels from the zoo as well as smaller critters from ordinary churchgoers' apartments. Other congregations have had similar services, but since the early 1990s the spectacle has spread to churches all over the country—at least three hundred churches in forty states and the District of Columbia, according to one 2004 estimate that cited only a partial list—and has become one of the more popular Sunday events of a parish year, a perennial local-news feature. The impact of such services on the gritty theological question of who has a soul is debatable. In some places, churches themselves acknowledge that the animal blessings are a way to fill dwindling pews and for parishes to compete for worshippers. But at the same time, filling a church with pets once a year has to have some effect on the beliefs of those in attendance. "Whereas rituals are often classified as marking the inclusion of those who belong and the exclusion of others, blessings of the animals seem to do something totally other than this; they include those who are most often excluded," religious scholar Laura Hobgood-Oster has written. "Of course, the next day they are excluded again, but are they excluded as fully as they were before the blessing?"

Others have taken up four-legged passage through the pearly gates as their own cause. In 2005, the writer Mary Buddemeyer-Porter followed her earlier *Will I See Fido in Heaven?* with a book called *Animals, Immortal Beings,* which collected quotations from religious luminaries like Pope John Paul II ("Animals possess a soul and men must love and feel solidarity with our smaller brethren") and Martin Luther ("Why, then, should there not be little dogs in the new earth, whose skin might be as fair as gold") to argue that religious texts could indeed be interpreted to allow animals in paradise. Not exactly, say critics. "Neither St. Francis nor the late pope believed that animals have souls in the full sense of the word or are destined for eternal life," the Reverend Richard McBrien, a Notre Dame theologian, said in one press account of the controversy. Added the Reverend Andrew Linzey from the University of Nottingham in England, "I think the idea that animals can make moral choices and should therefore be held responsible for their actions is absurd."

Back in Bach's Tuesday-night support group, many of the grievers also seem to feel like they're all alone. If the very existence of a full-time veterinary social worker offering sophisticated and respectful counseling to the bereaved demonstrates the triumph of American petmania, the experiences of many group members also highlight that culture's limits.

One of the participants in a December session was a guy named Bill Whiting, whose dog, Edna, had run away on Halloween night. After he put up flyers around town, he got a late-night call from two teenagers—"little monsters"—who demanded money and held up the phone to capture the yelps coming from what they said was his dog. A couple of hours later, they called back to say they had killed Edna. The second call came on his land line—the number on the dog's collar but not the one on his flyers. Naturally, the story of the dog torturers became a media cause célèbre. In short order, Whiting's story was on the Associated Press and Reuters newswires, Fox News, NBC, and CBS. He was contacted by pet detectives and pet psychics and a woman who said she'd fallen in love with him. Copious amounts of pop-psychological speculation followed, with sweeping conclusions reached about the differing views of animals of a white man from a gentrified neighborhood and a pair he believed to be black kids from less ritzy haunts. "I've got these skinhead people who get ahold of my e-mail or of my phone and say, you know, 'They're black. I'm going to kill them.' And I say, 'No!'" (Months later, telephone records led to the arrest of fifteen-year-old Victor Rodriguez, who was sentenced to juvenile prison for his role; no collaborator has been caught.)

248 · ONE NATION UNDER DOG

Far more common than Whiting's high-profile trauma, though, is the ineffable sense that the rest of the world doesn't get it. If your father dies, you can expect sympathy cards from coworkers, some time off from the boss, and many a memorial contribution from the gang at the office. But even as more people actually bring their pets to work, an animal's death—absolute, genuine devastation for the lonely souls in the group—elicits no similar reaction. "A lot of people are just like, you know, 'get over it' or 'just get another one,'" Bach says. "It's not as important in society's eyes. But for these people, maybe it's more important in their own eyes." In her field, they call it *disenfranchised grief,* the sense that you somehow don't have the right to feel so lousy about something.

During the time I spent with Bach, the disenfranchisement came in some surprising places. One morning, I watched her give a presentation to a classroom of veterinary students on the verge of entering the professional world. Bach walked through a presentation on the science of grief and the ways it intersects with the human-animal bond. She focused on how practicing vets could help, emphasizing empathetic formulations they could say to clients, like "Let's plan what to do next together" or "These are some very common fears/issues . . . you're not alone." Not exactly hard work, and the kind of conversation even the most coldhearted doctor could justify solely on the grounds that coming off as a caring individual would help keep a client in the business next time he or she got an animal. Maybe it was the approaching finals, but my sense was that Bach's presentation didn't find the most receptive audience in the lecture hall. "How do you guys feel about crying in front of clients?" she asked. Not so good, I suspected. Behind me, a pair of students were busy highlighting passages from a large-animal textbook.

One of the most eloquent visitors to Bach's group was a woman named Lynn Makowski. Makowski had a cat named Hitchcock. The cat had stayed with her through three cities, ten apartments, thirteen years. During their time together, Makowski had gotten her big job at a local museum and met the man who would become her husband. And, on the Wednesday before her wedding, Hitchcock went missing. The standard search, with its flurry of flyers and a Craigslist posting, ensued. No luck. On Saturday afternoon, she got married in a gazebo by the Delaware River. Her mind was back on the streets of her neighborhood, seeking out a thirteen-year-old brown tabby cat whose diabetes necessitated weekly blood tests and twice-daily insulin injections. She wanted to skip her honeymoon so she could keep looking. "But everybody—the family, my best friends, my sister who I'm closer to than anybody, even my husband—they were all like, 'You've gotta go,'" she said. "Nobody, across the board, said, 'You should stay.'"

Hitchcock never turned up, and Makowski wound up talking about him, half in the past tense and half in the present, at the Tuesday-night group. "To be honest, there's no other place I could go to talk about it," she said. "People think I'm the crazy cat lady. I need somewhere to talk . . . It's become such a big industry, with people thinking of their pets as their children and so on. But here there's nothing. I don't know if it's just how our society is so uncomfortable with death, or what." So, surrounded by strangers who seemed to get it, she laid out a picture of grief and guilt and loss. It may be a pet-crazed society, but she still felt all alone.

By the time Makowski spoke, I'd been coming to the group for several months. I'd accumulated more than enough material for the writing I wanted to do. My deadline was looming, and other work still needed to get done. And yet I kept going back, wondering how Makowski and Schmid and Whiting were all faring this week. My wife got to wondering whether there were some other issues I was working out at the group. I'd started doing my research on the new pet world—way back when—feeling mainly bemused about how I'd been sucked into the universe of dog walkers and pet hotels and veterinary antidepressants. I thought of it as a chronicle of absurdities, albeit absurdities in which I was a participant. I'd imagined the pet universe being full of people much farther gone than myself. My early expectations of the pet bereavement group, in particular, had involved crazy cat ladies rather than sophisticated grievers like Makowski, who sought support in the only place she could find it. Week after week, it was just terribly, terribly sad. I realized, after a while, that I was coming back again and again as a sort of communion. In a world where it's disappointingly rare to hear emotions discussed in terms that couldn't fit on a treacly Hallmark card, talking about pet mourning turned out to provide rare moments of genuine, thoughtful sharing.

And then, toward the end of a late-December session, a particularly difficult evening where people were talking about how hard it was to face the holidays after their loss, an unexpected thing happened: I piped up. I opened my yap to make some lame comment about my own Murphy and how bad I'd feel if something happened to him. I guess I'd been thinking about the most recent realization of my own dog saga: Murphy, never a speedster even in his prime, is slowing down. There's gray in his muzzle, and he gets cranky in ways he never used to. His sleeping has gone from eighteen or so hours a day to a solid twenty. He still bounds up the stairs in the morning to demand his walk, but sometimes when I call him to take him out for a last bathroom break before bed, it takes him a second longer to get from prone to standing. His hips, the vet tells us, will someday be a problem. Even though that's still a ways off, and even though I've spent the last couple of years learning a great deal about the medical interventions that will be able to save him from lameness, the prospect is still heartbreaking. He still runs like a dream—a lumbering, drooling, clumsy dream, but a dream all the same. I hate the notion that it won't always be thus.

Speaking in the group, needless to say, was not something I

was supposed to be doing. When I had first asked Bach if I could sit in, I'd made all the standard news-reporter promises about blending into the cinder-block walls and unobtrusively observing. Not participating is a stance that has been trained into me over a decade; I've been a journalist long enough that when I'm out at a concert as a private citizen, I have to remind myself that it's actually okay to clap. And anyway, if I was going to break the rules, it shouldn't by any logical measure have happened here. I'd covered murder scenes, fires, and two wars. After all that, how could a few hours of reminiscence about the dead dogs and cats of Philadelphia be the subject that brought me to the cusp of nonprofessional tears? Maybe in the same way live pets had gotten to the new friends in Ada Nieves's Meetup group, or the leash-law activists in San Francisco politics, or the big spenders at Pet Fashion Week, or the anxious clients who drive hours to visit VHUP's operating room. Though the specifics have changed, it's always been thus: Attachments to companion animals defy ordinary logic but conform perfectly to emotional logic. To talk about that attachment is to create common ground, a space where social rules against dog-park humping or fears about support-group sobbing are relaxed and even forgotten. It felt natural to start talking. So I did.

A moment later, my brain caught up to my mouth, and I realized with horror that I was talking about my happily alive-and-well dog in front of a roomful of people whose animals had died. So I quickly added something intended to sound authoritative about how my research showed that people shouldn't feel guilty about mourning these creatures we've all brought into our lives, and then I tried to shut up. My moment passed quickly. There were no journalism-ethics professors in the room to make note of my transgression—and no hard-bitten newsroom colleagues to cringe at its utterly saccharine content. Plus, there were a few more bereaved pet owners to hear from.

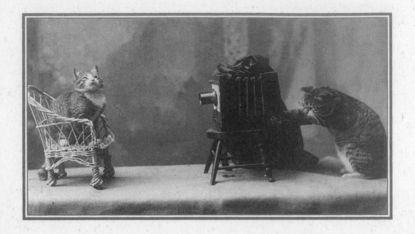

Our Pets, Ourselves

Given pets' enhanced status in the modern family, it should come as no surprise that pet portraiture is yet another booming subsector of the animal-services industry. Eight percent of dog owners told one survey that they've had, or plan to have, portraits made of their dogs; even more people opt for other items emblazoned with their animal's image. Finding a niche in "dogumentary" pictures, freelance photographers advertise like wedding photographers—and charge like them, too—for pictures that will last a lifetime. Less expensively, PetSmart advertises in-store portrait centers that do for pets what yesteryear's Sears photographers did for kids, complete with wacky props and backdrops.

Like several other aspects of the modern pet-spending boom, portraiture isn't so much new as it is newly democratized. Oil paintings of loyal dogs and manor lords predate photography; snapshots of well-heeled pets go back to the days of Mathew Brady. To our modern eyes, surviving nineteenth-century pet portraits have an oddly formal look. The children are well dressed; the pets, seated at their feet or comically positioned at eye level, appear unusually docile. Some of the stillness can be attributed to the requirements of photography in the age of slow film. But the appearance also speaks to the era and its ideas about how people and animals should behave. It was not a time of big hugs, sloppy kisses, and lounging on the living-room couch—for the kid or for the dog.

So what do our hard drives full of contemporary pet photos—on vacation! in the dog park! wearing sweaters! eating premium kibble!—say about this era? I've sought out the obvious and not-so-obvious ways that pet keeping has mirrored the economic, political, scientific, and social developments of our times. Pets are a global and timeless phenomenon, but the specific ways we treat our pets are sculpted by the broader currents of our history. Still, as I visited leash-law activists and day-spa entrepreneurs and veterinary miracle workers, I found myself wrestling with a question that seems to pop up whenever we discuss our generosity to animals: Is there something creepy about all of this? The lives of our pets, already shaped by the forces of contemporary culture, are also a subject of that culture's anxious self-doubts. Is modern petmania, we wonder, a sign of modern lunacy?

A pessimistic cultural critic might say yes, casting our culture of pet ownership as one of those odd public obsessions that characterize empires headed for a cliff—akin to seventeenth-century Dutch tulipmania or some inane dance craze of the roaring twenties. Like twenty-first-century pet portraitists, such a critic would be joining a venerable tradition: Pet party poopers existed well before the age of pet party planners. Ancient Rome's Plutarch attacked "persons who spend and lavish upon brute beasts that affection and kindness which nature has implanted in us to be bestowed upon those of our own kind"; twentieth-century Britain's George Orwell derided "the animal cult [that] runs right through the nation." In 1969, when few people had ever heard of a full-time professional dog walker, a writer named Kathleen Szasz dedicated an entire book to blasting what she called "Petishism," drawing comparisons between pet lovers and Nazis. "The 'humanization' of animals is often a means towards the 'dehumanization' of people one hates," she writes. Five years later, a dyspeptic *TIME* story declared pet spending out of control: "The U.S. pet set gets not only more nutritious meals but also better medical care and vastly more affection than the great majority of the world's people," it said. And that was when Iams was a small feed company.

Seeking out similar contradictions has grown even easier in the decades since. On one level, the contrasts can be staggering. I did my interviews with San Francisco's impassioned dog-park people at the same time as the cash-strapped state government announced plans to close several state parks designed for humans. The growth of veterinary insurance coincides with a crisis in human medicine, where 47 million American humans lack their own health insurance. Around the time I visited VHUP's brand-new 9,200-square-foot imaging center with its new linear accelerator, newspapers in Sri Lanka reported that the island nation of 19 million—hardly the world's poorest country—had also gotten its first such device. For people. Even if comparing domestic veterinary medicine to overseas human health care is a case of comparing apples to oranges, it remains deeply troubling to know that the hospital that pioneered the life-extending surgical miracle of the feline kidney transplant is located in a city where more than twenty thousand unwanted animals are euthanized each year.

No wonder, then, that the perpetual stream of gushing press accounts about pet spending is invariably followed, like a UPS truck being chased by an Akita, by letters such as this one sent to the *New York Times* in 2006: "Our dogs have a better standard of living than millions of people in other parts of the world. While I do understand the need for companionship, especially in New York, this dog obsession has gone too far. Have we isolated ourselves so much that we need dogs to start a conversation or meet people?"

I tend to disagree with the last-days-of-Rome interpretation, and not merely because Murphy has made a sucker out of me. True, the more extreme manifestations of modern pet culture—like pricey designer outfits whose couture credentials mean nothing to even the most genetically perfect Boston terrier—mimic a decadence we associate with the *Titanic* about ten minutes before it struck the iceberg. A society where people wait years for an au courant dog from a breeder even as hundreds of thousands of strays get put down every year certainly has some 'splaining to do. But to a large extent, the places where our pet keeping falls short of our professed values are themselves a reflection of our broader human shortcomings—materialism, inequality, poverty at home and abroad. Those things would be there with or without the time and money some of us devote to pets. It's a logical fallacy to imagine the symptom as the cause. School budgets, for example, don't get slashed because people decide they'd rather hire trainers for dogs than teachers for children; they get slashed because of political decisions. (Yes, you could argue that the tax cuts that cause such budget troubles are the same ones that put cash into the pockets of well-heeled pet spenders, but that's an awfully convoluted chain of causality.)

At the end of the day, the things I do for Murphy, the things you might do for your pet, are consumer choices. No one starts talking about third-world starvation when someone spends $3,000 on a flat-screen TV. Spend the same on a year's worth of high-end organic pet food and you're liable to get accused of taking food from the mouths of malnourished humans. I suspect that neither the pet-food buyer nor the flat-screen-TV buyer would say that this particular $3,000 expenditure is the only reason they don't send an equal sum to a food bank. Insofar as people make choices in order to spend time or money on their pet, the choice is among consumer options. It's not Murphy's meds versus pharmaceuticals for needy Sri Lankans; it's Murphy's meds versus a new video camera for, um, me. If we're going to start enumerating immoral consumer choices, I'd argue that spending money to care for a pet would rank near the bottom of the list.

On a philanthropic level, it can be a different story, with governments and donors choosing to devote money to animals that might indeed have gone to some other good cause. About a year after Leona Helmsley's multimillion-dollar bequest to her lapdog set off a torrent of nasty tabloid stories about the hotelier, a new revelation about Helmsley's will met with a much warmer reception. It turned out that Helmsley had also set up a charitable trust of between $5 billion and $8 billion that would be devoted to the welfare of dogs. The news immediately softened the reputation of a woman who had, in life and in death, served as a symbol of unbridled greed. For people uncomfortable with modern pet culture, though, Helmsley's dog-trust bequest ought to be far more disturbing than the $12 million she left her little Maltese. If it hadn't been for her love of dogs, that $12 million might have been added to some already-wealthy human Helmsley descendant's loot. The vastly larger sum she steered to charity, on the other hand, could have gone to human charitable causes had Helmsley not been a dog lover. Could the philanthropic impulses of Helmsley and other animal philanthropists have been better used in, say, the fight against HIV in sub-Saharan Africa?

Perhaps. But people donate to all sorts of causes. Some preserve art; others beautify roadways; others subsidize public television. If we weighed every act of generosity against a utilitarian standard of life and death, a great many worthy recipients—many of them far better funded than animal charities—would also have to be cut off. Like spending $10,000 on veterinary surgery for your beloved cat, an animal-charity donation may not be the single most altruistic gesture in history. In a world full of things we really should be ashamed of, though, I believe it remains a generous, loving act.

For whatever reason, it is spending on pets—more often than purchases of new televisions or donations to art museums—that prompts soul-searching about affluence and want. I suspect the contrasts will grow in the next few years. As I write this, in the summer of 2008, the stock market is tumbling and the press is full of doomsday predictions about the American economy. The pet industry's trade association has yet to register a drop in sales, which says something about our priorities in troubled times. But lots of people go broke betting that any one industry is truly recession proof. Either way, the juxtaposition of pet spending and human foreclosures will invite all sorts of easy criticism.

Still, I suspect pets will remain a better bellwether of our shifting culture than of our short-term economic cycle. I chalk it up to the same reason that the role of animals prompts so much anxious self-examination: Pets, and how we treat them, are a public reflection of our deepest individual values. The ways we express those values—whether they have to do with nurturing, family, generosity, or compassion—have changed dramatically over the years and will continue to change as the decades roll on. Yesteryear's stiff pet portrait in the sitting room is this year's e-mailed snapshot of Murphy drooling on the kitchen floor. What will society look like down the line? Just take a peek at the four-legged creature in the family picture. I guarantee you he'll be there.

Notes

A NOTE ON ANIMALS AND TERMINOLOGY

There are a lot of animals worth writing about in this country, but I'm focusing on just one class of them: pets. To define that group, I've relied on Thorstein Veblen, who made a distinction between animals with no specific economic purpose—pets—and the beasts of burden that were then far more common in American households. Of course, even today, there are shades of gray. One household's economically useless Labrador might be another household's economically worthwhile tool for guarding against burglars. But the basic idea still holds. Thus, except when they influence pet ownership, I've steered clear of discussing livestock or seeing-eye dogs or show dogs or commercial fighting dogs. It's not that they aren't interesting. It's just that when we spend time or money on a financial investment, it's a more or less rational economic choice. When we make significant changes in our spending on or bonding with a creature we keep for blissfully irrational reasons, it's a different thing entirely.

Likewise, while Americans have pets of all sorts, the bulk of the recent pet-care evolution centers on those old standbys the dog and the cat. I've thus focused on those animals to the exclusion of nearly all others. None of that, though, should be interpreted as a slight to owners of parrots or ferrets.

Speaking of which, in jurisdictions including the city of Boulder and the state of Rhode Island, people who have exotic and ordinary animals alike are not called owners. In the eyes of the law, they're *guardians*. To further muddy the picture, many scholars would describe the pets as *companion animals,* the word *pet* having been deemed patronizing. All of these terms are freighted with moral and legal implications. As an agnostic about those issues, I use them all interchangeably.

PROLOGUE: FROM DOGHOUSE TO OUR HOUSE

The book on adopting a dog was *Successful Dog Adoption,* by Sue Sternberg (Indianapolis: Howell Book House, 2003).

Media stories about pet luxury are an almost daily occurrence in news pages, business sections, and lifestyle articles, often under play-on-words headlines. Take these, all from just one month: "Gifts for Pets Are Cat's Meow," *Deseret Morning News* (Salt Lake City), November 21, 2007; "Pawty Hearty," *Arizona Republic,* November 17, 2007; "Haute Dogs and Cool Cats; Latest Trends in Pet Care Make Pampering Easy," *Dayton* (Ohio) *Daily News,* November 10, 2007; "It's a Ruff Life: Some Dogs Have Strollers," *Greenville* (S.C.) *News*, November 9, 2007; "Dog Peddling," *Washington Post,* November 8, 2007; and "Malls Wish You a Furry Christmas: Special Nights Set Aside for Pets to Visit Santa Claus," *Fort Worth Star-Telegram,* November 7, 2007. The *BusinessWeek* cover story ("The Pet Economy: Americans Now Spend $41 Billion on Their Pets. And a Lot of Humans Are Getting Rich") ran August 6, 2007, on p. 44.

For representative media-circus coverage of Leona Helmsley's will, see the cover of the August 29, 2007, *New York Post*. Headline: "Rich Bitch."

Most of the rundown of historic royal pet keeping comes from the brilliant *In the Company of Animals: A Study of Human-Animal Relationships,* by James Serpell (Cambridge: Canto, 1996), pp. 43–55. The story of Mary, Queen of Scots's beheading appears in *For the Love of Animals: The Rise of the Animal Protection Movement,* by Kathryn

Shevelow (New York: Henry Holt, 2008), p. 60. The information about King Charles II's lost dog and William and Mary's pugs comes from *The Animal Estate: The English and Other Creatures in the Victorian Age*, by Harriet Ritvo (Cambridge: Harvard University Press, 1997).

The passage about Parisian pet keeping appears in *The Beast in the Boudoir: Petkeeping in Nineteenth-Century Paris*, by Kathleen Kete (Berkeley: University of California Press, 1994). The taxes designed to dissuade proletarians from keeping dogs are discussed on pp. 40–48.

The Thorstein Veblen quote comes from his *The Theory of the Leisure Class*, unabridged version (Mineola: Dover Editions, 1994), p. 86.

The paragraph on American pet history owes much to the exhaustive *Pets in America: A History*, by Katherine C. Grier (Chapel Hill: University of North Carolina Press, 2006). Her discussion of pre-Columbian and early American pets comes on pp. 20–23; the bird craze is described on pp. 46–52; and FDR's dog is discussed on pp. 224–25. The passage on the political brouhaha over Fala's Aleutian journey comes from *Freedom from Fear: The American People in Depression and War, 1929–1945*, by David M. Kennedy (Oxford: Oxford University Press, 1999), p. 824.

The Swiss chalet doghouse is produced in South Carolina by La Petite Maison, Inc. See "Housing Boom Reaches Its Tail End," Newark *Star-Ledger*, November 16, 2006. The price comes from wellappointedhouse.com, which sells the chalet as well as "Colonial Mansion," "French Chateau," and "English Cottage" models.

CHAPTER ONE: THE $43-BILLION FUR BABY

The pet-ownership figures are from 2006 and 2000, and appear in the American Veterinary Medical Association's *U.S. Pet Ownership & Demographics Sourcebook* (Schaumburg, Ill.: AVMA, 2007). The human population figure comes from the U.S. Census Bureau's State & County QuickFacts, http://quickfacts.census.gov.

For Petco's purchase of stadium naming rights, see "What Is in a Name? A Lucrative $60 Million," *San Diego Union Tribune*, March 18, 2004.

The statistics on the size of the 2007 and 2008 pet expos were provided by the American Pet Products Manufacturers' Association. I interviewed its president, Bob Vetere, several times in 2007 and 2008. The APPMA's statistics about the size of the pet industry, as well as various sectors of it, can be found in the organization's 550-page *2007–2008 National Pet Owners Survey* (Greenwich: APPMA, 2007). In late 2008, it changed its name to the American Pet Products Association.

I interviewed Mike Dillon in June 2007 and April 2008.

The Packaged Facts projection about future pet industry growth comes from the firm's 2007 *Pet Supplies in the U.S.* report. The firm sells this report to businesses for $3,500.

Vetere made his statement comparing the pet industry to other industries at the Global Pet Expo press conference, February 15, 2008.

In 2006, according to the National Retail Hardware Association, hardware stores did $36.8 billion worth of business. However, stores classified as "Home Centers" and "Lumberyards" brought in $180.3 billion and $83.5 billion, respectively. Home Depot alone had $90.8 billion in sales. ("Retail D-I-Y Market Profile: 2007 Annual Report" by Dan Tratensek and Chris Jensen, *Hardware Retailing,* December 2007, pp. 25–34.)

The *Pet Business* stories appeared in the magazine's Show Daily on February 14 and February 15, 2008.

The history of pet spending is discussed in "Pet Stocks Can Endure Tough Markets," by Karen Richardson, *Wall Street Journal,* June 26, 2006. Both Mike Dillon, of *Pet Industry Weekly,* and David Lummis, of Packaged Facts, also discussed the surprising impact of September 11 and Hurricane Katrina.

The "mommy" and "daddy" data were compiled by the American Animal Hospital Association and appeared in the May 2002 *American Demographics*. The *Bark* magazine figure comes from its January/February 2008 issue.

VPI announced its top names in an August 22, 2007, press release. The full list of most popular dog names is: Max, Molly, Buddy, Bella, Lucy, Maggie, Daisy, Jake, Bailey, and Rocky. For cats, the top names are: Max, Chloe, Lucy, Tigger, Tiger, Smokey, Oliver, Bella, Sophie, and Princess. The Social Security Administration lists Jacob as that year's top name for boys and Isabella as the fourth most popular girls' name. Sophia (Sophie) ranked ninth for both human and feline females.

The statistics about childless households as a percentage of pet spending come from the 2007 Packaged Facts report *Premium Pet Demographics*. The figures about pet ownership among childless and nonchildless households come from the AVMA's 2007 sourcebook cited above.

The gift statistics appear in the APPMA's 2007 pet owners' survey cited above. It also reports that 8 percent of dog owners had commissioned portraits of their pets and 6 percent had thrown them holiday parties.

The statistic about human-only companies entering the pet market is cited in the 2007 Packaged Facts report *Pet Travel and Convenience Products*. I interviewed Shel Singh at the March 2007 H. H. Backer pet trade show in Atlantic City, New Jersey. I interviewed Keith Benson several times in 2007 and 2008.

The history of Petco is laid out in *Think Big, Act Small: How America's Best Performing Companies Keep the Start-Up Spirit Alive,* by Jason Jennings (New York: Portfolio, 2005). Chapter 8 focuses on Petco. The PetSmart figures come from the firm's 2008 annual financial report.

The statistics on chain stores and mass retailers as a percentage of the market can be found in the 2007 Packaged Facts report *Pet Supplies in the U.S.* and the 2006–2007 Pet Products News International *State of the Industry Report*.

Katherine Grier's exhibit is also collected in *At Home with Animals* (McKissick Museum, 2005).

David Lummis delivered his presentation on February 15, 2008, at the Global Pet Expo.

CHAPTER TWO: MAN'S BEST FRIENDSTER

Most of the scenes and interviews for this chapter come from my visit to the Chihuahua Meetup in New York in December 2007 and an earlier swim-party gathering in June 2007. I also interviewed Ada Nieves several other times in 2007 and 2008.

James Serpell discussed the tie between pet ownership and fraying social support networks in a presentation at the Winterthur Museum and Gardens, Winterthur, Delaware, in November 2007.

The research on dogs and hypertensive stockbrokers and heart-attack patients is discussed in "The Last Meow," by Burkhard Bilger, *New Yorker,* September 8, 2003. Nicholas Epley's article, "Creating Social Connection Through Inferential Reproduction: Loneliness and Perceived Agency in Gadgets, Gods, and Greyhounds," written with Scott Akalis, Adam Waytz, and John T. Cacioppo, appears in *Psychological Science,* vol. 19, no. 2, 2008, pp. 114–20.

"Dogs as Human Companions: A Review of the Relationship," by Lynete A. Hart, an essay in James Serpell, ed., *The Domestic Dog: Its Evolution, Behavior, and Interactions with People* (Cambridge: Cambridge University Press, 1995), provides a solid overview of the research. I interviewed Lisa Jane Hardy in October 2007 and April 2008.

The passage by Malcolm Gladwell is from *The Tipping Point: How Little Things Can Make a Big Difference* (New York: Little, Brown, 2000), p. 41.

The Dogster stats were retrieved from dogster.com/about in December 2007.

CHAPTER THREE: IT'S ME *AND* THE DOG

Except where noted, the scenes and interviews in this chapter were compiled on a reporting trip to San Francisco in January 2008.

The Gavin Newsom quote comes from "Lax Leash Law Has Some San Franciscans at End of Their Rope," by Chelsea Deweese, *Wall Street Journal,* November 25, 2005. Two years later, Newsom's onetime Green Party opponent in the mayoral election, Matt Gonzalez, told the *Los Angeles Times* that "the dog lobby has a Tammany Hall reality. Someone walks into your office and says 'I got 30 votes here, what can you do for me?' They walk precincts. It's the way the religious right does politics." ("S.F. Hot Under the Dog Collar," by John M. Glionna, February 17, 2007.) Gonzalez himself had the backing of a dog group called Mutts for Matt.

Arnold Levine's account of having feces put in his car comes from the same story.

The Ocean Beach Dog Web site is http://oceanbeachdog.home .mindspring.com, accessed in May 2008.

The role of the dog feces issue in Harvey Milk's political rise is described in *The Mayor of Castro Street,* by Randy Shilts (New York: St. Martin's, 1982). "It's symbolic of all the problems of irresponsibility we face in big, depersonalized, alienating urban societies," Milk said of uncleaned poop.

The statistics on San Francisco's canine population are cited in "S.F.'s Best Friend," by Meredith May, *San Francisco Chronicle,* June 17, 2007. Estimates of pet populations are inherently tricky because, although many places require pet licenses, many people fail to comply. The statistics on the city's child population and median home value come from the U.S. Census Bureau's 2006 American Community Survey for San Francisco, California.

David Kulick's quote appears in "Draft Plan for Dogs Provokes Outpouring," by Rachel Gordon, *San Francisco Chronicle,* August 23, 2001. Other coverage from the paper's archives includes: "Commission Fences in Dogs at S.F.'s Small Parks; Angry Pet Owners Pledge to Break Rule," by Heather Knight, May 9, 2002; "Supervisor's Proposal Would Unbuckle Dog Leash Law," by Rachel Gordon, October 4, 2002; "Dog-Eat-Dog Battle for Sunnyside Turf; Neighbors Squabble over Off-Leash Use," by Kathleen Sullivan, April 9, 2004; and "Dog Owners, Parents at Odds Over Space; Duboce Park Has Been Turned into a Battle Ground," by Carolyn Jones, April 1, 2005.

Richard Avanzino's statement is reported in "Canine Lovers Win Fight Over Off-Leash Walking," by Steve Rubenstein, *San Francisco Chronicle,* March 18, 1995, and "Fur Set to Fly Over Leash Law; SPCA Chief Calls for Dog Lovers' Protest at Ocean Beach," by Steve Rubenstein, *San Francisco Chronicle,* January 10, 1997.

Michelle Parris's story is covered in "Anger Unleashed: Dog Lovers Protest Pacifica Woman's Leash-Law Citation in S.F.," by Peter Fimrite, *San Francisco Chronicle,* November 13, 1997, and "Dog Walker's Case in Hands of Judge," by Peter Fimrite, *San Francisco Chronicle,* November 17, 1997.

I visited Sky Harbor airport in February 2008 and DBI in June 2007.

The research about pets as a factor in whether people flee domestic abuse was discussed in "Research on the Link Between Animal Abuse and Family Violence: Helping the Public to Understand What We Know as Well as Questions We Can't Yet Answer," a presentation at the American Humane conference in Alexandria, Virginia, on September 28, 2007, by Dr. Frank Ascione of Utah State University. The Naples facility is covered in "A Haven for Abuse Victims Who Keep Their Pets Close; Organizations Push Shelters to Offer On-site Boarding," by Sharon L. Peters, *USA Today,* March 18, 2008. Maine's groundbreaking law is cited in "The Case of the Battered Pet," by Barry Yeoman, *O: The Oprah Magazine,* June 2008.

The post-Katrina measure is discussed in "No Pet Left Behind: Accommodating Pets in Emergency Planning," by Hillary A. Leonard and Debra L. Scammon, *Journal of Public Policy and Marketing,* Spring

2007, and "In Crisis, No Pet Left Behind; Man's Best Friends to Be Protected," by Anne Gowen, *Washington Post,* February 22, 2007. Christina Coleman is quoted in "Residents Forced Out of Apartments Fear for Pets; Visit by Bush Delays Return Even More," by Jeff Shields, *Sun Sentinel* (Fort Lauderdale), September 15, 2001.

The Duboce Park renovations were discussed with me in an interview with David Troup of Duboce Park Dog. The ticket amounts are covered in "Barking Up That Same Old Tree; As New Set of Leash-Law Fights Heats Up, Even Those in Fray Tire of Seemingly Intractable Battles," by Ilene Lelchuk, *San Francisco Chronicle,* July 6, 2005.

I attended dog court on January 17, 2008.

Chapter Four: Trading Up

Except where noted, the scenes and interviews in this chapter come from my visit to Pet Fashion Week 2007, August 18–19, 2007.

I interviewed Janet Lee by phone after Pet Fashion Week, in August 2007. The research on overspending appears in "Does Excessive Buying for Self Relate to Spending on Pets?" by Nancy M. Ridgeway et al., *Journal of Business Research,* vol. 61, no. 5, May 2008, p. 392.

Details about Curious paper can be found at http://www.curious collection.com/.

The discussion of New Luxury comes from *Trading Up: Why Consumers Want New Luxury Goods—and How Companies Create Them,* by Michael J. Silverstein and Neil Fiske (New York: Portfolio, rev. ed. 2005). The quoted passage appears on p. 51.

I interviewed Mike Dillon several times in 2007 and 2008. The statistics about high earners come from the August 2007 Packaged Facts report *Premium Pet Demographics,* p. 3.

I visited Vicki Lynne Morgan's class at the County College of Morris in June 2007. Seth Kaplan showed me around the 2007 Global Pet Expo in Orlando. I visited his Long Island store in July 2007.

Chapter Five: Hip Replacements and Health Plans

Except where noted, the scenes and interviews from this chapter come from the week I spent shadowing Dr. Chick Weisse's team at the University of Pennsylvania's veterinary hospital.

The passage from *All Creatures Great and Small* (New York: St. Martin's Press, 1972) appears on p. 7.

The American Animal Hospital Association's 2004 pet-owner survey asked 1,220 respondents whether they would risk their life for their pets. Fifty-six percent said they were "very likely," and 37 percent said "somewhat likely." Only 7 percent chose the third option, "not at all likely." The prevalence of ACL surgery, including the *JAVMA* article, is cited in "An $80 Pet's $6,000 Bill; A Human Jock's Ailment Also Plagues Pooches," by Kevin Helliker, *Wall Street Journal,* April 11, 2006.

The insight into when cats became a vet-school focus comes from *Valuing Animals: Veterinarians and Their Patients in Modern America,* by Susan D. Jones (Baltimore: Johns Hopkins University Press, 2003), p. 136. Jones's book is a wonderfully comprehensive history by a uniquely qualified historian: She earned her Ph.D. in history only after earning her Doctor of Veterinary Medicine degree.

The statistics on women veterinary students were provided to me by the American Association of Veterinary Medical Colleges. See also "The Gender Shift in Veterinary Medicine: Cause and Effect," by Carin Smith, *Veterinary Clinics of America: Small Animal Practice,* March 2006 (Vol. 36, Issue 2, pp. 329–39). Statistics on postgraduate specialization were given to me by the American Veterinary Medical Association. The Missouri rural-vet legislation is reported in "Governor Pledges $500,000 to Ease Rural Vet Shortage; Missouri Lawmakers Jump on the Loan-Repayment Bandwagon," by Jennifer Fiala, *DVM Newsmagazine,* November 2007.

The total veterinary spending figure comes from the APPMA 2007 survey. The average veterinary salary was provided to me by the AVMA, as was the estimate of average student-loan debt. The July 2003 *Consumer Reports* story "Veterinary Care Without the Bite" is reprinted at http://www.consumerreports.org/Pets (accessed June 4, 2008). It is also discussed in *Tell Me Where It Hurts: A Day of Humor, Healing and Hope in My Life as an Animal Surgeon,* by Dr. Nick Trout (New York: Broadway Books, 2008).

I interviewed Reimer in March 2008.

I visited Metropolitan Veterinary Associates in November 2007.

The statistics for the growth of the veterinary chains are presented in "The New Era of Corporate Practice," by Brendan Howard, *Veterinary Economics,* November 1, 2007. VCA's revenues and stock performance are laid out in the *VCA Antech Inc. Annual Report,* SEC form 10-K (Los Angeles: VCA Antech, 2008).

Lilly announced its pet division in a press release titled "Eli Lilly and Company Enters Companion Animal Health Market," January 15, 2007. Reconcile's release is reported in "Eli Lilly Gets OK to Market Antidepressant to Dogs Who Act Up When Separated from Owners," Associated Press wire, April 25, 2007. Pfizer's two new drugs are discussed in "Animal Drug Sales Boom; Owners Drive Growth in Specialized Medicines," by Catherine Ho, *Detroit Free Press,* July 6, 2007. One estimate about pet obesity can be found in the American Veterinary Medical Association's April 1, 2008, *Collection Summary: Obesity in Dogs,* http://www.avma.org/avmacollections/obesity_dogs/summary.asp (accessed July 15, 2008).

The trends for geriatric animals were provided by AVMA.

The APPMA estimates that there are a total of 2 million pet insurance customers, the number presented at the 2008 Global Pet Expo press conference. A release announcing the numbers was called "Pet Pampering and Pet Health Insurance Drive Pet Industry Sales to Another All Time High" (APPMA, February 15, 2008). The growth-rate estimate comes from the May 2008 Packaged Facts report *Pet Insurance in North America,* executive summary, p. 3. Contrary to the APPMA, Packaged Facts estimates that only 850,000 pets are insured, but agrees that the field is on the verge of dramatic growth. The industry's history is also described in the document. Packaged Facts' David Lummis described the new players in an interview in April 2008. Lummis noted that the United States is well behind countries including Great Britain and Sweden in the percentage of pets who are insured, something he speculated could be due to people in those countries being more accustomed to collective medical care.

The animal beneficiaries of In Memory of Magic are all listed on the charity's Web site, imom.org. The specifics of the closed cases can be found at http://www.imom.org/pin/closed/index.htm (accessed June 5, 2008).

Chapter Six: Breeding the Perfect Beast

The 2008 Westminster Kennel Club show was held in Madison Square Garden on February 11 and 12, 2008.

Uno's postvictory schedule is described in "Uno Makes Westminster History," Associated Press, February 13, 2008, and "Star Treat-Ment," by Julia Szabo, *New York Post,* May 18, 2008. Schieffer spoke on *Meet the Press,* February 17, 2008.

I visited Amish country several times in May and June 2008.

The Pets of Bel Air scandal coverage includes "A Favorite Pet Store to Celebs Shut Down," celebritydogwatcher.com, December 12, 2007; "Richard Belzer Assists in Puppy Mill Protest," celebritydog watcher.com, December 20, 2007; "Humane Society Traces Expensive Pups to Pet Mills," by Rebecca Cathcart, *New York Times,* December 12, 2007; "Animal Group Says Westside Pet Shop Sold from Puppy Mills," by Carla Hall, *Los Angeles Times,* December 12, 2007; and "Hollywood Pet Shop Scandal!" by Johnny Dodd, *People,* January 21, 2008, p. 144.

I interviewed Bob Baker and Bill Smith several times in May and June 2008. Oprah Winfrey's puppy-mill show first aired on April 4, 2008.

The killing of the kennel dogs and its aftermath were reported in "Berks Kennel Owners Kill Their 80 Dogs," by Amy Worden, *The Philadelphia Inquirer,* August 13, 2008, and "With Shootings in Mind, Rendell Touts Kennel Bill," by Amy Worden, *Philadelphia Inquirer,* August 17, 2008. Ed Rendell described his efforts against puppy mills in remarks at the University of Pennsylvania's Veterinary School in December 2007.

There are countless books, and just as many theories, about the evolution of dogs. I was particularly influenced by a concise presentation by James Serpell at the Winterthur Museum in Delaware in November 2007. I also enjoyed the discussion in *Companion Animals in Society,* by Stephen Zawistowski (Clifton Park: Delmar Cencage, 2008), pp. 25–29, which describes the ideas of Raymond and Linda Coppinger in *Dogs: A New Understanding of Canine Origin, Behavior and Evolution* (Chicago: University of Chicago Press, 2001). The ideas about how dogs have evolved to mirror children in their effect on human adults' emotions are discussed in "Why Do People Love Their Pets?" by John Archer, *Evolution and Human Behavior,* vol. 18, no. 4, 1997, pp. 237–59. A less charitable (to the dogs) take appears in *The Truth About Dogs,* by Stephen Budiansky (New York: Penguin, 2000), and a skeptical look at breeders is featured in *Eminent Dogs, Dangerous Men,* by Donald McCaig (Guilford: Lyons Press, 1991).

I interviewed Hal Herzog in December 2007. His essays about dog breed popularity include "Forty-two Thousand and One Dalmatians: Fads, Social Contagion, and Dog Breed Popularity" (*Society and*

Animals, vol. 14, 2006, pp. 383–97), in which the statistics I cited appear, and "The Effects of Winning the Westminster Kennel Club Dog Show on Dog Breed Popularity" (*Journal of the American Veterinary Medical Association,* vol. 225, no. 3, August 2004, pp. 365–67).

The statistics on where dogs were acquired appear in the APPMA's 2007 pet owner survey.

I interviewed Steve Zawistowski several times in 2008.

I visited Beowulf in October 2007.

I visited PAWS in October 2007.

The Discovery/Petfinder deal is reported in "Animal Planet Buys Petfinder.com," by Meg James, *Los Angeles Times,* November 3, 2006. The crew from the Petfinder TV show appeared at Global Pet Expo 2008 and discussed the site's popularity with nonadopters.

PetSmart's transporting of unwanted animals is described in Zawistowski's *Companion Animals,* p. 81.

I interviewed Eve Yohalem in December 2007 and spoke with Simon Brodie several times in 2007 and 2008. Brodie's past legal troubles are reported in "'Designer Pet' Founder Guilty in British Scheme," by Penni Crabtree, *San Diego Union-Tribune,* October 28, 2006.

Allerca is cited as a top invention in *TIME's* November 13, 2006, issue, p. 66. The Toyger is featured in "Meet the Toyger: America's Next Supercat," by Kenneth Miller, *LIFE,* February 23, 2007, pp. 6–9. The criticism of hybrids is the subject of Jon Mooallem's brilliant "The Modern Kennel Conundrum," *New York Times Magazine,* February 4, 2007, p. 42. For the story of Booger II, see "American Pays $50,000 to Clone Dead Dog," by Anna Fifield, *Financial Times,* February 15, 2008.

Brodie shared with me examples of the hostile e-mails he had received.

I visited FlexPetz's Manhattan location in February 2008 and interviewed CEO Marlena Cervantes in January 2008. The company's Massachusetts troubles are cited in "Dog Rentals Irk Lawmakers; Company Plans Incursion into Mass., but Some Say It's Barking Up the Wrong Tree," by John P. Kelly, *Patriot Ledger,* March 11, 2008.

CHAPTER SEVEN: LEGAL BEAGLES

I interviewed Ben DeLong in December 2007.

The estimates on the size of the pet-food market are cited in the APPMA's 2007 *National Pet Owners Survey.*

The statistics on Menu's size and location come from the brand's corporate parent, Menu Foods Income Fund, and can be found at http://web.archive.org/web/20060515054228/www.menufoods.com/about_us/facilities.html.

Marty Becker's quote appears in "Pet Food Inquiry Expands," by Julie Schmit and Elizabeth Weise, *USA Today,* March 20, 2007.

The pet-food recall of early 2007 was the subject of a torrent of news coverage. One new-media Web site stood out: www.petconnection.com, whose tireless Gina Spadafori—herself a news industry veteran—and Becker, a veterinarian, first raised the alarm about the recall, directing panicked pet owners to reliable sources of information. *USA Today* also covered the scandal doggedly.

Robert Byrd spoke at an appropriations subcommittee hearing on April 12, 2007.

The number of fatalities remains deeply disputed. Because of delays in public announcements about the poisoning, many people may have been unaware of why their pet died until well after the fact.

The trail of the poison, and the continuing uncertainty over the numbers, are discussed in "Pet Detectives Work Hard, but Deaths Are Tough to Solve," by Elizabeth Weise and Julie Schmit, *USA Today,* April 6, 2007.

The rise of animal-law courses and Bob Barker's donations are described in "Beast Practices: High-Profile Cases Are Putting Plenty of Bite into the Lively Field of Animal Law," by Terry Carter, *American Bar Association Journal,* November 2007. A spokeswoman at the National Center for Animal Law told me she expects the number to rise.

The history of animal-cruelty laws is the subject of "Desecrating the Ark: Animal Abuse and the Law's Role in Prevention," by Margit Livingston, *Iowa Law Review,* vol. 87, no. 1, 2001. The New York law in question is N.Y. Rev. Stat. tit. 6, § 26 (1866). The emerging ideology of kindness is discussed in Grier's *Pets in America* as well as *Reckoning with the Beast: Animals, Pain, and Humanity in the Victorian Mind,* by James Turner (Baltimore: Johns Hopkins University Press, 1980). The Vermont law—and similar New York, Ohio, and Michigan measures—is also discussed in Livingston's *Iowa Law Review* article. In "The Calculus of Animal Valuation" (*Nebraska Law Review,* vol. 82, no. 3, 2004), she also notes that "under English common law individuals had only a very limited and qualified property interest in companion animals, such as dogs, cats, parrots, and singing birds. These animals were viewed as being kept at the owner's caprice, as having no intrinsic value, and as not being subject to an action for larceny."

I watched Livingston lecture about how the law has treated wrongful-death cases involving pets at an October 25, 2007, presentation at DePaul University College of Law cosponsored by the International Institute for Animal Law. The subject is also the focus of "Resolving Confusion in Pet Owner Tort Cases: Recognizing Pets' Anthropomorphic Qualities Under a Property Classification," by Lynn A. Epstein, *Southern Illinois Law Journal,* vol. 26, 2001; and "Recovery of 'Non-Economic' Damages for Wrongful Killing or Injury of Companion Animals: A Judicial and Legislative Trend," by Sonia S. Waisman and Barbara R. Newell, *Animal Law,* vol. 7, 2001.

The docket number for *Burgess v. Shampooch Pet Industries* is Kansas Court of Appeals 93698 (2006). Other cases involving significant payouts over wrongful pet deaths are discussed in "Jury Awards Dog Owner $39,000 in Malpractice Suit," by Jean-Paul Renaud, *Los Angeles Times,* February 24, 2004; and "Price of Killing Dog: $56,400," by Steve Mayes, *Oregonian,* June 1, 2006. The Kentucky horse case is *Burgess v. Taylor,* Kentucky Court of Appeals 44 S.W.3d 806 (2001).

I interviewed Phil Goldberg on June 2, 2008.

The history of contradictory rulings is highlighted in "The Future of Veterinary Malpractice Liability in the Care of Companion Animals," by Christopher Green, *Animal Law,* vol. 10, 2004. The reversed cases include a $40,000 verdict against a Texas Petco whose grooming salon allowed a schnauzer to escape and get hit by a car. In *Petco v. Schuster,* a Texas appeals court cut the payout by $35,000, to cover just replacement, training, and lawyers' fees.

Mary Ann Anzalone's case is *Anzalone v. Kragness* (Appellate Court of Illinois, First District, First Division, 826 N.E.2d 472, 2005). It is also discussed in "Court Sees More than One Way to Set Damages in Lawsuit for Dead Cat," by Steven P. Garmisa, *Chicago Daily Law Bulletin,* April 21, 2005, p. 1, and Livingston's "Calculus of Animal Valuation."

The tort-reform movement and Victor Schwartz's role are discussed in Stephanie Mencimer's *Blocking the Courthouse Door: How the Republican Party and Its Corporate Allies Are Taking Away Your Right to Sue* (New York: Free Press, 2006). His hiring by the Animal Health

Institute is reported in "Tort Watch for Animal Lovers," by Judy Sarasohn, *Washington Post,* December 29, 2005. His media accolades are described in a biography on the Web site of his firm, Shook, Hardy and Bacon, LLP. But that sketch leaves out a detail included in his article "Non-Economic Damages in Pet Litigation: The Serious Need to Preserve a Rational Rule," written with Emily J. Laird (*Pepperdine Law Review,* vol. 33, 2006): "Mr. Schwartz once owned two cats, Chat and Spinach. He believes that if Chat had lived the length of years of a human, Chat would have been admitted to a reasonably good law school. Spinach, on the other hand, would have been gainfully employed at a fast food chain."

The Perkins case is—hilariously—laid out in "To Love, Honor and Belly-Scratch; Marriages Come and Go. Judging by the Rising Number of Pet-Custody Disputes, Though, Some Passions Endure," by Sanjiv Bhattacharya, *Los Angeles Times Magazine,* January 9, 2005, p. 20. The same story contains the estimate about the rise in pet-custody litigation. The Helmsley coverage is described in notes above. I visited Palm Meow in January 2008. Perhaps the visit to retiree-heavy South Florida inspired me to lay out about twenty dollars for an Adams "Prepare a Last Will & Testament" CD. For the record, in the event of my untimely death, Murphy will go first to my in-laws, then to my wife's Auntie Lynn, and then to my uncle Frank. But he won't, alas, come with any money attached.

Chris Green, Victor Schwartz, and Jay Edelson all spoke alongside Margit Livingston at the aforementioned DePaul University session.

The advertising copy can be found on both the Pfizer and the Purina corporate Web sites.

The Menu settlement is presented in *in re: Pet Food Products Liability Legislation* in U.S. District Court, Camden, New Jersey, May 31, 2008.

CHAPTER EIGHT: TOY TOWN

Except where noted, my reporting about Starmark and Triple Crown Dog Academy occurred during a visit to Texas in July 2007.

The data about childless households and pets are from the 2007 AVMA *Sourcebook.*

The population figures for Hutto come from the U.S. Census Bureau's 2006 population estimates and 2000 and 1990 census figures.

Dr. Nicholas Dodman of Tufts University is probably the leading expert—and proponent—when it comes to the possibilities of veterinary antidepressants. He discusses them in *Puppy's First Steps: The Whole-Dog Approach to Raising a Happy, Healthy, Well-Behaved Puppy,* written with Lawrence Lindner (New York: Houghton Mifflin, 2007). He focuses more specifically on the issue of canine mental illness in *Dogs Behaving Badly* (New York: Bantam, 1999).

I interviewed Joe Markham in September 2007.

CHAPTER NINE: THE $100,000-A-YEAR DOG WALKER?

Except where noted, the scenes and information in this chapter come from my visits to Pet Chauffeur in July 2007, to Wag Hotel in January 2008, to the Groom Expo in September 2007, and to Petcetera by Lauren in March 2008.

The service-industry employment projections appear in "Occupational Employment Projections to 2016," by Arlene Dohm and Lynn Shniper, *Monthly Labor Review,* November 2007, p. 86. The journal is a publication of the federal Bureau of Labor Statistics. The BLS statistics on animal workers come from Bureau of Labor Statistics, U.S. Department of Labor, *Occupational Outlook Handbook, 2008–09 Edition,* "Animal Care and Service Workers," at http://www.bls.gov/oco/ ocos168.htm (accessed June 2, 2008). The $4 billion figure comes from the bureau's Consumer Expenditure Report, as cited in "Pet Industry 2008 Strategic Outlook," by Michael Dillon, Dillon Media LLC, February 2008.

I visited Rover Oaks in July 2007 and L.A. Dog Works in February 2008. In Palo Alto, Julia Cowles showed me Ralph's report card for January 16, 2008. The review of pet day-care facilities is "Day Care Is Going to the Dogs," by Anjali Athavaley and Lori Barrett, *Wall Street Journal,* June 28, 2008.

PetSmart's increased emphasis on services is discussed in PetSmart Inc., *2007 Annual Report,* SEC form 10-K (Phoenix: PetSmart, 2008), p. 3. The numbers on the growth of the boarding industry appear in the 2006 Marketresearch.com study "Pet Care Services in the U.S.," table 1-2.

The statistics on the grooming industry also come from that report, as do the figures on PetSmart and Petco. Petco's successes are discussed in its *2004 Annual Report,* SEC form 10-K (San Diego: Petco, 2005). Petco was purchased by a private-equity firm in 2006, so it is no longer required by the federal Securities and Exchange Commission to file the annual reports.

The statistics on outdoor pets come from the 2007 APPMA survey, pp. 53 and 154. The daytime stats are even more dramatic. In 2006, just 11 percent of dogs and 9 percent of cats were kept outside all day, down from 28 and 18 percent, respectively, eight years earlier. The percentage of dogs who sleep in their owner's bed and the growth of the grooming market are also cited in "Pet Care Services in the U.S.," table 1-6. The study of advertising is reported in "Animal-Companion Depictions in Women's Magazine Advertising," by Patricia F. Kennedy and Mary G. McGarvey, *Journal of Business Research,* vol. 61, no. 5, May 2008, p. 464.

The number of new grooming products and size of the shampoo market, as well as the growth of the grooming market, are cited in the 2005 Marketresearch.com study "Market Trends: Pet Grooming / Spa Products." The sizes and founding dates of the various pet-service trade associations were provided by the associations themselves.

Wages for animal service workers appear in the BLS "Animal Care and Service Workers" report cited above.

Chapter Ten: Trick or Treat

Except where noted, the reporting in this chapter comes from multiple interviews and training outings with Wendy Whiting and Leigh Siegfried in 2006, 2007, and 2008. I visited Whiting's session with the Monreals in November 2006. I visited Siegfried's sessions with Rick Cousins and Sue O'Brien in March 2007.

The training employment figures can be found in the BLS "Animal Care and Service Workers" report cited above and the BLS 2000 Industry-Occupation Employment Matrix. Bark Busters' statistics come from http://www.barkbusters.com/page.cfm/ID/4/FranchiseInfo/ (accessed June 2, 2008).

I interviewed Ian Dunbar in March 2008.

Colonel Konrad Most's book was reprinted in 2001 as *Training Dogs: A Manual* (Wenatchee, Wash.: Dogwise) and is discussed in "A Toast to Most: Konrad Most, a 1910 Pioneer in Animal Training," by Mary R. Burch and Duane Pickel, *Journal of Applied Behavior Analysis,* vol. 23, no. 2, summer 1990, pp, 263–64. Carl Spitz's role is described in *Handbook of Applied Dog Behavior and Training,* vol. 2, by Steven Lindsay (Ames: Iowa State University Press, 2001), p. 11. William

Koehler's manual is *The Koehler Method of Dog Training* (New York: Howell Book House, 1962). The passage is also cited in "Training a Dog with Treats, Not Tricks," by Adam Bryant, *New York Times,* March 14, 1996.

I interviewed Jean Donaldson in March 2008. Her book, *The Culture Clash* (2nd ed., Berkeley: James and Kenneth, 2005), includes a succinct history of recent dog-training developments and a compelling—and often hilarious—argument against pack theory. "The dog is supposedly staying up nights thinking of ways to stage a coup so you'd better keep him in place with plenty of coercion," she scoffs on p. 17.

Dunbar's lecture "Give Them a Scalpel and They Will Detect a Kiss," delivered in San Francisco in March 2005, has been released as a DVD by DogTec. Dunbar also provided the early numbers for APDT; the most recent membership figures come from the organization's Web site, http://www.apdt.com/about/who.aspx (visited June 2, 2008).

Cesar Millan's *Los Angeles Times* profile is "Redeeming Rover; Cesar Millan Helps Incorrigible Canines Roll Over a New Leaf, Find 'Fulfillment,'" by Bettijane Levine, September 25, 2002. *People*'s unsigned piece is "Ruffing It: Some Real Pit Bulls Live in Hollywood. Dog Disciplinarian Cesar Millan Gets Them in Line," December 9, 2002, p. 199.

Some examples of Millan's critics can be found in "The Snarls Don't Faze Trainer," by Sharon L. Peters, *USA Today,* May 31 2007; "The Dog Whisperer Should Just Shut Up," by Curtis Pesman, *Esquire,* October 2006, p. 182; and "Pack of Lies," by Mark Derr, *New York Times,* August 31, 2006. The Dunbar/Donaldson DVD is marketed by Dogtec.

The quoted sections from *Cesar's Way* (New York: Three Rivers, 2006) come from pp. 36, 25, 27, 28, 27, 56, 45, and 57, in order.

The "too stupid for words" passage is from p. 18 of *The Culture Clash*.

Chapter Eleven: From Alpo to Omega-3 Fatty Acids

I visited the Bogner plant and interviewed David Bogner in November 2007.

The no-kibble rule was on the list of rules e-mailed to me when I signed up for the Rawfeeding list on Yahoogroups.com.

The impact of the Menu recall on raw-food sales is noted in "Raw Pet Foods Are Popular, but . . . ," by Julie Schmit, *USA Today,* March 28,

2007. That same month, *Pet Food Industry* devoted its cover to the phenomenon, which it said represented 5 percent of the U.S. market. The future forecasts include the July 2007 Marketresearch.com report "Product Safety and Alternative Pet Foods."

The statistic on the current size of the pet-food market comes from the 2007 APPMA survey. The 1941 size is cited in "Birthing PFI and This Magazine," by Tim Phillips, *Petfood Industry Magazine,* October 2007.

An account of James Spratt's journey to England and the development of commercial pet food can be found in *The Lost History of the Canine Race: Our 15,000-Year Love Affair with Dogs,* by Mary Elizabeth Thurston (Kansas City: Andrews and McMeel, 1996). Spratt is also discussed in *Dog Shows and Doggy People,* by C. H. Lane (London: Hutchinson, 1902).

Webster Edgerly is discussed in "Hidden History of Ralston Heights," by Janet Six, *Archaeology*, May/June, 2004, and "They Eat What We Are," by Frederick Kaufman, *New York Times Magazine,* September 2, 2007. Interestingly, Edgerly is not mentioned in the Danforth biography on Purina's corporate Web site.

The Kasco advertisement is cited in Thurston's *Lost History,* p. 238. The significance of Dog Chow is noted in Grier's *Pets in America,* p. 283, and Phillips's "Birthing PFI." The statistic about new products appears in the May 2007 Marketresearch.com report "Global Pet Food Industry Outlook," figure 1-1.

The role of Hill's and Iams is discussed in "Iams and Hill's Wage a High-Fibre, Low-Cal War Against Ralston Purina and Carnation," by Laura Bird, *Adweek,* October 1, 1990, pp. 20–23. The broader evolution of the marketplace was described by Daniel Carey, a former Iams executive, whom I interviewed in December 2007.

The Iams purchase is the subject of "Procter & Gamble Is Buying Maker of Premium Pet Food," by Dana Canedy, *New York Times,* August 12, 1999. Mars's Nutro deal is reported in "Mars Inc. to Acquire Nutro Products Inc.," *Petfood Industry,* July 2, 2007. In early 2008, Alpo's decision to begin touting its beef as coming from black Angus cattle amused a group of Texas ranchers. "I don't think that your dog would care if it's from an Angus or a Hereford, or whatever," Donnell Brown told the *Fort Worth Star-Telegram.* "That product is mixed with corn, along with everything else. But if a buyer perceives it's a better value, because it's Angus, then they'll pay more." ("Ranchers Cash in on Black Angus Brand," by David Casstevens, January 27, 2008.)

The statistic about the largest pet-food firms appears in "Top Ten Global Petfood Leaders," by Jessica Taylor Bond, *Pet Food Industry,* January 2008, p. 19. The top two firms, Mars and Nestlé, control almost 50 percent of the global market. The U.S.-only figure was provided by the market-research firm Packaged Facts. The percentage of new food products labeled as "upscale" is cited in "The Premium Pet Demographic–Natural Pet Product Synergy," a presentation by Market Research Inc.'s David Lummis at Global Pet Expo 2008, February 15, 2008. Ol' Roy's status as the industry's best seller is reported in "Consumed: Ol' Roy," by Rob Walker, *New York Times Magazine,* February 22, 2004. The APPMA's Vetere and Market Research's Lummis confirmed that it retains that status.

In 1993, the Australian vet Ian Billinghurst published *BARF: Give Your Dog a Bone* (Lithgow, NSW: Ian Billinghurst, 1993).

Melinda Miller, Martin Goldstein, and Daniel Carey spoke at the Pet Food Nutrition seminar sponsored by Puppyworks/Petworks LLC at Mercy College, Dobbs Ferry, New York, on November 4, 2007.

Bravo!'s recall was announced in a September 18, 2007, press release that appeared on the FDA's Web site at http://www.fda.gov/oc/po/firmrecalls/bravo09_07.html (accessed August 13, 2008). The Wild Kitty recall was announced in a February 16, 2007, press release, at http://www.fda.gov/oc/po/firmrecalls/wildkitty02_07.html (accessed August 13, 2008).

Bierer spoke at a WholeMeals media luncheon at the 2008 Global Pet Expo in San Diego, February 15, 2008.

CHAPTER TWELVE: IT TAKES A VILLAGE TO RAISE A PUPPY

I visited the Lug-Nuts contest in Morningside Park on October 30, 2007. The same event is also the subject of the ESPN documentary *Don't Be Like Mike,* by Nik Kleinberg. Jane Kopelman described her program's history in a presentation at the 2007 American Humane convention in Alexandria, Virginia. I interviewed her several times in 2007 and 2008, and also interviewed Sternberg at the weight-pulling contest.

The idea of dividing APPMA's total spending by the total pet population comes from Grier's *Pets in America,* p. 316. "As a practice, pet keeping is cheap," she very persuasively argues. The Google Alert pointed me to this story: "Where Dogs Go to Relax," by Jean Spenner, *Saginaw News,* March 18, 2008.

The editorial about Vick appeared in the *Pittsburgh Post-Gazette* on August 25, 2007.

Elijah Anderson's discussion of dogs is in *Streetwise: Race, Class, and Change in an Urban Community* (Chicago: University of Chicago Press, 1990), pp. 222–28. The quoted passages appear on p. 222.

An authoritative study of why people relinquish dogs is "Characteristics of Shelter-Relinquished Animals and Their Owners Compared with Animals and Their Owners in U.S. Pet-Owning Households," by John C. New, Jr., et al., *Journal of Applied Animal Welfare Science,* vol. 3, no. 3, 2000, pp. 179–201. Other studies include "Human and Animal Factors Related to the Relinquishment of Dogs and Cats in 12 Selected Animal Shelters in the United States," by M. D. Salman et al., *Journal of Applied Animal Welfare Science,* vol. 1, no. 3, 1998, pp. 207–26, and "Reasons for Relinquishment of Companion Animals in U.S. Animal Shelters: Selected Health and Personal Issues," by Janet M. Scarlett et al., *Journal of Applied Animal Welfare Science,* vol. 2, no. 1, 1999, pp. 41–57. The National Council on Pet Population Study and Policy list of top reasons for animal relinquishment can be found at http://www.petpopulation.org/topten.html.

The major study of shelter statistics is described in "Population Dynamics, Overpopulation, and the Welfare of Companion Animals: New Insights on Old and New Data," by Stephen Zawistowski et al., *Journal of Applied Animal Welfare Science,* vol. 1, no. 3, 1998, pp. 193–206. It is also discussed in *Companion Animals in Society,* by Stephen Zawistowski (Clifton Park: Delmar Cencage, 2008). Zawistowski, a behaviorist and science adviser at the ASPCA, graciously shared advance copies of his book with me.

Ed Duvin's essay "In the Name of Mercy" appeared in *animalines* in 1989. It was reprinted at http://www.bestfriends.org/nomorehome lesspets/pdf/mercy.pdf (accessed June 4, 2008). He also sharply criticized shelters for the paucity of information about their populations and numbers of euthanasias. "Surrounded by the deaths of millions of precious beings, this industry has demonstrated neither the concern nor the competency to even validate the information upon which it bases life-and-death decisions," he wrote. In 2004, a group of shelter leaders signed the Asilomar Accords, which are supposed to standardize language and record keeping within the sprawling shelter world.

PETA's broadside appeared in the organization's fall 2005 newsletter, reprinted at http://www.peta.org/Living/AT-Fall2005/nokill.asp (accessed June 4, 2008). Nathan Winograd's book is *Redemption: The Myth of Pet Overpopulation and the No Kill Revolution in America* (Los Angeles: Almaden Books, 2007).

The statistics on the various cities' euthanasia rates come from Zawistowski's *Companion Animals,* p. 89.

India's pet fair is described in "It's Going to Be Your Pet Fair!" *Times of India,* March 1, 2008. China's spending increase, reported by the market-research group Euromonitor International, appears in "Dogs and Cats Benefit as Wealth in China Increases," by Joseph Chaney, *International Herald Tribune,* March 18, 2008. That story also discusses dog meat sales. Beijing's pet population is discussed in "China Says Hello Baristas, So Long Wok Repairmen; Fast-Changing Economy Needs New Job Titles," by Craig Simons, *Atlanta Journal Constitution,* October 15, 2005.

The Los Angeles bill is discussed in "Law to Require Altered Pets; L.A. Council Gives Initial OK to Mandating Sterilization of Dogs and Cats at 4 Months or Older," by Carla Hall, *Los Angeles Times,* February 2, 2008. Chaining dogs is prohibited in cities including Miami, New Orleans, and Fort Worth, according to http://www.unchainyourdog.org/Laws.htm, the Web site of a group that promotes such laws (accessed June 4, 2008).

Florida's "Doggie Dining Bill," including the scene when it was signed, is described in "Gov. Bush Signs Bill Allowing Dogs to Eat Outside at Restaurant," by Travis Reed, Associated Press state and local newswire, June 2, 2006.

CHAPTER THIRTEEN: THE AMERICAN WAY OF PET DEATH

Except where noted, the scenes reported in this chapter come from multiple visits I made to the pet-loss bereavement group between September and December 2007.

The statistic about the total number of pet deaths a year appears in "Birth and Death Rate Estimates of Cats and Dogs in U.S. Households and Related Factors," by John C. New, Jr., et al., *Journal of Applied Animal Welfare Science,* vol. 7, no. 4, 2004, p. 230.

Katherine Grier discusses Hartsdale in *Pets in America,* pp. 111–12.

Ralph Bunche's story is recounted in *Ralph Bunche: An American Odyssey,* by Brian Urquhart (New York: W. W. Norton, 1993), p. 109.

I visited Fairwinds in February 2008 and interviewed Donna Rae Yuritic in March.

I interviewed Wallace Sife and Jerry Dahm in March 2008. Coverage of Paul Dahm's plans to file a lawsuit can be found on the Britton Web site at http://www.legendofrainbowbridge.com/. Coverage of Dahm's lawsuit can be found in "Oh, Dear Abby," by Matt Sabo, *Oregonian,* September 27, 2000. Bill Rudy, the attorney who represented "Dear Abby" in the "Rainbow Bridge" matter, confirmed in August 2008 that the settlement was confidential.

For a discussion of the growing popularity of animal blessings, see "Ritual Blessings with Companion Animals," by Susan L. Holak, *Journal of Business Research,* vol. 61, no. 5, May, 2008. Laura Hobgood-Oster's quotation and the estimate of how many churches bless animals appear in her article "Animals Re-Enter the Christian (and Interfaith) Sanctuary: Blessings of Animals in the U.S.," *Earth Ethics,* vol. 12, no. 2, Fall, 2004, pp. 27–30.

Mary Buddemeyer-Porter's books are *Will I See Fido in Heaven?* (Manchester, Mo.: Eden, 1995) and *Animals, Immortal Beings* (Manchester, Mo.: Eden, 2005). Richard McBrien and Andrew Linzey are among those who argue against her position in "Writers and Theologians Explore the Spirited Question of Pets' Afterlife," by Denise Flaim, *Newsday,* July 18, 2000.

EPILOGUE: OUR PETS, OURSELVES

The pet-portrait statistics appear in the APPMA's 2007 survey, p. 26.

Old-time pet portraits are discussed in Grier's *Pets in America,* pp. 96–103. A beautiful array of such pictures can be found in *The Best Dog in the World: Vintage Portraits of Children and Their Dogs,* by Donna Long (Berkeley: Ten Speed Press, 2007).

The Plutarch and Orwell quotes are both cited in Serpell's *In the Company of Animals,* on pp. 24 and 59, respectively. Also see Kathleen Szasz, *Petishism* (New York: Holt, Rinehart, 1969). The cited passage appears on p. 99. The *TIME* story, "The Great American Animal Farm," appeared in the December 23, 1974, issue.

Sri Lanka's linear accelerator is reported in "Radiation Treatment at

Ceylinco Healthcare Opens in September," by Shirajiv Sirimane, Sri Lanka *Daily News,* August 15, 2007, online at http://www.dailynews .lk/2007/08/15/bus11.asp (accessed June 5, 2008). Philadelphia's euthanasia ratio is cited in Zawistowski's *Companion Animals,* p. 89.

The anti-dog letter appeared on the letters page of the *New York Times* on December 10, 2006.

Leona Helmsley's charitable gift is reported in "Helmsley Left Dogs Billions in Her Will," by Stephanie Strom, *New York Times,* July 2, 2008.

Acknowledgments

My journey into the new world of American petdom started with a dog and a cat who remain clueless about the help they gave me. But the same loving logic that leads some people to insist on new seasonal sweaters for their fashion-indifferent pets obliges me to single out Murphy and Amelia here. Thanks.

Writing this book also required the help of a lot of humans. Since each of my thirteen chapters focuses on a different realm of the pet universe, that left me with thirteen different sets of people to pester with what must have seemed like clueless questions. Unlike my pets, they had a choice in whether or not to help with my reporting. I'm grateful they chose to do so.

The people who let me in on their personal worlds, their professional worlds—and their pets—included Bob Vetere, Ada Nieves, John Denny, Ann Farrow, Arthur Feinstein, Carl Friedman, Bill Herndon, Karin Hu, Linda McKay, Brent Plater,

Sally Stephens, Nancy Stafford, David Troup, Matt Zlatunich, Jennifer Kistulentz, Julia Cowles, Bjorn Gärdsby, Janet Lee, Carlos Tribino, Sue Dolbow, Mary Ann Sparano, Allyson Berent, Marilyn Dunn, Chick Weisse, Gail Luciani, Jordan Reese, Julie Banyacski, James Buckman, James Dougherty, Karen Farver, Paul Orsini, Catherine Popovitch, Milen Velinov, Milena Velinova, Mark and Michelle Halmo, Bob Baker, Marsha Perelman, Simon Brodie, Marlena Cervantes, Chris Haddix, Terri Gianetti, Ted Swedalla, Daisy Okas, Betsy Moran Legnini, Bill Smith, Susan Barrish, Vicki Smith Doyle, Ken Majewski, Rochelle Michalek, Cherie Travis, Jay Edelson, Margit Livingston, Victor Schwartz, Ben DeLong, Dawn Majerczyk, Claire Moomjian, Keith Benson, Joe Markham, Stacy Alldredge, Lauren Huston, Ian Dunbar, David Lang, Ritu Raj, Steve Smith, Pat Bentz, Jessy Gabriel, Wendy Whiting, Leigh Siegfried, Melinda Miller, David Bogner, Dan Carey, Jane Kopelman, Kiska Icard, Randy Blauvelt, Marie Wheatley, Elizabeth Vaughan, Donna Yuritic, Christina Bach, Merry Klimek, Lynn Makowski, Marlena Schmid, and Kim Levin.

Throughout my research, I also relied on help from people who have to write and think for a living about various topics covered in this book. My understanding of the pet economy was greatly aided by people like Mike Dillon, Tom Ehart, David Lummis, and Vicki Lynne Morgan. I'm especially indebted to Tatjana Meerman, the publisher of marketresearch.com, who helped me access far more research material than I'd otherwise have found. Phil Arkow of American Humane, Frank Ascione of Utah State University, Sharon Curtis Granskog and David Kirkpatrick of the AVMA, Lisa Greenhill of the AAVMC, Ledy Vankavage at the ASPCA, Kevin McCarron of the Bureau of Labor Statistics, Lisa Jane Hardy, and Dr. Aubrey Fine all steered me to helpful pieces of research. Though much of his work focuses on the many, many pets who don't live the luxurious lives I've described in this book, Steve

Zawistowski of the ASPCA very generously shared drafts of his own book and helped me ponder pet life and pet death. Marion Nestle and Malden Neshiem helped explain pet food's contents to me even as they scrambled toward deadlines of their own. Hal Herzog of West Carolina University talked me through his fascinating research on breeds. Katherine Grier, who literally wrote the book on American pet history, delivered a presentation on cats that I was lucky enough to see at the opening of her wonderful exhibit on the history of the very products I was writing about. In the burgeoning galaxy of pet-oriented media, I benefited from my conversations with Susan Chaney at *Dog Fancy,* Brian Hutchins at *Pet Products News,* Claudia Kawczynska at *The Bark,* Kristi Reimer at *Veterinary Economics,* Craig Rexford at *Pet Business,* and Gina Spadafori at petconnection.com. And back at my neighborhood dog park, one of the regulars was a nice British man with a dog named Atticus. Only after I started researching this book did I learn that he was James Serpell, perhaps the smartest thinker when it comes to the bond at the center of this book. He nicely let me interrupt that bond from time to time as I pestered him with questions during Atticus's morning romps.

A number of friends and colleagues, in and out of journalism, also helped this project by steering me to helpful information, suggesting topics I should cover, or just letting me swipe office supplies. I thank Catherine Bonier, Meredith Broussard, Jason Cherkis, Jason Fagone, Melissa Farris, Tom Fitzgerald, Marcia Gelbart, David Grazian, John Grogan, Kaitlin Gurney, Emilie Lounsberry, Catherine Lucey, Holly Maher, Meredith May, Michael McCormick, Stephanie Mencimer, Aaron Mettey, David Plotz, Natalie Pompilio, Jeff Shields, John Shiffman, John Sullivan, Ben Wallace, and Amy Worden. Ryan Donnell and Darrow Montgomery took beautiful pictures. Jason Neugent and Charlotte Walker helped keep track of my two- and four-legged family. Several editors published pieces that sprang from the reporting I did for this book: Tom McGrath and Larry Platt at *Philadelphia,* Avery Rome at *Obit,* and Frank Foer, Adam Kushner, Britt Peterson, and Ben Wasserstein at *The New Republic.* As I traveled to report this book, I was also able to lean on the hospitality of a lot of friends and relatives who offered beds, meals, rides, advice, or company: Todd Robinson, Jason Zinoman, Agnes Dunogué, Chris, Kim, and Ruby Thom(p)son, Jennifer, Peter, Thomas, and William Nelson, Frank and Christine Currie, Marc and Megara Vogl, Janice Meerman, Jeff Ruhser, Becky Katkin, Richard Meachem, Clara Jeffrey, Kevin Arnovitz, and Ruben Fleischer.

I also got advice and help from friends and colleagues who read part of my proposal and my book drafts, or who schlepped through the entire thing: Jordan Barnett, Patrick Kerkstra, Andy Putz, Amanda Ripley, Hank Stuever, Michael Tortorello, and Marc Vogl.

My agent, Larry Weissman, took the time to craft a winning book idea and make sure its spirit survived the challenges to come. Larry has an intuitive understanding of that place where reporting, narrative, and argument intersect, which makes him the perfect partner for a journalist writing his first book. That Larry's own partner, Sacha, is a wordsmith who helped buff my proposal to a high shine only made things better. At Holt, I'm grateful to Christine Kopprasch for helping keep me on schedule and on track. During the years I was working on this project, I was especially lucky to work with an ambitious and talented editor, David Patterson, who put his own blood, sweat, and tears into making this the best book it could be.

This book started with a conversation I had at a Halloween party with Sasha Issenberg, who, typically, was denouncing the very idea of having a pet. And though he's never gotten used to having Murphy greet him at my door, he's been a championship friend over the years, a feat that's included reading drafts of my work, offering suggestions about a subject he's proudly ignorant of, and serving as an all-purpose literary adviser.

The luckiest journalists have bosses early in their careers who, often through sheer terror, manage to install themselves permanently in underlings' brains. I had two of them, David Carr and Erik Wemple, who hired me at *Washington City Paper* when I was twenty-three. A dozen years later, both of them read and offered helpful thoughts on this book. But I hope they realize that they were also there, perched in my subconscious, screaming imprecations against sloppy writing or lazy thinking, as I wrote every word.

Eleanor Rose Hawkins Schaffer, who showed up a day after I handed in my first three chapters, did little other than look cute and distract me while I came down the home stretch. That I loved her all the more for it gets at a central lesson of this book: We'll do all sorts of things for family, two-legged, four-legged, or still learning to crawl. I've been the recipient of just that largesse from my wonderful circle of relations. My in-laws, the Hawkinses, first got me thinking about this unlikely subject when they used to make fun of all the kooky things we did for Murphy. More recently, they've provided babysitting, room and board, infusions of airline miles—and, most important, a feeling that however badly this project seemed to be going, someone was excited on my behalf. I got the same feeling from the vast universe of Curries and Bruners and Schaffers, all of whom have a way of making you feel more important than you are. My brother, Chris, and my parents, Howie and Tezi, are as supportive a family as I could ask for. I'd like to think they had a hand in my professional life: My brother's congenital aversion to bull, my mother's meticulous intelligence, and my dad's invention of the "secret story" all made me the writer I am.

Mostly, though, this book exists because of Keltie Hawkins.

I've been dreaming of writing a book acknowledgment to her since about our second date, though it took me so long that my thanks now include gratitude for her doing so much of the diaper changing while I was upstairs swearing at the computer. Keltie read the manuscript, came up with the title, and managed not to brain me as I lumbered toward my deadline. Earlier, she was the one who first wanted to get a dog, which we did at the most inconvenient possible time. Her logic was that more love is always a good thing. That's the logic that defines her—and I hope I'll eventually soak up enough of it to become a person who deserves her. For now: Thanks.

Illustration Credits

About the Author

A former staff writer at *The Philadelphia Inquirer, U.S. News and World Report,* and *Washington City Paper,* Michael Schaffer has also written for *The Washington Post, Slate,* and *The New Republic.* He lives in Philadelphia with his wife, Keltie Hawkins, and their daughter, Eleanor. They insist that their own pets, Murphy the Saint Bernard and Amelia the black cat, are not freakishly pampered.